PENGUIN TRAVEL LIBRARY

Voices of the Old Sea

Norman Lewis has written thirteen novels and seven non-fiction works. *A Dragon Apparent* and *Golden Earth* are considered classics of travel and *Naples '44* has been described as one of the ten outstanding books about the Second World War. Lewis travels extensively and as far as possible off the beaten track in search of inspiration for his work. Apart from writing books his main interest lies in the study of the cultures of so-called primitive peoples. He regards as his principle achievement the world reaction to an article written by him entitled 'Genocide in Brazil', which was published in the *Sunday Times*. This account, after a long personal investigation, of the near-extermination of the Indians of that country led to a change in the Brazilian law relating to the treatment of Indians, and the formation of organizations such as Survival International, dedicated to the protection of aboriginal people. *A Suitable Case for Corruption*, *The Sicilian Specialist* and an autobiographical volume, *Jackdaw Cake*, are also published by Penguin. His most recent work is *The Missionaries* (1988), which brings together his own experiences of missionaries and their activities in Asia and Latin America.

Norman Lewis lives with his family in Essex.

Norman Lewis

Voices of the Old Sea

Penguin Books

PENGUIN BOOKS

Published by the Penguin Group
27 Wrights Lane, London W8 5TZ, England
Viking Penguin Inc., 40 West 23rd Street, New York, New York 10010, USA
Penguin Books Australia Ltd, Ringwood, Victoria, Australia
Penguin Books Canada Ltd, 2801 John Street, Markham, Ontario, Canada L3R 1B4
Penguin Books (NZ) Ltd, 182–190 Wairau Road, Auckland 10, New Zealand

Penguin Books Ltd, Registered Offices: Harmondsworth, Middlesex, England

First published by Hamish Hamilton 1984
First published in the United States of America by Viking 1985
Published in Penguin Books 1985
3 5 7 9 10 8 6 4 2

Printed and bound in Great Britain by
Cox & Wyman Ltd, Reading
Typeset in Bembo

Foreword

After three war years in the Army overseas I looked for the familiar in England, but found change. Perhaps it was the search for vanished times that drew me back to Spain, which in some ways I knew better than my own country – a second homeland to be revisited when I could. Here the past, I suspected, would have been embalmed, and outside influence held at bay in a country absorbed in its domestic tragedy. It was a conjecture that proved largely to be true. The Spain I returned to was still recognisable as that of Lorca, of Albéniz and of De Falla, still as nostalgically backward-looking as ever, still magnificent, still invested with all its ancient virtues and ancient defects.

Following a preliminary reconnaissance of the whole peninsula I settled for reasons that are made evident in this book in the remote fishing village of Farol. I had had medical advice to lead as active a life as possible, so I took out a licence and became a part-time fisherman, a pursuit which not only consumed the energies but provided the opportunity for close association with men not wholly freed from the customs of the Celto-Iberian past.

By the end of my third season it was clear that Spain's spiritual and cultural isolation was at an end, overwhelmed by the great alien invasion from the North of money and freedoms. Spain became the most visited tourist country in the world, and slowly, as the foreigners poured in, its identity was submerged, its life-style altered more in a single decade than in the previous century. Now – twenty-five years after my first memorable season among its uncorrupted fisherfolk – it is as remote from Lorca as the Romancero Gitano is from the Spain of El Cid Campeador, and the Reconquista.

Cómo le puedo decir? Esto es
seguro — aquí hemos estado siempre,
y aquí tenemos siempre que estar,
escuchando las voces del viejo mar.

(When asked how the great changes that had taken place were likely to affect his future, a fisherman replied, 'How can anyone say? One thing is certain. Here we have always been, and here, whatever happens, we shall remain, listening to the voices of the old sea.')

Season One

1

When I went to live in Farol the grandmother who owned the house gave me a cat. 'Don't feed it,' she said. 'Don't take any notice of it. It can sleep in the shed and it'll keep the rats away.' Farol was full of cats, for which reason it was often called Pueblo de los Gatos – 'cat village'. There were several hundred of them living in whatever accommodation they could find in the village, and in caves in the hill behind it. They were an ugly breed, skinny with long legs and small, pointed heads. You saw little of them in the daytime, but after dark they were everywhere. The story was that Don Alberto, the local landowner who was also a bit of an historian, claimed that they had always been there and produced a fanciful theory, based on some reference made to them by an early traveller, that they had some connection with the sacred cats of Ancient Egypt. Mentioning this, the fishermen of Farol would screw their fingers into their temples and roll their eyes in derision as if to say, what will he come up with next? Their story was that the cats had been imported in the old days to clean up the mess left when they degutted fish on the spot before packing them up to be sent away. No one in this part of the world would ever kill a domestic animal, so their numbers soon got out of control. In addition to scavenging round the boats, they hunted lizards, frogs, anything that they deemed edible, including fat-bodied moths attracted to the oleanders on summer evenings, which they snatched out of the air with their paws. Whenever the cat became too old or sick to have about the place it would be put in a bag and taken to the cork forest and there abandoned. The people who owned this part of the forest lived in the village of Sort, about five kilometres away. They had no cats but were overrun by dogs, and as they, too, were squeamish about taking life they brought down unwanted animals, borrowed a boat, and left them to die of hunger and thirst on an island a hundred yards or so off-shore.

It soon became clear that the Grandmother was a person of exceptional power and influence in the village. All the domestic aspects of life – and largely the financial ones too – came under the control here of the women, 'dominated', to use the local word, by the Grandmother, just as the males were dominated by the five senior fishermen owning the major shares in the big boats. In each case the domination was subtle and indirect, a matter rather of leadership accorded to experience and vision.

The Grandmother had gathered a little respect in deference to her money but most of it was based on sheer spiritual qualities. She was large, dignified and slow-moving, dressed perpetually in black, with the face of a Borgia pope, a majestic nose and a defiant chin, sprouting an occasional bristle. A muscular slackening of an eyelid had left one eye half-closed, so that she appeared at all times to be on the verge of a wink. Her voice was husky and confiding, although in a moment of impatience she was likely to burst into an authoritarian bellow. Everything she said carried instant conviction, and the villagers said that she was inclined to make God's mind up for him, because whenever people left a loophole of doubt about future intentions by adding the pious formula 'if God is willing', she would decide the matter there and then with a shout of '*Si que quiere*' – of course he's willing.

As a matter of course the Grandmother meddled in family affairs of others. She provided instruction on the mechanics of family planning, investigated the household budgets of newly married couples to decide when they could hope (if ever) to afford a child, and put forward a suitable name as soon as it was born. All the names suggested for male children were taken from a book she possessed on the generals of antiquity, and the village was full of inoffensive little boys called Julio César, Carlos Magna (Charlemagne), Mambró (Marlborough) and Napoleón. And one luckless child was doomed to go through life bearing the name Esprit de Cor (esprit de corps) who, someone had assured the Grandmother, was the greatest commander of them all.

Above all the Grandmother was an expert on herbal remedies, and the villagers saved on the doctor's fees by prescriptions provided after a scrutiny of their faeces and urine. '*Mear claro y cagar duro*' (clear piss and hard shit), she claimed – quoting a saying attributed to Lope de Vega – were at the base of health and prosperity. She also offered a sporadic supply of the urine of a woman who had recently given birth, locally regarded as effective in the treatment of conjunctivitis and certain skin ailments – although in a village where the birth-rate must

4

have been one of the lowest in the world, it was rare for a donor to be available.

My room in the Grandmother's house was odd-shaped and full of sharp edges, with a ceiling slanting up in four triangles to a centre point, and dormer windows throwing segments of light and shade across walls and floor. In Farol they were nervous of the use of colour, so it was all stark white, and living in this room was rather like living inside a crystal, in which the Grandmother, when she came on the scene, appeared as a black, geometrical shape.

A tiny cubicle contained a charcoal-burning stove, and another a floor of ceramic tiles. It was a feature of the house that illuminated a nook in the Grandmother's mind inhabited by poetic fancies, for the tiles' pattern – made to the Grandmother's own design – depicted flowers on intertwining stems, growing from a central hole beside which a powerful disinfectant in an amphora-shaped container had been placed.

I was taken into the garden to admire another feature of the accommodation: three strands of barbed-wire twisted together round the top of the wall, cut from a roll the Grandmother had bought as an extravagance. Beyond the wall a rampart of sunflowers besieged by goldfinches hung their heads, and through their stalks I could see the beach with glossy, translucent pebbles glittering among the coarse limestone chips, and a rank of purple and yellow fishing boats leaning on it. I asked the price, and the Grandmother's eyes became misted with introspection. She passed her tongue very slowly in a clockwise direction round her teeth inside the lips, and said five pesetas a day. 'Here,' she said, 'you will enjoy great tranquillity.'

This proved true, and to find the place had been an immense stroke of luck. I spent my first week in Farol, to which I had been drawn by its reputation of being the least accessible coastal village in north-east Spain, in the fonda – the village inn – being driven out largely by the smell of cats. The fonda was run by two shy, silent brothers I never saw except at mealtimes when one or other of them would bring the food, drop the plate on the table, head averted, and scuttle away. The food was always tinned sardines – a luxury in this place where they sometimes caught fresh sardines by the ton – and hard-boiled eggs. The brothers kept sixteen cats in their cellar, and had taken four more away and left them in the cork forest only the week before I arrived.

My room in the Grandmother's house had been occupied until a few days before my arrival by the Grandmother's eldest daughter, her son-in-law and their two small children, who – as I was later told – had been hugely relieved, after some years of living in the shadow of the Grandmother's personality, to be able finally to make their escape. There were fifty or more such houses in Farol, built in an irregular and misaligned fashion into a narrow zig-zag of streets, and a few more squeezed where space could be found among the semi-circle of massive rocks almost enclosing the village. Standing aloof were several mansions originally belonging to rich cork merchants who came here for their holidays at the end of the last century, all in varying states of decrepitude, and decorated with stone coats of arms to which their owners had not been entitled. Farol catered for the basic needs with a small, decayed church, a ship-chandler's, a butcher's shop, a general store selling a wide range of goods from moustache wax to hard black chocolate kept in a sack, that had to be broken up with a hammer, and a single book – Alonso Barros' *Eight Thousand Familiar Sayings and Moral Proverbs*, published in 1598 – of which almost every house possessed a copy, and by which people regulated their lives. There was a bar, too, which offered a thin, acidulous wine from the barrel at a half-peseta a glass, or a bottled wine called Inocente, claimed on its label to contain calming vitamins. The bar was notable for its display of the mummified corpse of a dugong, known locally as 'the mermaid'. This grotesquely patched and repaired object with its mournful glass eyes, sewn-on leather breasts and a flap covering its sexual parts was believed to vary its expression – whether pensive, sceptical or malicious – according to the weather, and it was noticeable that strangers who took refuge in the bar from the horrors of the fonda where they were obliged to put up – generally agreed to be the worst in Spain – seated themselves so as not to be depressed by the sight of this macabre trophy.

It was at a long table placed under the mermaid that the principal fishermen met in the early evening to discuss the events and the adventures of the day. This they did in blank verse, for although the people of Farol were indifferent to music, to painting, indeed to art forms of all kinds, they were profoundly ensnared by the power of words.

6

Catalan, their workaday language, was put aside at such sessions in favour of Castillian, its cadences esteemed by the fishermen as more suited to poetic expression. The men of Farol hoarded words as their children collected the coloured pebbles on the beach. Their versifying seemed to be spontaneous. When one man had had his say, another would leap into the pause that followed with an opening line, then wait for nods or grunts of approval to continue. Thus:

Ayer los chubascos me agarráron, pero hoy . . . [a murmur of '*Sigue, sigue*' – 'go on, go on']
Yesterday the storms clawed at me, but today . . .
La suerte me corrió.
Luck ran at my side.
Al amanacer visité la marea
At dawn I visted the tide
Y viendo que el día no llevaba malicia –
And seeing that the day bore no malice –
Cogí la barca, y me fuí –
I took the boat, and I went –
Pa' dentro del mar, donde las grandes olas se movían. ('Sigue, sigue.')
Into the deep sea, where the great waves moved.
Y allí en la claridad del agua, solo, aislado,
There in the clarity of water, alone, alone,
Ví tantos fantásmas vivaces,
I saw many lively ghosts,
No de los sin habla, que comen las almas,
Not of the kind without tongues, eaters of souls,
Pero de los que cantan con voces dulces del alba.
But those that sing with the sweet voices of the dawn.

It was impermissible to eavesdrop on these sessions, unthinkable to be seen taking notes, and at the approach of someone, like myself, outside the bardic circle the noble flow of Castillian came to an end to be replaced by the disjointed rhythms of Catalan. So engrained had the habit of speaking in blank verse become, that it often asserted itself in the most mundane of discussions, and a fisherman found it hard to discard metrical rhythm even when ordering his necessities at the ship–chandler's, or buying a round of drinks.

In a village enjoying the brand of democracy, the absence of status–

seeking imposed by a manageable, shared-out poverty, a few notables emerged in addition to the Grandmother.

The formal head of the community, the Alcalde, an outsider who had been imposed on the village, had been almost forgiven for what he was by convincing the villagers that he had been a Nationalist not by choice, but by the geographical accident of having been born in Nationalist-occupied territory. Shopkeepers in Farol acted as bankers, supplying goods on credit throughout the winter in anticipation of sardines and tunny to be caught in summer, and were therefore entitled to some grudging respect. Inevitably the butcher wielded power through his control of the rare meat supplies – more importantly of the blood hot from the veins of slaughtered animals, given to sickly children. My next-door neighbour attracted attention to himself in a community that hardly understood the usages of property through his marriage to a rich peasant girl, who had brought him some fields and trees he had never seen. The five senior fishermen expected to be listened to when any matter relating to the village weal came under discussion. Don Ignacio, the priest, in so far as he could be considered a villager, was well thought of on the whole, largely because he had lived with a mistress quite openly, and had learned to mind his own business.

The other person of consequence would have been seen by most outsiders as a prostitute although a villager might have pretended, or even felt surprise at such a suggestion. Sa Cordovesa, possessor of a delicate beauty and charm, had arrived as a child refugee from Andalusia, and now conducted multiple affairs with discretion, even dignity, behind the cover of making up cheap dresses. By common consent the community put on blinkers in this matter, a posture of self-defence adopted to cope as painlessly as possible with a situation in which most men could expect to reach the age of thirty before they could afford to marry. Taking refuge in self-deception, Farol invested Sa Cordovesa with a kind of subjective virtue. She had allies – such as the Grandmother – by the dozen, and was made welcome in any house. It was not long before I discovered that there had been a succession of Sa Cordovesas in the past. Farol had solved a social problem in its own unobtrusive way.

This was the view of Farol, cut off more by secret human design than by the accidents of nature and, by reason of its continuing isolation, a repository of past custom and attitudes of mind. Life had been always hard – an existence pared to the bone – and local opinion was that it was getting harder, purely because mysterious changes in the sea were directing the fish elsewhere. In most years catches were a little sparser than the year before, but there were optimists who believed that the decline was not necessarily irreversible, and they awaited in hope the end of the cycle of lean years.

The fishermen were totally absorbed by the sea, oblivious almost of the activities of those who lived by the land, wholly ignorant of the fact that only a few miles away a catastrophe was in the making. Three miles back from the shore the cork-oak forest began – hundreds of thousands of majestic trees, spreading their quilt of foliage into the foothills, and up and over the slopes into the low peaks of the sierra. The great wealth of cork belonged to the days before the invention of the metal bottle top, but even now, with slumped sales and low prices, the oaks provided a livelihood for hundreds of tree-owning peasant cultivators from Sort, the neighbouring village of dogs, and many other forest hamlets.

In the year before my arrival in 1948, people in Sort began to notice that something was happening to the trees, that the early spring foliage had changed colour and was withering. Word of their neighbours' alarm reached Farol, but the fishermen shrugged their shoulders and went on preparing their lines or mending their nets. It was impossible for them to understand that their destiny could be in any way linked with that of peasants with whom they had little contact and from whom they were separated by huge differences of temperament and tradition. For the fishermen of Farol the peasants of Sort might have been the inhabitants of a distant planet rather than of a village five kilometres away, and they found it difficult to interest themselves in their fate, whatever misfortune might have befallen them.

2

My increasing involvement in village life was helped by a friendship struck up with Sebastian, the Grandmother's second son-in-law, who was married to her young daughter, Elvira, both of them living in her house. Sebastian was bold and romantic-looking, with flashing eyes and the face of a corsair, but his striking apearance fronted for a character that was hesitant and meek, and he was firmly under the Grandmother's thumb, and plotted endlessly to break the chains she had lain upon him.

He had come from Figueras, his home-town, to work as a carpenter-mason at Farol, and the Grandmother's Elvira, captivated by his looks, had demanded him from her mother, who had agreed to underwrite a marriage that would have been otherwise impossible. The state fixed Sebastian's wages at 21 pesetas a day, and without the Grandmother's subsidy and the provision of a furnished room in her house it would have taken Sebastian six or seven years to save the 10,000 pesetas custom required of a man before marriage could be contracted.

Elvira was rather ugly, an inheritor of the Grandmother's over-masculine features although little of her intelligence, but she and Sebastian got on well enough. Elvira had had a narrow escape in the matter of names, for in the epoch following the fall of the monarchy when Spaniards came to hear something about socialism, the Grandmother had called her first Libertad (Liberty), and then Juana de Arco (Joan of Arc), but even Don Ignacio – who wanted to keep everybody happy – had felt obliged to turn these names down at the christening. The Grandmother's less than benevolent despotism saw to it that the marriage was conducted on her own terms. Because they could not afford children it was the practice of many fishermen to restrict the opportunities for begetting them by sleeping with their wives only in the siesta hours, between two and four in the afternoon, and Sebastian received orders to subscribe to this custom, otherwise occupying a bed on the verandah at the back of the house. She also commanded him to learn to fish in his spare time in order to increase his income and thus struggle upwards towards the financial independence which he so earnestly desired. This he did although, lacking both experience and skill, he was able to practise the art only in its lowliest form.

The fact that Sebastian and I were both *forasteros*, strangers, outsiders, who might have come as well from Barcelona as from England, drew us together. He, at least, had a foot in the door and held it open for me but, although he had lived for four years in the Grandmother's house, he was not accepted as a villager. Every evening, work over, he took a boat and fished for calamares, which he sold for a peseta or two to the Grandmother. Only if he caught more than one fish – this happened on average one evening out of three – was he allowed to keep the extra money himself. His problem was that he could not manage the boat efficiently and fish at the same time, and that no fisherman – probably from reasons of superstition, he thought – would go out with him.

We sat in the bar under the despairing glare of the mermaid, our mouths atingle with the Alcalde's tart wine that left the teeth discoloured after a single glass, and discussed a project that had occurred to him. 'How long are you staying with us?' he asked.

'As long as the money lasts out.' I explained the currency restrictions in force. 'A month. Two months. Depending on how things go.'

'You could come fishing with me. Between us we could catch five or six calamares a night. The Grandmother would buy your share, or she'd take it in payment for the room.'

I told him that the last thing I wanted to do was to tread on the fishermen's toes.

'You wouldn't worry them,' he said. 'No one fishes for calamares. It's too boring.'

'I'm very anxious to get along well with these people,' I told him.

'No problem,' he said. 'You only have to remember two things. Don't wear leather shoes – certainly never in a boat – and don't stand on the beach and watch when the boats are coming in. If they've caught nothing they'll say you brought them bad luck. If they like you they'll ask you to give a hand pulling up the boats. When that happens you're in.'

On our first calamar fishing expedition we put Sebastian's leaky twelve-foot dinghy into the water soon after five, then rowed for an hour along the shore to avoid any possible collision of interests with the fishermen. As ever in this deep clear water over rock, the sea was a polished interweave of sombre but refulgent colours that contained no blue. Past every headland the view opened on a new adventure of riven cliffs and pinnacles, of caves sucking at the water, of rock strata twisted and kneaded like old-fashioned toffee. Boulders of colossal proportions had fallen everywhere from the cliffs and we threaded through a maze of them over water possessed of a surging, muscled vivacity to reach an inlet where the fishing would take place, and where the shallows were of such transparency that the weeds under us showed through, like the fronds, the fanned-out petals and the plumes of a William Morris design.

The implement used in this least creative of all kinds of fishing was a lure composed of a circular base plate of bright metal from which curved some twenty inch-long hooks. The lure was lowered on a line until it touched bottom and then after a few seconds jerked upwards. No bait was used. If a calamar happened to be in the neighbourhood it would be attracted by the shining metal, and caught by one or more tentacles. In this way, manoeuvring the boat with one arm and raising and lowering the lure with the other we covered the narrow triangle of water at the end of the inlet until the shadow of a cliff closed like a curtain over the water and the fishing came to an end. We went back to the village with six small calamares of which I had caught two, and Sebastian four. These the Grandmother accepted without comment, showing some cautious approval, however, by including a small piece of extremely bony fish with the evening meal of rice and onions she supplied for two pesetas. In addition she presented me with a rare starfish and a knot of fossilised wood, indicating where they should be hung on the walls to produce the most attractive shadows. Yet a further gift was a glass jar full of translucent pebbles, green and yellow in colour, to be found by the thousand on the beach. 'To make the place seem more like home,' she explained.

Encouraged by this first small success, we went out with the boat every evening for some weeks whenever the weather permitted. Slowly our average catch improved, not so much because we became more expert in handling the lure, for there was no art concealed in its use, but because we gained in knowledge of the habits of the calamar, and where and when it was most likely to be found. In the first week we doubled our catch, so that the Grandmother felt obliged to knock half the price off my board and lodgings. So far so good, and Sebastian and I now began to consider ways in which we could expand our fishing activities.

As a matter of course we turned to the Grandmother for her advice, but the counsel offered little more than a restatement of commercial principles.

'Don't bring me anything but noble fish,' the Grandmother said. *Noble* was the favoured adjective in local use to express approbation – *indecente*, its opposite. 'I am not in the market,' she went on, 'for fish of indecent appearance, for example eels of any description.' There was a pause for the wag of an admonishing finger. 'Nor are fish with stings or poisonous spines, including rays or arañas, of any interest, in fact the reverse, and I have no truck with anything notorious for feeding on offal or any filth that can be found. Octopus aren't welcome here except at times of general shortage.'

We hoped for some positive lead but there was none. 'As for catching your fish,' the Grandmother said, 'what do you expect me to tell you? Watch what the others do, and copy them in an intelligent fashion.'

We studied the experts, but success eluded us. In three evenings of line fishing, using the correct bait generously provided by the next-door neighbour, we caught only one strangely bewhiskered dogfish which the Grandmother declined to buy on grounds of indecency. A further attempt at diversification was even less successful, as we borrowed a small net, wrapped it, as instructed, round the base of a submerged rock, and not only took no fish, but wrecked the net, at a cost of fifty pesetas for its repair. So it was back to the tedious business of calamar fishing, with its small but dependable return, and in the end we became so accomplished at this that we consistently doubled our average catch of the first few days, and the Grandmother ceased to charge rent.

In this way we continued, unadventurously, until Sebastian suggested that we should try diving masks and a speargun made up by the local mechanic from an illustration he had seen. Mysteriously this had appeared in a magazine devoted to religious topics, and the picture showing a Japanese spearing a fish was supposed to illustrate an article on the life and miraculous works of the Blessed Egideo of Naples. It was the speciality of this saintly personage (whose reputation I happened coincidentally to be aware of, having recently spent a year in that city) to bring 'off' fish to marketable life, as recorded on twenty-seven separate occasions in the *Ufficio Prova* of the Vatican.

Like most Mediterranean people who spend their lives in close association with the sea, Sebastian could not swim and became nervous and unsteady in water reaching up to his chest. It was only because he was of peasant or artisan origins that he could even contemplate learning to dive and becoming an underwater fisherman. In my three seasons on this coast I never saw or heard of a fisherman by birth and background who could bring himself to do so. Some primordial restraint held them back from such investigations (and *violations* – as they put it) of the mystery of the sea. 'I hold the sea,' said a fisherman in the Alcalde's bar, 'to be the father and the mother from which we all come, and therefore to be treated with every respect.' It is significant that in Spanish the sea can be equally *el* mar, or *la* mar, masculine or feminine, grandly and uniquely unisexual, above and beyond all creation.

For our experiments with the mask and speargun we selected a sheltered spot where the rocky sea bed sloped down in a series of wide, shallow steps providing a succession of graded depths from about three feet to fifty feet. Sebastian fought off his panic, put on a mask and took the gun and began to wade about in the shallows. He pushed his face under the water, made his choice of the brilliantly striped or spotted wrasse wiggling about in the weed, poked the trident of his gun down and eventually skewered a fish.

After some minutes of this I left him, to explore the deeper water. A number of technical difficulties prevented the fishermen from putting down their nets in this spot, and swimming on I entered a new and wholly extraordinary submarine world, an underwater preserve that might have remained unchanged for thousands of years.

Everything in this sunny scene, every form and colour, was fresh. The panorama was one of the sea-gouged and polished bedrock, splashed all over with scarlet and ochreous algae, with its sierras, its jungles of weed and its teeming population of fish. Apart from the birds, the visible life of our world is largely restricted to surfaces. Here limitless stratification encouraged a dense marine populace with fish of all sizes from darting coloured particles to enormous bull-headed meros stacked at varying depths to feed, to circulate in a slow ruminative way, to rise or sink with a gentle ripple of fin or a flicker of tail.

I recognised many of these fish, and knew them by their local name, but many were unknown to me. They were on the whole indifferent to my presence but curiosity impelled some to move in for a closer inspection and an occasional *servia* – a large pelagic fish constantly on the move – would circle me several times before drifting away. Fish seen in this way were saturated with colour which faded instantly in death. Escorvais, weighing up to four pounds, presented themselves heraldically in static family groups outside the caverns in which they lived, glowing with purplish incandescence in the water, seeming actually to emit light, no trace of which would remain by the time – tarnished and flaccid – they reached the fishmonger's slab.

I turned back, making for shallow water through bead-curtains and chain mail of fish; fish sable and silver, fish glistening like Lorca's small, stabbing knives, fish that sparkled in their shoal in unison, off and on, like an advertising sign, as with a common impulse they changed the angles of their bodies to the light. As the seabed came closer and more clearly defined, I could see the small fidgetting movement of crabs, crustaceans and molluscs in its crevices. A moray slid a little way out of its fissure to watch me with its demented stare, and a family of mullet prepared, if unmolested, to socialise even with humans, turned to accompany me into shallow water.

While I had been away Sebastian, still nervous and unsure of his footing, the water up to his armpits, had speared a dozen wrasse and had them dangling from a wire carrier tied to his waist. In the boat they made a couple of limp handfuls, but for Sebastian they were full of promise of things to come.

I told him of the big fish I had seen.

'How big?'

I had already caught the fisherman's habit of exaggeration. 'Big as mules. Get your friend to make you a better gun and we might get some.'

'I'll talk to him about it,' Sebastian said. 'Looks as though I shall have to learn to swim.'

3

The Grandmother had a suggestion to make. It was the custom in the cat village to wash the tiled floor of every room in the morning of every day. I had not done this, and she pointed out that it was no part of her bargain that she should do it. She therefore suggested that a woman called Carmela should come in for an hour every day to do this and any other tidying up that had to be done, at a cost of two pesetas.

Carmela was another odd person out. She had arrived as a refugee from the deep south, had been in trouble with the police and claimed to have a sick child to look after, who nobody had ever seen, for whom she was always scrounging food. Carmela proved to be fiftyish, boss-eyed with straggling grey hair, and dressed perpetually in a faded and shapeless party frock with frills. She arrived, scrubbed the floor with high vigour, polished the jar with the precious stones, picked the cat up by the scruff of the neck and threw it into the street, begged for a crust left over from the previous day, wrapped it in a grubby cloth, stuffed it down the front of her dress and went. Before she left she offered to procure for me all or part of a rabbit, which I knew, her reputation being what it was, would be poached on somebody's property in the cork-oak forest. I conferred with Sebastian on this matter, and it was agreed that we could afford to take half each. In this way it was left.

Two days later Carmela arrived with the rabbit which she split down the middle, and Sebastian and I paid her eight pesetas each for our halves. It turned out that part of the deal was that she should do the cooking for me on this occasion, and while she chopped up the rabbit I was sent to the village shop to buy an earthenware casserole, a fistful of charcoal and a tablespoonful or so of black-market olive oil. Although an outsider she was as emphatic as a cat villager on the subject of colour, and the casserole was turned down on the grounds that it was too brown, and it had to be changed. It later occurred to me that these trips backwards and forwards to the shop might have been part of a process of mystification, a kind of three-card trick, by which odds and ends of the meal were spirited away, for when the cooking, done on a tiny charcoal fire on the balcony, was at an end, the quantity of rabbit that remained seemed small.

Carmela was positive, dictatorial and taciturn, but when she spoke at all it was to some purpose. On this occasion it was to mention that with every week that passed she had to go deeper and deeper into the forest to snare her rabbits. This she believed to be due to the loss of cover. Last year a number of oaks had failed to produce any foliage, and this shadeless, denuded area was spreading. The gist of her argument was, if you wanted to eat rabbits, now was the time. The way things were going this time next year there wouldn't be a rabbit to be had anywhere.

My next-door neighbour Juan was the only man in Farol who should at least have had some slight interest in the fate of the oaks, for his wife, Francesca, had brought fifty oaks as her dowry to this dowry-less village, and another seventy had passed to her as her inheritance on her father's death. She was a lively, high-stepping, intelligent woman who wore a silk dress on all occasions, and had strutted about in high-heeled shoes until the Grandmother had warned her in a tactful fashion that all articles made from leather were taboo in the village. On a later occasion, and in my presence, the Grandmother tackled her, in a pretendedly jocular way, on the matter of her attire. 'I shit on God,' the Grandmother said (it was the mildest of Catalan oaths, rarely out of her mouth). 'Why do you go in for these colours?'

Francesca returned the triumphant smile of youth. 'To draw attention to myself,' she said. 'When I'm older – say thirty-five – I'll be into greys and browns, and when I'm fifty it'll be black for good, heaven help us. Let's make hay while the sun shines. Who wants to look at an old woman?'

Her gaunt but imposing young husband, who always seemed on the verge of prophetic utterance, said he felt himself tainted by property acquired in this way. He had put off visiting the trees and the few barren acres that had gone with them, although agreeing to accompany his wife on mushroom-hunting trips in the vicinity, from which they returned with basketfuls of the celebrated *amanita caesaria*, used by one or more Roman empresses to poison their husbands.

Francesca confirmed that the trees were ailing, about half those on her property being affected. She was worried about the possible loss of revenue from cork, but even more so by the fact that only about half the normal crop of mushrooms had come up the last autumn. Like the rabbits the mushrooms needed cover and shade. Sort was full of men who had spent their life with trees, and knew all that was to be known about cork oaks, and these men were of the opinion that Sort was facing a tragedy. In 1947 oaks all over southern Europe had suffered attack by the caterpillars of the winter moth due to their hatching on the precise day (a coincidence occurring roughly twice in every century) when the leaf buds first appeared. The majority of the oaks eventually recovered from this loss of foliage, but in the Pyreneean forests many trees weakened in this way contracted a virus disease from which they subsequently died. Juan and the rest of the fishermen withheld their sympathy. It was solidly believed that every peasant had a boxful of thousand-peseta notes buried under his floor. 'They'll never go short of anything. Let them live on their fat,' was the general verdict.

The first signs of hard times in Sort was that their dogs were clearly getting even less food than usual, and therefore becoming more venturesome in their forays into Farol territory where they managed to catch and devour not only an occasional cat, which no one grudged them, but a chicken here and there, which was a grave and unpardonable offence.

Whereas the cats of Farol needed no more than the presence and companionship of man, the dogs of Sort were not wholly independent in the matter of feeding themselves. Their function was to hunt game in the forest, and they were rewarded with the skins, the heads and the feet of the rabbits they caught. Apart from that they had to make do with the sparse offal to be picked up about the village, and rare cannibal feasts when one of their own kind perished through accident or disease.

Unlike the people of Sort, who were individualists, those of Farol, accustomed to the communal enterprises of the sea, lost no opportunity to work as a team. In both villages women helped to make ends meet by keeping chickens. These, in Sort, would be shut up in cages at night, suspended from trees to keep them out of the reach of the dogs, or the rare fox that ventured into the village once in a while. In Farol although this kind of protection was less essential a communal coop had been built for the use largely of the aged and infirm, and a week after my arrival a pack of famished dogs from Sort managed to break into this and carry off many of the hens.

This was a calamity for which there was no redress. Sort denied responsibility. A peasant from the dog village who had driven a cartload of vegetables over to Farol to barter for fish, was tackled in the Alcalde's bar about what was to be done. His reply was, 'How do you know they were our dogs? You can't tell one dog from another.'

The fishermen, who were given to informal meetings, held one on the spot, after which they told the man he could take his vegetables back. At a second meeting reprisals were decided upon. The view was that if the Sort people were not prepared to cut down on their dog population, the fishermen would have to take their own measures to reduce their numbers. But how? It was impossible to conceive of anybody taking an axe or a club and killing a dog outright and the idea of using rat poison went against the grain. The final solution was to procure a number of dried sea-sponges, and fry these in olive oil to provide a flavour irresistible to dogs. When a few days later the animals had recovered from the surfeit of chickens the sponges were put out for them on the periphery of the village. It was a time-honoured method and as ever successful. The dogs gorged themselves on the dried sponges which swelled up as they absorbed the gastric juices until in the end their stomachs ruptured. A dog that had come too late on the scene to partake of the fatal meal, was trapped, and then as a traditional gesture of defiance and contempt, castrated and sent home with a black ribbon tied round its neck. The black ribbon symbolised cowardice.

After that the Sort people kept their dogs under control by fastening them to heavy logs which they had to drag about wherever they went. From this time on, the relationship between Sort and Farol – never more than a watchful neutrality – fell into decline, and both communities suffered from the loss of a local market for their produce.

4

The deepening rift between the cat and dog villages manifested itself in many ways. For the time being the villagers of Sort ceased to eat fish, and those of Farol – who grew no crops of any kind – went short of vegetables. A minority of affluent peasants in Sort still favoured a negotiated peace, and took it upon themselves to drive over to Farol on the Saturday night hoping to open up a dialogue with the fishermen, whom they expected to find in the Alcalde's bar. The moment was ill-chosen, for they arrived in the middle of the final of a contest for the most telling blank-verse description of a dramatic episode in the fishing life. The mood in and around the bar was one of impassioned oblivion. No one was drinking, but a falling tear occasionally missed an empty glass, and the peasants, fidgeting uneasily in their corner, were overlooked. Their mood sobered from cautious optimism to well-tried patience, but by the time the boy the Alcalde employed arrived to take their order, the drift to belligerence had begun. They ordered *palo* – a murky local version of sherry, tasting more of liquorice than the solera – but the Alcalde, having judged the contest, and declared the winner, came full of apologies to say that his barrel was empty. The peasants got to their feet, clumped as if across ploughed land to the door, spat on the threshold and departed.

Next day Sort's reaction took the form of raising a barrier across a footpath through village land used by the fishermen as a short cut to the main road. A right of way had been established here, following a feud between two families when a funeral party taking the head of one household to his grave had suddenly switched direction to cross its enemies' land, thus by irrevocable custom cutting the land in two. The ruling of the Alcalde of Sort was now that the right of way thus established had belonged only to those persons legally resident in Sort, and that outsiders such as the cat people had abused customary law by including themselves in the privilege. This was a blow indeed to the fishermen because it meant that heavy crates of fish would have to be trundled in future for an extra kilometre before they could be loaded into the truck carrying them to town.

The people of Sort were nominally Christian, but those of Farol hardly that, since custom permitted no male member of the fishing community to attend Mass. When they stood in need of guidance, whether spiritual or mundane, both villages had recourse to the same clairvoyant, the Curandero of Ripoll. The Curandero settled disputes of all kinds, particularly in the case of the peasants, those arising from inheritances. He fixed the women up with birth-control devices made up from sponges and, if his arrival happened to coincide with the all-important tunny-fishing season, he accompanied the boats to sea, 'smelt out' the shoals of fish, and showed the fishermen where to cast their lines.

The view was gaining ground now in the cat village that if ever they were to eat onions, cucumber and vegetable marrows again, a conciliatory arrangement would have to be reached with Sort, and it occurred to them that since the Curandero was so successful in healing breaches between families he might prove equally valuable as a mediator between the two communities.

A slight problem existed in that, although this man was spoken of as the Curandero of Ripoll, no one had ever been allowed to know his real name, much less any address where he might be reached – if he possessed such a thing. The tunny-fishing season was now about to begin, and it was believed that he might already have installed himself in one of the coastal villages, so the people of Farol clubbed together to provide funds for one of the men to go in search of him. A few days later he was back with the message that the Curandero was on his way.

The fact that I should have been entrusted with confidential information passed on by Sebastian was an encouraging sign of my steadily improving status in the village. It remained a drawback to be a foreigner, but with every week as my face became more familiar, it was less of one. I had to appear to share local prejudices. 'Take your hat off when you pass the church,' Sebastian said, 'but don't go inside. Stay away from the bar when the police are there. Don't try to buy a fisherman a drink. Wait until they ask you to have one.' There were so many social pitfalls, so many ways to be avoided of doing the wrong thing. Working cautiously, tentatively, towards what I hoped might some day be full acceptance by the community, I never made a move without taking Sebastian's or the Grandmother's advice.

The Curandero arrived on what was known here as the Feast of the

August Virgin, and elsewhere as the Feast of the Assumption, when peasants in interior villages and hamlets knocked off work for once, put on their stiff holiday clothing, made up picnics and came down to spend a few hours on the beach. A lonely shore became for a day an animated one, with children doing what they could to dig castles in the coarse unsuitable sand, their parents paddling a little uncertainly in a few inches of water, hoping thus to absorb benefits supposed to be conferred by the minerals it contained, and picknickers doing their best to enjoy themselves although continually molested by scrounging cats.

In this lively scene comings and goings that would have drawn attention at other times passed unnoticed. When the Curandero arrived by rowing boat a small party of fishermen waited to welcome him. Every man wore a hat, although some hats had been borrowed for the occasion. As the Curandero stepped down from the boat all the hats came off. The Curandero smiled and nodded. He had a round, boyish face with pink cheeks and blue eyes. He wore a holiday-maker's imitation suede jacket, a hair-net intended to conceal the scars in his scalp, and pads clasped like a telephonist's headphones over his ears. A year or two before a priest of Llobregat had denounced him for smuggling condoms in from France, and was said actually to have assisted in the terrible beating given him by the police who had broken both his eardrums and caused permanent damage to his kidneys.

A strip of matting had been laid down across the sand leading from the boat to a roughly made shelter put up in an hour or so from bamboo poles and palm thatching. Here the Curandero met the various families who had claimed the privilege of putting him up in their houses. He was given a glass of the local vinegary wine with a gold half-sovereign in its bottom. This he held in his mouth for a moment before transferring it to his pocket. A chair and table were carried in and he was invited to sit down to a meal of saffron rice, while the principal males stood smiling self-consciously in the background, hats in hand. Children were brought to be patted on the head, but the women kept out of the way.

After the reception the Curandero was led hobbling away to the first house where he would lodge. Little more was seen of him from that moment, as he felt obliged to keep out of sight of the police, who would have asked for nothing better than an excuse to give him a second beating. The fishermen explained the difficulties that had arisen in their relations with Sort, and the Curandero said he would do all he could to settle the matter in an amicable way. The three days he spent in Farol were devoted to dispensing herbal medicines, casting horoscopes – which the fishermen could not have enough of – but above all providing counsel on all matters relating to marital relations and family planning. In this way his authority superseded that of the Grandmother's who was forced to take a back seat for the duration of his visit.

In many areas of Mediterranean poverty – a poverty I had become familiar with – large families are the thing, and it is a proud, although almost everyday accomplishment for a woman to have borne ten children by the time she is thirty-five. The economic facts are that children in a city offering endless opportunities for low-grade, low-paid employment, are an insurance against economic disaster, and from the age of eight upwards many of them work to contribute small sums to the family budget.

In an impoverished fishing village the sea is the only employer and the resources it provides are strictly finite. A family of fifteen children in Naples may be something to boast about. In Farol where many families remained voluntarily childless, one-child families were common, and any number of children in excess of two was rare and to be deplored. The cat people kept their families down by postponing marriages until the late twenties, by sexual abstinence – many couples infrequently occupied the same bed – and by the devices furnished by the Curandero. Every time he arrived he took time off to go on a hunt for the small, densely-textured local variety of sponge to be hooked out of fairly shallow water, thereafter cleaning, and shaping, and offering each specimen with a supply of prophylactic ointment made up from lard impregnated with crushed hemlock.

The sponges were collected, prepared and delivered within a couple of days but before turning his attention to settling the dispute with Sort there was another small diplomatic mission for the Curandero to attend to.

Farol had just been deprived of the presence and valuable services of Sa Cordovesa, whom I had so often seen seated by her door, eyes cast down, as demure and composed as a Madonna over her sewing. She had been snapped up by an admiral, whose name, as he said, meant stag and who was on a visit to the area while undertaking a coastal survey. The admiral spent a single night at the fonda, spotted Sa Cordovesa in the morning, proposed marriage by the early afternoon, and carried her off on the evening bus.

By the happiest of chances another beautiful girl had come to live in the village shortly before Sa Cordovesa's loss, and the fishermen asked the Curandero whether she should be encouraged to stay. This young lady was known as Maria Cabritas because she had herded goats in Sort where she had been bred and born. Maria was a beauty of film-star quality with the fairest of blond hair framing her face in tender ringlets, and enormous innocent eyes. She had come by a French fashion magazine from which she copied the dresses worn as she trailed through the bushes and brambles after her goats. In Sort she had been brought before the Alcalde charged with immorality – an imprisonable offence – and the Alcalde, who had a soft spot for her, instead of handing her over to the police, had told her and her mother to go and live somewhere else. So they had moved in to Farol and been allowed to set up temporary home in one of the ruined houses belonging to the departed cork families Sebastian had been engaged in renovating for the past few years.

The fishermen wanted the Curandero's advice on the advisability of encouraging Maria Cabritas and her mother to take up residence on a permanent basis. At the back of their minds they clearly hoped that Maria might be persuaded to take over Sa Cordovesa's role, but Sebastian reported that they were a little troubled over the extreme fairness of her hair and complexion – a rarity indeed in this part of the world, and taken by some to indicate the possession of the evil eye. The Curandero saw the girl, cast her horoscope and returned with an enthusiastic report. Thus the matter was settled and when Maria, dressed in the latest Paris style and clutching her French magazine, took her goats to pasture along the cliff tracks overlooking the village, she was usually followed at a discreet distance by one or more admirers, although so far no one had received the slightest encouragement that would have inspired an aspirant even to address a hopeful word to her.

Having dispensed with the routine domestic problems of the cat village, the Curandero went to Sort where, as ever, a number of disputes awaited his arbitration. On the whole the richer the families the more bitter and prolonged were their quarrels, particularly when there were a number of children to squabble over inheritance. These feuds could be carried to absurd lengths, and the Curandero reported back to Farol an instance where a large farmhouse of the traditional kind had been divided up in such a way that one son was able to cut off access to the stairs, compelling the co-heirs, his brothers and sisters, to reach their bedrooms by ladders.

The mortality of a year had left a number of inheritances to be settled. In each case the estate (after ceaseless bickering and recrimination) had been divided up into theoretically equal parts, and the Curandero sat under a tree, with the dogs straining at their logs to get at him, and held the straws to be drawn, after which each heir would be entitled to choose his or her part in order of the length of the straw. Nothing on the face of it could have been fairer or more democratic, but manoeuvring behind the scenes often made a farce of the procedure. Returning this year the Curandero faced the grievances of a small queue of heirs complaining that some way had been found to diddle them out of their fair share of the inheritance. Congratulating the cat people later on their delivery from the scourge of property, the Curandero mentioned that, on his observation, the brothers in any family always seemed to end up with the lion's share of whatever had been left, and that however much land the sisters finally came by, it was usually found to be deficient in some way, or without access to water.

The problem with the most pressing priority for the dog people was that of the cork oaks. In their most recent effort to arrest the course of whatever disease or malefic influence it was that looked like wiping out the forest, they had arranged for a full-scale open-air religious service of exorcism and intercession to be conducted by their own priest with the support of the priests of three other parishes, and everything in the way of such accessories as holy images and banners they could provide. A procession had been formed, led by the priests and escorted by acolytes chanting and swinging censers. It was considered dishonourable here, as in other parts of Spain,* to assist in carrying the banners in a religious procession, which could lead to broken-off engagements and, in the case of married men, suspicion of cuckoldry. In this case old men immune from such threats had to be employed, and two collapsed under the strain of carrying the standards up the mountainside, one of them suffering a heart attack.

*Anda, que no te quiero,
Porque llevaste
El dia de San Marcos
El estandarte.
Go away, I don't love you,
Because on San Marcos' Day, you carried the standard.
(Traditional song from La Solana in La Mancha)

This episode provoked much derision among the atheists of Farol, and the Curandero seemed shocked when told of it. He pretended at first to lose all interest in the affair, telling the villagers that he did not wish to meddle, and recommending them to wait and see if the Church provided a miracle. In the end he was mollified and agreed to do what he could. Due to his old injuries he could only walk with difficulty and had to be carried in a chair to the place called the Shrine of Saint Agata on the fringe of the cork forest. He made it clear that he could not hold out much hope of saving the trees, but assured the villagers that he would at least tell them plainly one way or another what fate had in store for them.

St Agata's shrine was the scene of a dismal fiesta of the local kind held by the dog people on the third of May every year. The shrine was a small stone ruin in a field wired off to keep out the goats, and all that happened for the fiesta was that the villagers went up to it, traipsed round the field twelve times – the men going in one direction, and the women the other – and then ate the sandwiches they had brought and went home. The Curandero's party passed the first of the trees before reaching the shrine, and here he asked to be put down. He limped round the tree, sniffed at the trunk, broke off a twig and examined it, and crushed a prematurely withered leaf between thumb and forefinger. His manner was silent and abstracted, and the general feeling was that he was still put out over the business of the procession. When they arrived at the shrine the villagers had been hoping for some sort of performance from him. They would have felt reassured to see him froth at the mouth or fall into a trance and prophesy a satisfactory outcome of the dilemma, and if he'd poured out the sherry they'd brought along on the ground, by way of a libation, it would have been better than nothing. All the Curandero did was to poke his head inside the ruin while the little crowd of villagers stood by, twisting their hands. After that, he said, 'The spirit's gone. Let's get back,' and that was the end of the matter.

This left the villagers in too depressed a frame of mind to object when the Curandero told them that as they might need all the help they could get from the people of Farol in the bleak years that lay ahead, they had better make their peace with them while they could. The outcome was that the dog people called off their ban on the fishermen's use of the short-cut through their village lands, and in return the cat people invited their neighbours to take part in the annual fiesta of Farol, held in September. This, too, was an exceedingly dull affair, involving a seemingly meaningless ritual in which both villagers and strangers alike linked arms to prance three or four times up and down the village street – an exercise followed by the inevitable consumption of stale sandwiches.

These matters now disposed of, the Curandero was free to apply his gifts to the more important procedures of preparation for the great annual tunny fishing upon which the meagre fortunes and dubious prosperity of Farol so much depended.

It turned out that the tunny fishing was likely to be held up until some days later than had been hoped. The Curandero observed the direction and change in the winds, was taken in a boat to test the temperature of the currents, worked out an astrological chart, consulted the tarot cards, and announced in the end that it would be another week before the shoals reached that part of the sea.

The delay caused some alarm. We were reaching the end of August and nobody could remember a year when the tunny had failed to arrive by the beginning of the month. For five years in succession Farol had experienced the renewed calamity of the non-appearance of the spring sardine shoals, and the depressing viewpoint was gaining ground that these would never be seen again. It was remembered that fate seemed even to have gone out of its way to prevent the village from deriving benefit from the last sardine harvest. The fishermen assured themselves that nothing would go right when a fox was sighted in the village shortly before the event. This was the most dreaded of all omens. What happened was that the sardines showed up in their millions on Good Friday – a day when the government decreed that activity of any kind came to an absolute standstill. On this day Sebastian said that anyone could have walked down to the water's edge, carrying a pail, dipped it into the water and lifted it out full of fish. By Saturday the shoals were thinning and heading away, and a mediocre catch had to be taken by sea to Palamos, where with a chance of the fish going stale it had to be auctioned off on the Monday at less than a quarter the expected price.

In the lean years that followed, life in Farol, under its brisk and well-scrubbed aspect, became a matter of planned survival. Even when there were fish to be caught the fishermen began to suffer more and more from natural wear and tear to their gear. The boats had been laid up to deteriorate during the war, since when it had been impossible to buy tackle. Nets were wearing out, and most of the boats spent several weeks in every season out of the water under repair. The fishermen were hardly better off now than their counterparts would have been in the Middle Ages, because the engines fitted to the large boats had suffered a process of cannibalisation over the last eight years until valves and pistons and crankshafts were at an end, and only one boat remained with an engine that still ran in a spasmodic and fitful fashion.

Now the unspoken thought in most minds was, what was to happen to them all if the tunny stayed away? There was no cash left, and the fishermen had been living on credit for six months. The shopkeepers, the Alcalde who kept the supply of wine going, and the men who sold hooks, line, caulking material, varnish, carbide for the acetylene lamps, oil and petrol, were all heavily in debt to their own suppliers and faced ruin if the fishermen were compelled to default. This was a village under the threat of death.

While Farol waited, the Curandero covered his charts with diagrams of the stars in their courses, with cubic sections, parabolas and mystic rays, and the fishermen fussed about putting finishing touches to their preparations. I carried on my patient campaign for full acceptance into the fishing community, making myself useful in small and unobtrusive ways, always ready to help haul a boat up on the beach or bail out one that was leaking. Such assistance was taken for granted – no one was ever thanked in Farol for anything – but I now found myself sometimes invited to join a group drinking in the bar. My Spanish was fairly fluent and my neighbour Juan helped me with Catalan, produced a vocabulary of fishing terms, and listed some sixty kinds of fish by name. The problem here was that the Spanish name for almost everything was quite different from its name in the Catalan dialect in local use, which in itself differed from Catalan as spoken in the city.

Juan fished with the palangre, the local version of the paternoster line. It had been a great social break-through when he had invited me one evening in the most casual fashion to join him, and thereafter I helped him wherever I could – an exercise which inevitably cost a night's sleep. Alsono de Barros' *Familiar Sayings and Moral Proverbs* – bible of these remote villages offering practical as well as moral counsel on every human predicament from nymphomania to foot-rot in sheep – makes pessimistic reference in three separate instances to line-fishing as opposed to the use of nets. '*The man who fishes with the hook eats more than he catches*,' says Barros; it is an opinion still shared by most fishermen throughout the Mediterranean. However net-fishing on the whole requires corporate effort, whereas line fishing is suited to reflective and solitary temperaments, of the kind Juan possessed.

His boat carried sixteen lines, most meticulously coiled in shallow baskets, each line having between thirty-nine and forty-seven hooks, totalling nearly a thousand hooks. Preparations were endless. When there were fresh sardines to be had these were the best bait, but these days sardines were caught once in a blue moon. In their absence hermit crabs were the best substitute, but a preliminary operation had to be mounted to catch them, and they were only to be fished in sufficient numbers a mile out to sea. A small, specialised type of lobster pot used for the hermit crabs was put down in great numbers the night before going out with the palangres. Baiting up the hooks took us from 2 a.m. to 4 a.m., after which we went out and put down the sixteen lines, which would be taken up three or four hours later. On our first trip out with the palangres Juan caught forty-two fish and sold them for 60 pesetas. I took nothing from him for which I knew he was grateful, although it would have been bad form to say so. He was pleased to have me with him because I kept fairly quiet, and he mentioned that most of the fishermen were forever spouting poetry, which got on his nerves. Some brief allusion was made to the cork trees, and he told me that he and Francesca had given up any hope of further income from Sort, and from that time on he expected to be as poor as any other fisherman.

Juan introduced me after this to a senior fisherman called Simon, who had been selected to 'dominate' one of the boats once the tunny fishing started. Simon had been involved as a boy in the terrific catastrophe of the freak storm of 11 January 1922 which had suddenly blown up out of a clear and calm sky to drown hundreds of fishermen all along the Spanish coast. He had been one of three survivors of twelve men of Farol caught at sea when the storm overtook them. He had been blown half way to Italy and picked up, semi-conscious and unable to give any account of himself, by an Italian ship on its way to South America, from which he had returned as if from the dead two months later. Since then he had been regarded as saturated with what the Arabs called *baraka* – communicable good luck, and was hardly ever seen unaccompanied by two or three companions who kept as close to him as they could in the hope of benefiting from some auspicious current flowing from his body.

Simon, a wasted but still commanding presence, questioned me about my habits and beliefs, warned me of the disciplines imposed on tunny fishers, including the usual embargo on sexual relations on the preceding night, and the obligation to maintain a Trappist-like silence until the moment when the actual fishing began. With Juan's sponsorship I was able to pass the test and Simon said that he would speak to the other 'part-holders' in the boat, and see if they would agree to taking me along.

'Make sure you don't wear a leather belt in the boat,' Juan had warned me, adding the story that in his father's lifetime a man in a tunny boat who was found to have secreted a leather wallet, supposedly containing a charm, had been thrown into the sea, and drowned.

Storms were a matter of weekly occurrence during the winter months, many of them comparable in vigour to those battering the Atlantic coasts of northern Europe at that season. In summer they were short-lived, freakish and rare, but one blew up, taking Farol by surprise, during this period of apprehensive waiting during the last days of August.

It also caught a number of fish off their guard. Large and highly esteemed species such as the Mediterranean sea bass feed close to the rocks in heavy seas, favoured by the reduced visibility in their raids on small fish. Like incautious drivers in a fog they are subject to accident, and often stun or kill themselves by high-speed collision with the rocks. In winter such casualties add to the gleanings of the sea provided by fish stranded in rock pools, helping the fishing community to eke out an existence at a time when the weather puts a stop to normal operations. Sudden deaths among fish from such causes are infrequent in summer, although they happen once in a while. As soon as this particular storm blew itself out Sebastian and I went out in his boat on a routine spear-fishing trip, and visiting a sheltered inlet among the rocks we found a magnificent dentol lying dead on the bottom in shallow water.

The dentol, a form of sea bream, is a fish of exceptional and striking beauty, large and solitary and weighing up to 25 pounds, daubed on its back just below the head with a glowing iridescent purple patch – a lustre that begins to fade as soon as it is caught, and becomes invisible by the time it reaches the slab. Seeing this fish drifting so very slowly, as it always does through the soft, powdery haze of deep water, it is hard to believe that it does not actively radiate light, rather than reflect it. Dentols were never taken in the nets and there was only one young fisherman in Farol who had inherited the almost mysterious skill of catching them by line. The fish we had come upon was a relatively small one of its kind, weighing some seven or eight pounds, but for us it was a great prize, and I recovered it with a shallow easy dive, and a harpoon shot into the spine at a range of two or three inches.

Sebastian passed his share over to the Grandmother, with whom he was beginning to build up a substantial credit, but as I had speared enough spiny little rock fish to cover my rent for that day, my half went to Carmela. She accepted this sizeable piece of fish with perhaps the slightest relaxation of her expression of stony indifference, and quite amazingly managed as usual before going off to stow it away out of sight somewhere about her person. Gratitude must have stirred somewhere under the layers of acrimony and suspicion, for next day she turned up with a small turtle, as she claimed it to be, although I was never altogether sure that it was not a tortoise, which she insisted that she would cook for my lunch. The stipulation was that I should absent myself while the culinary preparations went ahead, so I strolled as far as the bar, sat under the stuffed mermaid for a *palo*, waited for a half-hour, then returned. 'If you'd have seen it before it was ready your mind would have been prejudiced,' she said. 'All meat is good, but sometimes you must forget where it comes from. When we were hungry in Alicante we ate dog when we could. The idea was a bad one, but it was better than rabbit. Oh yes, much better. You will eat this and enjoy it.' I did.

Slowly the true facts about Carmela had come out. First of all I learned that she was under some sort of loose police supervision, and that she was frequently harassed by being awakened in the middle of the night for a search of the shack she lived in, or to be called in for questioning. We finished what was left of the dish, the delicate medallions of white meat flavoured with garlic and marjoram that could have been fillet of pork, while she explained how all this had come about.

The story was that at the beginning of the Civil War she had been on a visit to the island of Ibiza, at that time still in Government hands. One Sunday afternoon while parading in conformity with local custom along the seafront, the crowd of which she was a member had come under attack by Italian planes supporting the Nationalist rebels. Everybody thought, she said, that the planes were on their own side, and she and her friends and many others had stopped to wave and cheer. At the end of the front the planes banked, turned and came in low for their bombing run. The result was devastation, and Carmela had been blown through a café window accompanied by the headless corpse of a friend. She had escaped with minor damage.

Next day a number of Fascist sympathisers already held in prison were put up against the wall and shot. Anybody who felt like watching this spectacle was invited to do so, and Carmela had gone along. She described the episode in her usual matter-of-fact way, noting that the firing squad took aim at the eyes of the men they executed. Somehow Carmela's presence had been remembered, and ever since the Nationalists had taken over, she had been under constant suspicion.

5

On the first of September the Curandero told the fishermen that all his prognostications were complete and that they should be prepared with their bait for the fishing that would begin next day. Tunny was fished with a species of sand-eel called sonsos as live bait. It was believed in Farol that sonsos existed only in the coarse shell-impregnated sand to be found in the immediate neighbourhood of the village, and it was a theory that their presence even in the far past had been the sole reason for establishing the village where it was. As usual Farol depended on the expertise of a single family to provide this vital resource. There were said to be only two other fishermen in the province who knew how to catch sonsos and they were forced to travel long distances to Farol when sonsos were in local demand.

The bait fishing involved its own ritual which was quite inexplicable even to the fishermen who practised it. Several boats, operating under the instructions of the specialist, swept the sea-bed with shallow nets, and while this was going on custom insisted that the fishermen keep up a tremendous outcry, as one man after another would boast of his capabilities in the fields of fishing and lovemaking and the others would respond with a chorus of mockery and oaths.

I was not allowed in a boat, but permitted to stand at the water's edge and watch while this happened. It was a morning of flat calm with the sea a little misted, like glass that had been breathed upon, the boats' keels slicing the water cleanly and a dribble of fire twisting in their wake. The fishermen's shouts of pretended rage and scorn came ringing across the tympanum of the surface, the filthiness of ritual oaths cleansed in the extreme purity of the surroundings.

By an unlucky chance a Spanish family of holiday-makers, wretchedly lodged and fed at the fonda, had chosen on this day to hire a boat for an outing. They had blundered into this scene, actually fouling one of the nets. They were driven away with the most terrible imprecations – although next day the fishermen made amends by sending a present of fish to the fonda.

That night all the men took baths, scrubbing themselves most carefully with abrasive green soap. Most of them went straight to bed after this, to keep themselves intact from injurious influences.

In the morning we were at the water's edge, very quiet, all communication reduced to gestures. Simon was already in the bows of the boat he dominated and Juan and I climbed in in silence. There were five of us and I took one of the oars. It was an 'old sea', a slow heave of water following a distant storm that had blown itself out, and a curl of low cloud on the horizon which was thinning out presented no threat. The men were tight-lipped, with thin, forced smiles, like prisoners awaiting sentence, and I noticed that one was trembling. We dipped our oars in the water with great care to avoid splashing, as the tunny were credited with an acute sense of hearing. As the fishermen put it, one crept up on them. Should we find the tunny shoal, our problem would be the shortage of tackle. There was a scarcity of everything, of line, even of hooks. If a line gave way a valuable and irreplaceable tunny-hook went with the fish. Juan was down to his last three hooks.

The boat with the Curandero led the small fleet of seven. The Curandero wore his hair-net, his earpads and his wellingtons, but out of deference to the fishermen's suspicion of something meant to resemble leather, he had left his imitation suede jacket behind. I was told later by one of the men in his boat that he had kept his eyes closed and guided the boats towards the tunny by smelling them out. He claimed not to be able to smell the fish once they were in the boat.

The mysterious intuitions of nature seemed attuned to what was to happen. Grey mullet, scavengers among sewage in shallow water, were slithering just under the surface in pursuit of the boats, and great squawking gulls – hardly ever seen along this coast – had dropped out of the sky to flap about just over our heads. Back on the beach which, by custom, should have been deserted at this moment, a solitary horseman had appeared, identifiable as a *guardia civil*. His small, sombre profile provoked uneasiness. A mounted policeman could only be an officer, and what could a man of such rank and power want with a wholly unimportant fishing village such as Farol?

The Curandero raised his hand and we stopped rowing. There was nothing to be seen in the water other than circling mullet but the Curandero blew his conch-shell, a sullen and melancholic hoot as a signal for the fishing to start. There were three inches of sand in the bottom of each boat, and over it three inches of water. The sonsos, carried in canvas bags to the boats, had been tipped into the water, and the lively ones, the '*vivos*' – those to be used for baiting the hooks – had instantly burrowed into the sand, from which their tiny watchful heads projected. Those sonsos lacking the energy to burrow into the sand continued to swim about in a lethargic fashion, and my friends scooped up handfuls of these to throw them as hard as they could in all directions into the sea. We listened in the silence to the spatter of the bait hitting the water, then the fishermen baited their hooks with lively sonsos, hooking them through the lower part of the body, and threw out their lines.

The fish struck instantly, setting off a great outcry in the boat. It was impossible to hold the lines until the tunny's first efforts to escape and survive had begun to slacken, and the seventy-five gauge nylon line wound on cork bobbins that lay free by the gunwales went out in great whipping snatches, thirty feet at a time and in a fraction of a second, with the corks bouncing and spinning in the air. The tunny were the fastest fish in the sea, believed in their first dash for freedom when they felt the hook to reach a hundred kilometres an hour, and the fishermen made no attempt to hold them until they reached the bottom of one of their tremendous dives. We had thrown out three lines and three fish had struck. The fish hit bottom, and the men took the lines and hung on with agony in their faces as the line cut into their hands, opening old sores, and the blood began to flow.

Almost in the same moment all the other boats had hooked fish, and a great confusion began, because some small boats were being towed in all directions, even gyrating like leaves in a whirlpool, and the proper sickle-shaped tunny fishing formation had broken up. To this disorder was added the fouling and crossing of lines and the extravagant underwater knots tied in them as the tunny twisted and turned, shot under the boats and encircled them as they came closer to the surface with the loss of their first ebullient energy. Now they came into sight; great gliding metallic shapes, appearing strangely inanimate although still possessed of great reserves of power.

In our boat, a kind of demented ballet was being performed, with Simon the dominator who should have restored order distracted by his struggle with a monstrous fish. The most skilled and important task of all was to pull out the boat's drain plug at regular intervals to allow fresh water to flow over and revive the sonsos, after which the man who performed this urgent duty would replace the plug and bail out. But the man who should have done this, Pablo, had a fish on his line and could not bring it in. Pablo was the man who had been trembling, and now he was close to tears. I hauled in the line with him, and my hands, too, were bleeding. 'There's too much at stake,' he said. 'If I catch fish I get married, and if I don't, that's it.' I took the line from him while he went to deal with the sonsos. There were three of us hauling side by side, with the boat listing over, and you could see the fish held quite still about thirty yards away, their silver slaked in the blue. We were flying kites together in the deep sky with our hands full of blood.

The fish gave up unexpectedly, like toys with motors that had suddenly run down. I pulled Pablo's fish straight into the boat's side and Simon gaffed it through the tough skin over the backbone, bringing it up with a jerk and a lift into the gunwale, spattering us all over with its black-red gore, balancing it for a moment before letting it crash down into the bottom of the boat. Here it lay, an unconvincing manufactured object in cheap-looking tin-plate with the brassiness showing through, and straight grooved lines fanning out from the corner of the jaw where the hook had held across eyeball and cheek. A failing mechanical aftermath opened and closed its mouth, very slowly three or four times, after which it moved no more.

Tunny were coming in now one after another and because the fresh water and bailing procedures had gone by the board, the sonsos could hardly be seen for blood, but there was nothing at this late stage to be done, for said the fishermen, to have bailed out this water saturated with blood would have frightened the fish away. The men went on fishing with whatever bait they could find. Confusion and fury worsened, an oar was broken, a precious, hopelessly tangled line had to be cut, one of Simon's fingers was half-severed, and another man had cracked a rib.

Suddenly the shoal had thinned, the shouting died down, until we could hear the echoless babel over the water from the other boats, and this, too, died away. The Curandero blew on his conch shell again signalling that the fishing was at an end. It was unwise, unlucky to push on with the fishing until the very last fish had been induced to take the hook. The fish had to be 'left with hope'. All the remaining sonsos, plus a bagful of bogas brought along for that purpose, were tipped into the sea by way of a token recompense, and the boats turned back, leaving a lace-cap of seagulls settled on the water to mark the place where the fishing had taken place. It had been a good fishing, leaving the men physically drained and a little emotional in their relief, and one or two of them were wiping their eyes with the bloody cloths used to clean their hooks before rebaiting them.

Back on the beach the solitary horseman had ridden away, carrying with him the menace of his presence, and now it was in order for the villagers, to whom the Curandero had signalled with another blast of his conch-shell that fish had been caught, to congregate at the water's edge. Our boat was so laden down with the catch that Simon could never have brought it in to shore in heavy seas. We had thirty-two fish of which Juan had caught nine weighing between thirty and fifty pounds apiece – his record catch. The fish had now to be sold with the minimum of delay. It was a commercial transaction too big for the Grandmother to handle, and a buyer from France with tinted spectacles and a tartan shirt was waiting. His discouraging news was that tunny fishing had been going on all along the coast for the past two days, threatening the market with a glut. At the beginning of the week one of Juan's fifty pound fish would have fetched 500 pesetas at the canning factory. Now the price was down to 150 pesetas and likely to fall further. The man's lorry was parked at the junction of the short cut and the main road, and the fishermen wheeled their fish on barrows and hand-carts to where it awaited them. The buyer and his assistant weighed the fish, then the buyer took out an enormous bundle of thousand-peseta notes and paid them off. The amount received by every man was enough to settle his accumulated debts. With whatever was left over family men, as they always did, would buy new clothes of the best quality to be found for their wives and children. From this point on they started again financially from scratch and the shops and the man who supplied their tackle would re-open their credit accounts.

They were a race of optimists, and suddenly every man of the cat village was sure that the sardines would be back once more in the coming spring.

6

The police captain, who had been watching the tunny fishing from the beach, was on an annual tour of inspection of the area of his command and he pranced up and down on a beautiful horse with arched neck, flowing mane and incredibly fine limbs. He wore a patent leather hat from the early part of the last century and under it his face was classic, but slightly unearthly – that of a centaur. There were starred reflections everywhere on his splendid harness, his polished boots and his silver stars as he pranced about, and the morning after the great tunny fishing trip, there was a sharp, authoritarian rapping on my door, and he was there.

He came in, took off his kid gloves, sat down on an uncomfortable chair of local manufacture, reached for my passport and began to copy down its details in a strong but careful hand into his gold-tooled, black leather book. He spoke hard but mellifluous Castillian, with strong emphasis, as a man of education, on the subjunctive. If a classic statue could have spoken it would have been with the marbled resonance of this voice. What was I doing here? he asked, and I told him I was on holiday.

In a place like this? He looked through the window at the vacant beach. The fishermen were sleeping off the exhaustion of the previous day and had pulled the boats out of the water and gone off without bothering to clean up the mess. A number of cats like mangy little grey tigers were doing what they could to remedy this.

'It's quiet,' I told him, 'and that suits me.'

'Why do you like it quiet?'

'I've had enough of crowds. There aren't any distractions.'

'No,' said the captain, 'there are no distractions. Nobody comes to a place like this unless they have to. I certainly would not. The sea has no appeal for me. You must not think that Spain is like this.'

'I don't.'

'I can tell you of better places to spend your holidays. Places where there is some life. These people are not even real Spaniards. How long do you intend to stay?'

'As long as I can.'

The police captain picked up his gloves and put them on, stretching them carefully over his fingers. 'I saw you out in one of the boats yesterday. They are not allowed to carry anyone who is not a member of the registered crew.'

'I'm sorry. I didn't know.'

'Your visa has a month to run. To be able to stay here you must comply with the laws. When it expires you must leave the country. If you want to come back I would choose some other place.'

The Alcalde of Sort had put an empty house at the captain's disposal and given him a servant to look after him, and later in the day this woman appeared in Farol trying to buy fish for his supper. She was told that no boats had gone out, which was true, but her story when she got back to Sort was that she had met with a point-blank refusal. The captain, it was heard at Farol, had been furious.

It turned out that this man was very religious. Very little was said in private in either village that did not soon become a matter for public gossip, and it appeared that the old woman who looked after our priest had been hanging about in the background when the captain called on him, and made a careful record of their conversation, which she reported to Carmela, who passed it on to me.

The question was raised as to the church-going habits of the villagers. The priest said, 'They're not very devout in this part of the world. At least not openly.'

'But surely you have some sort of congregation?'

'The Alcalde, the shopkeeper and his wife come most Sundays, the town clerk puts in an appearance once in a while.'

'And that's all?'

'As a general rule. People who go to confession, for example, are distrusted by their neighbours who believe that they must have committed crimes that need to be confessed.'

'Don't they realise that we are all born in sin?'

'Nothing will make them accept it. I used to preach "all we like sheep have gone astray," and they'd walk straight out of the church. The fishing population is subject to a kind of taboo. They mean no harm, but it's impermissible to make any reference to religious matters except in a blasphemous way.'

The Captain shook his head in wonderment. 'What do you put that down to?'

'Many of the people in these villages are really pagans. The Inquisition used to carry out expeditions up and down the coast as late as 200 years ago. It didn't do much good.'

'Do they worship anything?'

'Conceivably the sun, in an off-hand sort of way. It's the only thing I've ever heard a fisherman admit to having any real reverence for.'

'And this is a Christian country,' the Captain said.

'In the hinterland, perhaps,' Don Ignacio said. 'To some extent.'

The captain told the priest that he would have liked to enter the Church himself, and, according to the priest's housekeeper, seemed eager to discuss religious topics in general. The old woman told Carmela that she knew her master well enough to realise that few things bored him more, and that all he really wanted to talk about was archaeology, about which the captain knew or cared nothing.

The captain thoroughly approved of Sort, and one of the reasons he had chosen to stay there was the story published in the papers about the way the villagers had resisted the FAI. The anarchists had gone round collecting the wooden saints in the churches for burning, but the dog people had buried their saint and only dug it up again after the Nationalist victory. It was an episode for which the cat people expressed nothing but contempt.

With this prejudice in their favour the captain set out to make himself agreeable to his hosts, and certain official duties to be performed were carried out in a perfunctory way. On two occasions, one eleven and the other sixteen years previously, murders had been committed in which it was suspected in each case that wives had pushed their husbands down dry wells – 'the final solution', as such domestic killings were referred to in the local jocular way. These murders remained unsolved, and since in the interim one suspect wife had died and the other emigrated, the captain announced that he proposed to cease investigations and close the cases.

In Farol he showed himself less sympathetic; once again his enquiries were into a mysterious disappearance, this time of a local man who had suddenly dropped out of sight within days of the end of the war, just as advancing Nationalist troops were about to overrun the village. The young man in question lived alone in some state in a pretentious house built on the outskirts of the village. This had been abandoned for some years and had now fallen into ruin. He announced himself to be the illegitimate son of a ducal family, and let it be known that he had been provided with substantial funds and packed away out of sight under the threat of cutting off all support if he caused any trouble. The impression I got from the fishermen was that they believed him to be not quite right in the head, and that he had succeeded in making himself generally objectionable at a time when no one could afford to fall out with his neighbours. He drew attention to himself at a time when self-effacement would have been preferred; by aping grand manners he annoyed a people with no cause to have any affection for the rich.

The captain called on the Alcalde of Farol and gave him six months to find out what had happened to the man or lose his job. He made it clear that Farol was a place he thoroughly disliked. His last action was to go down to the fishermen's boats and check on their names, most of which he said struck him as detestable. He particularly disliked the pagan name *Afrodite*, and was puzzled about *La Dudosa* ('The Doubtful Girl' – doubtful about what?), *Una Grande Liebre* ('A Great Hare' – is this some joke?) and *Inteligencia* (faith is what we demand of Spaniards, not intelligence). The owners of these boats were summoned, ordered to paint out their names and rename them after the saints. The man who called his boat 'A Great Hare' was questioned for half an hour as to the possibility of concealed motives, but the captain could get nothing out of him, and concluded he was mad. The captain checked on the boats' registration numbers. Odd numbers were considered lucky, and even ones unlucky and to be avoided; thus registration numbers containing more than their fair share of threes and sevens were noted down in his book to be changed at the Comandancia de la Marina, so as to teach their present holders not to be superstitious.

Simon was asked to explain the significance of the wavy lines painted on the prow of his boat.

'They represent waves, in a formalised way.'

'In my opinion they contravene the regulations. Better get rid of them,' the captain said. He called over another fisherman. 'What purpose do you imagine those eyes on your boat serve?'

'We regard them as a sign against evil. Well, say a defence.'

'The evil eye, as you call it, doesn't exist,' the captain said. 'Evil is in men's hearts. Paint them out. While you're about it, there's no such saint as Santurce. Change the name to San Faustino.'

The police captain went finally prancing away on his fine horse to be seen no more that year, and Farol settled to relative calm. As soon as he was out of sight the Curandero emerged from Farol's equivalent of a priest's hole and a boat was ready to carry him off to his next port of call. I was told that the fisherman who had risked naming his boat 'A Great Hare' had had a most lucky escape, due purely to the captain's ignorance of the dangerous joke the name recalled. The Nationalist slogan had been *España – una, grande, libre* ('Spain united, great, free'), and the Republican prisoners held in camps at the end of the war and forced to chant this over and over again, sometimes for hours on end, had been accumstomed to inject sly derision into the procedure by changing the *libre* into *liebre*, so that the slogan came out 'Spain – a great hare'. In this part of the world the hare was considered the most disgusting of animals, with homosexual proclivities and prone to syphilis.

Following the captain's warning I applied for a fishing licence, kept out of the big, registered boats, but went fishing as before with Sebastian and Juan, as their boats did not come under the ban. I also made some progress with the difficult and demanding art of sea-fishing with rod and line, in this way occasionally catching a fish that fulfilled the high standards the Grandmother set.

My standing in the village continued to improve, until one day the Alcalde set aside a fine ruin of a chair outside his bar for my personal use, in this way denoting the conferment of native status. It had helped to follow the rules closely, and to make myself useful when I could, and not only to the fishermen, but unexpectedly to their wives and the shopkeepers in the matter of keeping accounts. Although Geoffrey of Ipswich may have introduced arithmetic into England after his thirteenth-century visit to Barcelona, few rural Catalans could now even add up, let alone multiply or divide. This meant that I was constantly in demand, particularly in the general shop, where a woman might have bought five or six articles – each likely to involve centavos as well as pesetas – and the shopkeeper went very slowly up and down his counter, scratching his ears and shaking his head disconsolately before addressing himself to the huge problem of totting up the account.

In the meanwhile I made investigatory sorties outside the limits of Farol. One was to visit a settlement of charcoal burners, who live their own mysterious and isolated lives in the cork forest. For the first time I began to understand the real nature, the drama, the calamity that had overtaken the oaks. We climbed into the foothills through a landscape once robust, now turned fragile and delicate. So many thousands of trees once almost solidly massed against the slopes, seemed now to be fading away, the once dense greens replaced by the smoky browns and the lavender-greys of death.

Sebastian and I found a group of charcoal burners squatting near a huge pile of turfs used to cover the wood with the fire smouldering beneath, their wine bottles close to hand. So great was the community's dependence upon them for its fuel that they could make their own rules in the matter of payment for their services. Any landowner who contracted charcoal burners was obliged to provide each man with two litres of wine and one and a half kilograms of bread a day. The charcoal burners, once their fire had been lit, had little more to do for twelve hours or so until the charcoal was ready, and for most of this time they stayed drunk. They glanced up at us a little nervously then looked away, a most mysterious people, mongoloid in appearance, with little hair on their bodies and speaking a language among themselves of which no one understood a word. The tree- owners' loss was their gain and great times were in store for them, as it was clear that from now on there would be little shortage of wood.

We paid visits to one or two of the bigger peasants in the Sort area, and I learned from them a little more about the peasant attitude to life. Unlike the much poorer fishermen who lived in hope of huge catches, if not next week, then the week after that, the peasants were imbued with pessimism, so deeply rooted – so cultivated, almost – that they insisted on going to fairs and buying china ornaments with cynical proverbs on them, and sticking them all round their houses to remind them of the unpleasant facts of their lives which, since there was no escaping them, they might as well learn to live with. At the back of this attitude may have been the fact that in cultivating the earth there were never windfalls to be hoped for. Bad weather could ruin a man, but good weather never more than slightly and predictably increased his income. The peasants, therefore, unlike the fishermen were addicted to gambling and games of chance. They were also subject to boredom that frequently degenerated into melancholia. Sebastian and I called on a man who had suddenly announced to his friends that he had had enough of life. He had done as well as a peasant of his standing could do, and was highly thought of and went short of nothing, but all he could say was 'life bores me'. He got up to shake hands with us, offered us a drink, then sat down, smiling a little vacantly. We asked a few polite questions and he answered them intelligently enough, but he had nothing to say to us. When we were outside Sebastian said, 'There are plenty like him. Soon he'll stop eating, and that will be the end.'

7

Most of the land surrounding the village was owned by a reactionary aristocrat known as Don Alberto. Don Alberto was a lover of all things of the past and to get into his house one had to go through an extraordinary farce. There was no bell or knocker on the door, and visitors were forced to stand there and call out in a loud voice '*ave Maria purisima*', this being an ancient custom of this part of the country observed by no one but Don Alberto. At this, a crone in black would shoot the bolts and open the door. This woman had been Don Alberto's beautiful mistress in the days of both their youth, when they had lived in Madrid and she had been presented at court and painted by a court painter.

We sat in an enormous sepulchral room on three chairs which were its only furniture and sipped Don Alberto's stale *rancio – palo* aged in the cask, and thicker, sicklier and more liverish than the young version of the wine. Don Alberto got on to his favourite subject – the glories of things gone by. He was a tall, incredibly thin man who creaked a little when he moved, bald-headed with a tuft of grey hair behind each ear, and strangely enthusiastic eyes. In indication of a life of leisure he normally went about in pyjamas having extreme broad stripes, like those of a Devil's Island convict, worn with a large and floppy beret. His English, learned from a Scotch nanny, was excellent and he read nothing but the Latin classics and obituary notices. Even the climate had radically changed, he said. He remembered a childhood refreshed with the soft rains of spring and autumn that rarely ceased to fall, and the scent of dampness, he said, was still in his nostrils. Now the tyranny of the sun was harsher than that of politicians. 'The loss of rainfall is the cause of half our troubles,' Don Alberto said. 'This country will never be the same again.'

Don Alberto was a Spaniard cast in the mould of Don Quixote, austere and romantic, full of fancies and living on air. The peasants, in their estimation of human character, never applied that nebulous word 'good' to a man. A big bodied, tough, successful peasant who set the standard was *concreto* – solid. Don Alberto they would have categorised as *noble*, if he had not been a bit of a figure of fun. Anyone

45

could get the better of him in financial matters, and this diminished him a little in their eyes. In local share-cropping arrangements, for example, the tenant expected to get a third of the produce, and the landlord two-thirds, but in Don Alberto's case the situation was reversed, not out of generosity on his part, but because it was beneath him to argue.

My first meeting with Don Alberto was at the house of the priest of Farol, Don Ignacio, who invited me because Don Alberto was an authority on local folk customs, in which he knew I was interested. Don Ignacio, too, was an educated man who spoke English very well and as resolutely as Don Alberto he had turned his back on the present. It was his habit to slip away whenever he could to an archaeological dig on a Roman site near Ampurias. When this happened he posted a notice on the church door to say that he was suffering from an attack of tonsillitis, and had gone to bed.

Don Ignacio's house was bare and claustrophobic as Don Alberto's, and he lived uncomfortably attended by an old woman virtually interchangeable in appearance from the one who looked after the old landowner, who fed him on gruel made from the disgusting-looking araña fish that none of the fishermen or their families would touch. This grey-haired, slatternly old creature was generally accepted – as in the case of Don Alberto's housekeeper – to have been his mistress, and in so far as the priest enjoyed any prestige it was based on this legend, or historic fact.

There were cats everywhere about Don Ignacio's house when I arrived, their eyes gleaming in the gloom. Some of them were staggering about the place, clearly drunk, for, in accordance with custom, although the priest gave them no food, he put down a saucerful of *rancio* for them at frequent intervals. To help them to endure their condition, as he said. 'It must be terrible to be without a soul.'

Inevitably the two men were on their favourite topic – the decadence of modern times. Don Alberto blamed the cinema which displayed the godlessness and luxury of the rich to the poor, and the widespread consumption of tomatoes – recently introduced into local agriculture – which reduced fertility and lowered the birthrate. He wondered if this were not part of a conspiracy to reduce families and ultimately destroy the influence of feudal landowners like himself by depriving them of their workforce.

Don Ignacio took a liberal standpoint in this argument, pointing out that he knew of twenty couples in Farol, who had been waiting years to get married and could not do so because they could not save up the 10,000 pesetas regarded as the minimum capital required to embark on marriage.

Don Alberto didn't see that money came into it. He remembered when people had been far worse off than now, when landowners had lessened their day labourers' appetites by baking earth with their bread. If he himself still had a pine-branch put in the dough it was because they had got used to the flavour. Marriages in the old days in villages like Farol were on the basis of total poverty. And what was wrong with that? Wasn't it obvious that the poor were purer in heart than the rich? Weren't Jesus and his disciples poor men?

The priest seemed embarrassed at the direction the argument was taking, but agreed that the rich these days were a pretty immoral lot. Black marketeers all of them, Don Alberto said, and the priest agreed. It had become a nation of black marketeers.

Don Ignacio appealed to Don Alberto for his advice as a specialist, as to what to do to liven up the Farol annual fiesta due to be held in some two weeks' time. Both men agreed that this was a thoroughly spiritless affair, and that if the people of Sort were to be invited to join in they ought to feel convinced that they were going to enjoy themselves.

Don Alberto's attempt to revamp the fiesta of Midsummer's Eve, the Verbena of San Juan, at Sort had not been an entire success. He had learned from his researches that as recently as fifty years before, the custom had been for the village boys to chase after the girls, slashing at their legs with bundles of lighted brushwood. Just as in the case of rites held elsewhere at the same time when youths and maidens trudged barefoot through glowing embers, it was a mysterious fact that no one was ever hurt. The revived festival in Sort was less remarkable in this way, because the magic failed to work, and a number of girls were slightly scorched. 'Something went wrong,' Don Alberto admitted. 'We've lost faith. We don't believe in ourselves the way we did.' Profoundly boring as both men found the Farol fiesta in its present form they were both convinced that there was no reason why it could not be turned into a success. They were full of ideas.

'Fireworks,' Don Alberto said. 'Now that's something to draw the crowds.'

'I'm sure you're right. If we can get hold of any, and get a permit in time,' Don Ignacio agreed.

'A procession with floats, fancy dress, with prizes to be won for the best costumes, a magic lantern show, free wine, dancing in the street.'

'A circus would be the thing. Clowns, a fat lady. A wall of death. Admission free for children. A small one's just opened up near Ampurias where I'm investigating a third-century villa. I could speak to them about it.'

'I wish you would,' Don Alberto said. 'They'll never have had a fiesta like it in this village before.'

When I mentioned these plans to Sebastian later in the day, he laughed. 'They're crazy, the pair of them. Just wait and see what happens when the time comes.'

8

Enquiries into the histories of the cat and dog villages revealed extraordinary facts. They were dramatically different in atmosphere and character from each other in every way, but they were also quite alien in their customs from the body of Spain that enclosed them, of which they seemed to know so little. The people of both villages were conscious of this separateness, but the only explanation they could offer was their long physical isolation at the end of a windy and precipitous dirt road that became often impassable in winter.

What seemed to have been kept from them was the fact that – as Don Alberto coolly admitted – this isolation was by no means accidental, and had been contrived by his own family in complicity with three great cork-owning families of the area, two of which had now disappeared, leaving as their memorial only three vast crumbling mansions on the outskirts of Farol.

All these dynastic fortunes had been founded at the beginning of the last century when seven cork-processing factories were supplied with fresh-cut cork coming from as far away as Portugal. The corks, poured out by the million, were exported to France – the best variety, from local trees, going to the champagne area. The invention of the metal bottle-top had brought this epoch, almost overnight, to an end.

Don Alberto, and on another occasion Don Ignacio, described the little feudal enclave that had been carved out here for the production of an amenable workforce protected from all disruptive influences. The atrocious road along which no bridges could be built across the mountain torrents kept out all but hardy and adventurous travellers. When the local authorities sent piles of road-building materials prior to beginning work the cork barons ordered them to be shovelled away, and when – only a few years before the outbreak of war – the peasants of Sort got together to widen a dangerous corner, dynamite was used to start a landslide and put an end to their efforts.

Don Alberto de Soto and his family before him owned nine-tenths of the worthwhile agricultural land and the cork barons owned the mountains, but Don Alberto said that mistakes had been made in the past in his father's and his grandfather's time by rewarding workers for especially meritorious service by selling them small plots of land, thus creating a kind of upthrusting and unreliable middle class, and the cork families had made the same mistake with what were seen as unprofitable trees. Otherwise the old feudal consortium, founded he insisted as much on ideological as economic factors, had held together well. People longed for firm leadership and limited horizons, he said, especially in a country with a chronic addiction to political discord. The little empire ruled over by the four families was paternalistic, if despotic. Don Alberto's great-great-grandfather, founder of his family's fortunes, might have put earth in his peons' bread, but at least there was plenty of bread, and no one ever starved to death on his estates as they did in considerable numbers elsewhere in Spain at that period. He handed out bonuses for large families, imported an ex-bandit from the Sierra de Gredos to keep order, and when one of the peons killed this man, arranged for him to be publicly garrotted, and the labourers were given a day off work to allow them to attend the ceremony.

The system immediately prior to the war had remained roughly as before. The Republic had spawned a number of political parties and aggroupments, all of them obnoxious to the rulers of Sort and Farol, but their agents and propagandists had been warned to keep their noses out, or to expect to have them bloodied. When the going rate for a peon was 6 pesetas a day, Don Alberto was still able to pay only 4 pesetas, but he was unusual among his breed of men in providing some minimal help in case of sickness or in old age. All that Don Alberto did he most sincerely believed was for the good of his people.

He was naturally pessimistic about the future. By dint of saving and scraping and picking up a duro (5 pesetas in the old money) here and a duro there the peons his great-great-grandfather had taken over in Sort had slowly scraped together enough capital to organise their own class system. At the top a few pear-shaped men, with long finger nails to prove they did no work, owned a hundred or so cork oaks and grew sweet peppers, cabbages and maize on a few hundred acres of land. At the bottom of this pyramid the village muleteer, self-employed and therefore working for half the minimum wage decreed by the state, had trained his mule to deposit its manure only at the door of the inn, for which he received a glass of wine twice a day.

The near-collapse of the cork industry which had forced the young men of the village of Sort to seek work elsewhere or to emigrate had helped to bring about what Don Alberto saw as a deplorable state of affairs.

All however was not lost, because about a year before my arrival the heir to the last surviving cork business in the area, an exceedingly energetic young man, had found an overseas market for first-quality cork, bought up for an old song a number of moribund cork enterprises, and was seen as well on his way to founding a new cork empire. Sentiment had impelled him to give orders for the old house at Sort to be put in order with the intention of using it as his headquarters whenever in the area. It was this project on which Sebastian and a number of builder's labourers had been engaged, and the work of restoration was on the point of completion. Puig de Mont, the new cork magnate, proposed to arrive for the ceremony of taking possession at the end of the month, and it was hoped that this would coincide with the fiesta on the twenty-third. Don Alberto's dream, his fondest hope was that this event would herald the rebirth of the industry, the re-opening in modernised form of the factories, the reclamation of so many promising lads from disordered and aimless lives and the restoration of at least some semblance of the decencies of the past.

Don Alberto mentioned his intention – although he did not wish it generally known – to import a band to welcome the saviour of the area in a fitting manner, and as he stepped down from the car that had brought him, the band would strike up *See the Conquering Hero Comes* – the Spanish and English versions of which are almost identical.

9

There were two *pescas grandes*, main catches, to be expected in the year. The first and most important of these, the spring catch of sardines, normally happened in March, immediately following which – if the catch proved satisfactory – a number of long-deferred marriages would take place. These were in church, in surroundings for which the fisherman bridegroom felt an intense superstitious aversion which led occasionally to extraordinary scenes. Filled up with brandy, reeling and staggering and supported on one side by his mother-in-law-to-be and on the other by his bride, he would be escorted to within sight of the church door, after which, with final shouts of encouragement, all the males of the party would turn round and go back, leaving only a few hard-bitten old women to carry on and enter the church.

Don Ignacio, highly sensitive to the embarrassment provoked by the occasion, kept the service short and sweet, and was sufficiently understanding not to insist on celebrating Mass before getting on with the ceremony, which the priest of Sort always did. This priest had been known to dismiss couples whose responses he found unsatisfactory, claiming in one case that the groom had muttered incantations and counter-charms under his breath. When Don Ignacio had finished with the couple, he got rid of them abruptly without offering to shake the groom's hand, and was quick to turn away so as not to see him spit ritually into the wind as they went. Normally the couple went back to the mother-in-law's house, where in many cases they would continue to live. Because of the windfall of pesetas brought by the sardines in March, most children were born in Farol under the sign of Sagittarius in December.

For several years the first *pesca grande* had not taken place, reducing the annual income of the village by about one third. The second *pesca grande*, that of the tunny, had been only moderately successful, leading to two marriages, and the final hope for an eventually prosperous year lay in the *pesca minor*, the 'small catch' provided by autumn sardine shoals that arrived with fair punctuality. The first shoals were reported on 16 September in the first quarter of the moon – a time when, although no one could explain why, few fish were ever taken.

Between them the men of the village sold fifty-one cases for 69 pesetas a case – an incredibly low price, as a case of sardines at this time of year were expected to fetch 250 pesetas. The fishermen suspected that they had been the victims of a market rigged by *gente comprada* – petty racketeers who bred like flies in this highly favourable environment. As a matter of passing interest, no one could be found in the village with enough arithmetic to work out fairly rapidly the total sum due to them for this transaction, and I had to be called in.

From that time on only small quantities of sardines were taken. I went out with Juan, and we fished all night and caught less than a case. There was no market for these small and sporadic catches of fish, most of which were eaten in the village, or exchanged for vegetables. The Farol method of cooking fresh sardines may have been unusual. They were salted and kept in a cool place for four days, and after that always grilled.

At this time the village of Sort made its wine. The grapes were always cut on 20 September, and I was invited by Don Alberto to take part in treading them next day. A room in one of the village houses containing an enormous tub was used for this purpose. The grapes were tipped into the tub to a depth of almost two feet, and – while the women were excluded in the street outside – the men marched in, took off their rope-soled alpargatas, rolled up their trousers and the treading began. There were no concessions even to basic hygiene. The splendid reddish-purple grapes claimed by Don Alberto to be of Roman origin were thick with dust when they went into the tub, and in many cases sprays of leaves were attached to the grape-stems, and there was an overpowering stench from the alpargatas strewn about the floor.

In the meanwhile two men wearing black and white patched shirts and armed with short batons pushed through the line of women in the street, and began to whack out at each other, uttering weird cries while a third man, similarly dressed, played a pipe. This was another of Don Alberto's folkloric revivals, which the villagers found absurd. Don Alberto said that his arthritis prevented him from joining in the treading, but he was in attendance, seated on his aged Levis two-stroke motorcycle and looking like a praying mantis. The Alcalde, an illiterate ex-goatherd with a row of pure gold teeth, was also there, and the priest of Sort, a saturnine and unshaven fanatic much disliked by his parishioners, prowled menacingly in the background. There were no representatives from Farol.

After we had traipsed round the tub for about a half-hour the trodden mass was shovelled out to be transferred to several large barrels in which it would stand to ferment for three days. Following that, the grape juice would be drained off and poured into a number of small barrels prepared by washing them out in hot wine. As soon as each barrel was filled to the top a mouse would be dropped in, held under the surface until drowned, and then removed. Finally, just as a bitter branch was added to the baker's dough, a small branch from the vine was added to each barrel, to impart a vinegary flavour. The original intention had been to make the wine less palatable to the peons who would drink it, but it was a device that no longer served its purpose as all local wine-drinkers including Don Alberto himself had acquired a taste for the flavour.

The wine would continue to ferment until 11 November, and on St Martin's day the barrels would be plugged. From that time on it was ready to drink. This year Don Alberto had planned a ritual wine-tasting, with pipes and drums by peasants wearing the old stocking-type caps, breeches and gaiters, and seamstresses had been put to work to produce these garments copied from a picture on an old soap calendar.

Following the wine-treading Don Alberto and I were invited to the house of the Alcalde who had done well out of the war and was no longer dependent upon goats, but still had a small herd of them about the house, kept on as pets. The goats lived in a room adjoining the one in which we were received, and the Alcalde was delighted to be able to entertain us by opening the door and calling them one by one, by name, into our presence. Each goat came through, trotted up to us, held its paw to be shaken and went tripping back. One of them paused for a second, parted its rear legs, and let go a stream of urine before doing this. This caused both men some amusement, and Don Alberto was delighted by the performance as a whole. It occurred to me, subjected to what I should once have found the overpowering fetor of these surroundings, but which now provoked in me no disgust, that I had made considerable progress in the last two months.

With only three days to go to the fiesta the strangers invited by Don Alberto appeared in the cat village and began to put up a large tent on the beach. This was his circus, but which turned out to be no more than a travelling theatre of the kind which still survived where there were no cinemas within reach – a sad and seedy affair providing the barest of subsistence for ageing and talentless players who had come to the end of the road.

A garish poster covered the front, of monsters and devils and man-eating tigers and a man in a baloon, and under it a notice read: *The Palace of Illusions, A Spectacular Parade of Great Luxury*. The sweet, sad, shallow music of the far south came through the tent's opening all the long late summer's afternoon and aged actresses, ravaged by the years and exposure to the sun, hung about despondently in carpet slippers, kimonos and beach suits in appalling taste. A blood-red ticket box plastered all over with handbills of performances that had taken place many years before in important towns bore a placard that urged, 'Hurry! Don't delay a moment. The spectacle is about to start, and few places remain.' but nobody went to the theatre, because nobody in Farol felt they could afford to throw four pesetas away in entertainments of this kind. They had also realised that these people were gypsies and they disliked and mistrusted gypsies and everything to do with them. This antipathy was irrational and reflected no more than a national prejudice, for it was unlikely that any member of the community had ever spoken to a gypsy, but for all that it was deep-seated. When Carmela seized a cat up by the tail, swung it round her head and hurled it through the window, or dropped a mouse sizzling into the nearest fire it was always with a cry of hatred: '*gitano*!'

I asked her and the Grandmother to list their objections, and they were these:

1) they were treacherous and unpredictable;
2) they dressed flashily and were given to boasting;
3) they preferred to live in caves (which was true);
4) no male gypsy ever worked if he could find a girl to pimp on. Having found a girl to keep him he spent his life sleeping or playing the guitar.

In the course of this enquiry it came out that many things regarded by foreigners as typical of Spain, such as flamenco dancing, were held in contempt by the cat people because of their gypsy origins.

I was in the bar with Juan and Sebastian when a young man from the beach theatre came in with a guitar and began to sing *cante flamenco*. This annoyed my friends, and after a moment or two Juan said, almost in an undertone, 'May the devil shit out your soul.'

The gypsy heard him and immediately got up to go. Juan was conscience-stricken at having given offence, so he went after the man and stopped him at the door. He said later that he felt terribly embarrassed because although he was ashamed he couldn't bring himself to apologise. In the end he asked the man, 'Why do you sing like that?'

'To frighten fear,' the gypsy told him.

This was the kind of way any Spaniard liked to hear a man talk and Juan began to take a liking to him.

'Who wrote the words of that copla? You?'

'No, a man called Lorca,' the gypsy said.

'Well, I like it anyway. From your part of the world is he?'

'Nearby. He died.'

'I'm sorry to hear that,' Juan said, 'because he was a man I would have liked to meet. Anyway, come and meet my friends, and have a drink.'

Next day Maria Cabritas reported a sad incident to the Grandmother when she went to buy fish. The people of Farol were very proud of taking care of the old and needy, which they did in a tactful and unobtrusive way. In this season the boats went out shortly after dawn to put down the nets for *bogas*, a fish about twice the size of a sardine which could only be taken in the first hours of daylight, after the dolphins which continually pursued them had gone. The boats normally beached with their catch at about eight and, watching this scene from my window, I could expect to see two or three old ladies, all of them widows, loitering in the vicinity close to the water's edge. The fishermen had worked out a system for giving without seeming to give, and in this way avoiding all possibility of humiliating the taker. Every day a number of fish would be left as if overlooked in the boats, and while fishermen turned their backs, ostensibly occupying themselves with their gear, the women would go over to the boats and help themselves to all the fish they could carry in their hands.

Maria Cabritas told the Grandmother that she had been taking a short cut along the beach with her goats that morning when she had noticed one of the women from the theatre standing with the old ladies waiting for the boats, and when the moment came for them to help themselves to the fish she went with them. She wrapped the fish she picked up in her scarf, walked back up the beach, and then sat on the sea wall to look at the fish, and at that moment several cats attacked her. Maria said she was screaming and trying to fight the cats off, but they were climbing all over her. They tore the fish out of her hands and ran away, and the woman sat down on the wall again, covered her face with her hands and began to weep.

The fishermen were extremely upset to hear about this. Someone said, the players must be starving but we didn't know. That night a case of sardines was taken down to the beach and pushed just inside the. opening of the tent, and next day most of the wives and children of the village attended the performance and did their best to enjoy it. There was renewed talk about getting rid of some of the cats and the village half-wit was paid a small sum to round up about fifty of them and take them up to the forest. It transpired that he released them too close to home for in the next few days most of them – recognisable from their various disfigurements – were back in circulation.

29 September, the day of the fiesta, dawned. It had become clear to Don Alberto that little or nothing was going to be done to turn this into a more joyous occasion than any of its predecessors.

Nobody in the cat village would agree to put out flags, nor for one flimsy excuse or other would they allow confetti to be used. At most they gave grudging assent for a few fireworks being let off late at night. The underlying feeling he picked up – although no one put this in so many words – was, what business is this of yours? You don't live here.

The idea of a fancy-dress procession was dismissed with incredulous laughter, and fishermen who mentioned this suggestion to me said, 'You listen, and pretend to go along with him. It's all you can do. In the first place, where's the fancy dress coming from? I've worn these same things you see me in now for the past three years.'

We went together to discuss the matter of a free issue of wine with the Alcalde.

'We have to buy our wine from your friends up the road,' the Alcalde told Don Alberto, 'and what we've got left over from last year's gone sour. It's undrinkable.' As for dancing in the street that idea was instantly knocked on the head. 'Why not leave the thing as it is?' the Alcalde said. 'You won't find anyone in this village who even knows how to waltz.' His advice to Don Alberto was to forget the magic lantern show, because – although he might not have noticed it – they'd spruced up the old slaughterhouse dating from the times when people could afford to eat meat, put seats in it, and now put on a movie show once a fortnight. This meant that no one bothered about magic lanterns any longer.

When Don Alberto got onto his motorcycle and puttered down to the beach he found the gypsies' tent had been taken down, and they were packing up their gear ready to move off. Their manager told him their takings for three days had been just over 200 pesetas, and he was bitter and derisive, as gypsies are wont to be when things are not going their way, about the false hopes Don Alberto had encouraged.

Don Ignacio had a suggestion to make and we went to his house where he showed us a collection of bric-à-brac collected on one or another of his archaeological digs. There were numerous pieces of broken clay pottery, fragments of glass, a foot of Roman drainpipe, a third of an infant skull, and many more nondescript and unidentifiable objects. The only sound and undamaged item he described in an awe-hushed voice as a third-century inkwell – held as if it had been a jewelled egg from an imperial Russian collection. His proposal was that this dismal paraphernalia could form the basis of an exhibition, certain to attract excited crowds who could be charged an entrance fee of 2 pesetas – to go to church funds. When Don Alberto turned this down he suggested an entertainment by a local lad who could imitate crickets, bullfrogs, the kind of snuffling and whining that the hungry hounds of Sort constantly kept up, and the screechings the local cats gave out when busy with their nuptial routine. Don Alberto shook his head at this, too, mentioning a music-hall attraction he had witnessed in Barcelona some years before, featuring a man able to fart simple tunes. He imagined he must be dead by now.

All that remained of the original plans for enlivening the day was the band, whose members arrived by bus in good time on the morning of the twenty-sixth, in their greyish, once purple tunics, their braided caps and carying their cornets, trombones, a single tuba and an enormous drum.

Their first engagement – quite independent of any commitment to the fiesta – was to welcome young Puig de Mont, who was to arrive on this very day to claim his family domain. Huge efforts had been made under Don Alberto's urgings to clear the calamitous road down to Sort of major obstacles and to fill in the atrocious potholes so that an expertly-driven car could reach the village. Work on the old house had been finished with only hours to spare, Sebastian and his team having worked overnight by the aid of flares. An alfresco meal was to be served, for which a trestle table had been set up in the street outside the Puig de Mønt mansion door, and the Alcalde, backed by the pear-shaped old men lined up in order of importance, waited for the appearance of the car to give the signal for the band to strike up.

A moment later a ripple of excitement spread through the crowd as a shining Mercedes with folded down hood and two outside exhaust pipes, turned the corner. It stopped and Don Federico Puig de Mont stepped down. He patted the dust from his grey flannels, shook hands all round and was conducted to the table. The band crashed into *See the Conquering Hero Comes*. A photographer brought in from a nearby town held up a contraption like a small bird-table heaped with magnesium powder which he exploded, and the women squeaked with excitement in the background and were hushed.

The band galloped through the *Conquering Hero* and launched out into the Triumphal March from *Aïda*. The great man sat down, and the village dignitaries, every man of whom wore a black hat, borrowed or otherwise, took their places. One or two important women had been allowed to huddle unobtrusively in the background, and at the end of the street two Civil Guards, rifles slung, and neck-protectors of white cloth suspended from the backs of their hats, looked from the waist up remarkably like sphinxes.

An enormous dish piled with goat's flesh embedded in a mountain of soggy rice was brought to the table, and several of Don Federico's neighbours began a struggle, with rice flying in all directions, for the honour of piling food on his plate. I sat facing the guest of honour, flanked by the notables across the table, and it suddenly struck me that apart from Don Federico all these men were cast in the same mould. Don Alberto could have been almost the twin brother of the illiterate Alcalde, and even the pear-shaped men with immensely long finger-nails and several chins appeared as self-indulgent members of the same family. Thinking further about this it occurred to me that Don Alberto and Don Ignacio, the priest, were physically practically indistinguishable – the products of a severe and dominant environment – and that so strong was this racial imprint that it cut across the classes, to the point that no one who didn't know them would have been surprised to see the cadaverous muleteer of Sort puttering about the place perched on Don Alberto's motorcycle, or Don Alberto hastily dragging a mule in the direction of a tavern outside which it would punctually deposit its dung in payment for its master's glass of wine.

The face of Don Federico Puig de Mont was from the portrait gallery of a different world, remaining in appearance and gesture wholly apart from those who surrounded him, a man with his feet set on a different path. He was measured and coolly correct in all that he did, sampling the greasy rice and sipping the turbid wine with no change of expression. He bore with the blare of the band's trumpet, almost in his eardrums, showed no signs of being affected in any way by the peasant heartiness – put on to some extent in the hope of concealing fear – the belching and farting that went on all round him, accepted with a nod of gratitude the fleshy titbit recovered by a gnarled paw from the dish and dropped on his plate. A hen landed squawking on one end of the table and began to peck at the spilled rice, and Don Federico never glanced in its direction. He had trained himself to handle any situation.

A visit to the trees was next on the agenda, but shortly before this, after the fiery aniseed liqueur had been poured out, Don Federico's agent slipped a paper in front of him. The agent had been sent to Sort three days in advance of this visit, had carried out an inspection of several square miles of forest, and this was his report. Don Federico's brows knitted as he digested the facts it contained, and when he had finished, he took out his pen, jotted down a number of figures, and did a few simple sums.

We all then went to see the trees, following roughly the direction taken by the Curandero a few days before. Loking down into the first valley where the oaks began, the bare earth was the colour of milk chocolate paled by exposure to the sun in a shop window, and covered by an interlacing pattern of fine black branches stripped of the last of their leaves. It was a day when from some freak of the local atmosphere having to do with wind direction and humidity, the sky appeared purple rather than blue, and although we were a mile from the village, all its sounds, such as the donkey's braying, and even the children at play which would normally have been muffled in foliage, reached us with an almost piercing clarity.

Don Federico and his agent had drawn close together, and the members of the party from the village seemed to have moved away from them a little apprehensively. Everyone stopped while the agent opened a knife and cut a piece of cork from a tree. Both men examined it in silence and Don Federico shook his head.

After this we went back downhill to the village, where nobody could find anything to say. When we reached the little square where Don Federico had left the car the two men shook hands all round, and Don Federico gave the Alcalde a slap on the shoulder and said, 'Well, we'll be letting you know.' Then they got into the car, waved from the window and drove away.

Don Alberto said to the Alcalde, 'I suppose you know what happened?'

'I have a good idea,' the Alcalde said.

'He's changed his mind, and he's pulling out,' Don Alberto said. 'Until now I've gone on hoping that something could be salvaged from this. Now I see it can't. There's no money to be made here any longer.'

'If that's so, we're finished,' the Alcalde said.

As an outsider I had been excluded – as in fact almost all the males of Farol were – from the principal part of the fiesta, which had taken part in the early morning, and as an outsider I should not even have been aware of its existence. The fiesta as a whole was generally referred to as Sa Cova – 'The Cave'. There was a central feature, a mystery, which was kept a close secret in the village, and it was considered unlucky to make any reference to it in ordinary conversation. This took place in a cave, the existence of which would actually be denied if a stranger started asking embarrassing questions. Carmela had made some vague illusion to there being 'something more to Sa Cova than met the eye' but, having been born elsewhere, could provide no details. Sebastian was in the same position, though his wife gave him some reluctant account of the matter.

Elvira explained to him that every year at the end of the fiesta, a 'candidate' was chosen from among the young village girls to head the festivities for the year to come. The selection was based upon consensus of opinion and sometimes, when no decision could be reached, the straws would be drawn. Appointment brought great prestige to the girl and to the family thus honoured. Sebastian said that his wife seemed sour about it all, because there had never been any question of her candidacy being put forward. This chosen one as she was called was normally between 5 and 10 years of age, pretty and intelligent (and if she had fair hair, so much the better). Sponsors – all of them women – would be appointed from other families – and they would help with any expenses that might arise in preparing the child for the fiesta. The year for her would be one of privilege and full of small attentions. It was the custom for all the women and children of Farol to be provided with new clothes to wear on 26 September, and the chosen one was dressed in white as if for a first communion and lent or given a few pieces of inexpensive jewellery for the occasion. On the morning of the fiesta she would be expected to eat a small specially baked chocolate cake.

Then the Romería – the short sea pilgrimage – would begin. The child and her mother would get into a boat in charge of a man who was not her father and, followed by several other boats, all of them full of women most carefully turned out in their new clothes, the procession would set out along the coast. The boats would then row several miles to a cave at the bottom of a cliff when the chosen one and her retinue of women would be put ashore, and while the men waited in the boats the women would go into the cave. Once inside the mother smacked the child quite lightly, the child pretended to cry, and that was the end of the thing. Back in the village there would be a general rush to embrace and kiss the girl, and the men were not excluded from this. It was meaningless, absolutely meaningless, Sebastian said, but it was far and away the most important event of the year for the people of Farol.

In theory no male villager had ever entered the cave, but, being an outsider, Sebastian saw no reason why the prohibition should apply in his case and one day, when he was sure that the coast was clear, he had gone there. He noted that as in many other sea caves the water was of great transparency and brilliance, and that the vestibule of the cave was suffused with a strange, blue light. The rocky floor sloping up from the water was very smooth, as if polished over the centuries perhaps by innumerable feet. The cave contained nothing but the stumps of a few broken stalagmites, but there were sooty markings on the wall that might have been caused by lamp smoke, and seemed to form some sort of pattern. He was suddenly overcome, he said, by a sensation of doom, as if he were in the presence of evil. He added, 'But then I am very imaginative, and susceptible to atmospheres.'

The main pre-occupation of those villagers who did not go on the sea pilgrimage was the preparation of food; obligatory messes demanded by tradition, many of them unpalatable to those who tried them for the first time. The Farol people, condemned on the whole to plain food and little of it, were not only heavy-handed on the spices on festive occasions, but had the extraordinary habit of putting chocolate into almost everything – a habit Don Alberto was convinced had been picked up in Mexico from seafaring forbears. The chocolate was kept by the shopkeepers in a canvas bag hanging from the rafters away from the rats. It had to breathe, he said. When anybody ordered a supply he got out a lump and broke it up with a hammer. After many years of breathing the surface pores had turned white, but the freshly exposed surfaces of the chocolate were almost black. Its flavour was penetrating and bitter. The most festive of all festive dishes was calamares cooked in their own ink, with chocolate and saffron, and it was at this moment that I realised why the Grandmother had been so insistent that Sebastian and I should bring her all the fish that we could catch.

Those who could find no calamares had to fall back on meat, rarely to be had in Farol and, even when available, of the poorest quality. As a rare flavour for this special occasion the wholesale butchers had provided a quantity of offal: hearts, lights, liver, stomach and sexual parts (the last ordered from the butcher's wife wordlessly, with the gesture of a bell-ringer pulling on his rope). A number of families would sit down to a stew called *asadura* made from these ingredients, its slightly repellent flavour masked by a large quantity of peppers cooked in the dish.

For the lucky few with a little spare cash left over from the proceeds of the tunny fishing, or whose credit was better than average at the butcher's, there were chickens and rabbits. The chickens were old boilers. Their flesh was given to sickly children as were the odds and ends of giblets an elderly hen provided, plus its head – shorn of beak – and the feet which were put on display in saucers along the counter as if they had been offerings at a shrine. Rabbits had become scarce and dear, and the butcher's wife used all her native artistry on the small number she had to offer. They were suspended in heraldic fashion along the length of her counter, legs widespread to show a brilliant little banner of liver at the entrance to each vacant abdomen, fear-obsessed eyes bulging from their sockets, a tiny white rosette pinned to the tip of each ear. It was a national law that all rabbits had to be shown thus, complete with identifiable heads, to prevent fraudulent substitution by cats.

I had visited the butcher's shop with Carmela shortly after it had opened for business that morning and we had found the butcher's wife all ready for the fiesta under her blood smirched apron, with hair piled in rolls straight from the curlers, her rows of pearls and her new silk dress. She was pink and hearty, with pouting, cherry-red lips and her big, smooth arms flecked with the tiniest of vermilion spots, as if her skin were in harmony with her environment. Carmela warned me to look away as she took up her cleaver and began to hack a small bit here and another there from the unrecognisable animal tissue on the counter. When Carmela picked up her purchase wrapped in a newspaper sheet containing nothing but religious information, it squelched faintly, and she let out a cry of '*todo es bueno!*' – it's all good food', her frequently repeated motto.

Nobody did anything strenuous on the day of Sa Cova. The big meal started at 2 p.m., and went on until about 3.30, after which most people went to bed. In the period of the siesta anything went, and sex-starved husbands made the most of it. Taking a brisk walk that afternoon in an effort to quell the heartburn, it was impossible to overlook the matrimonial rumpus behind shuttered windows in the otherwise silent street.

At about five things began to move again. The villagers got up, washed, threw the washing water out of the window, then dressed with great care for the early evening promenade due to begin when at least half the street was in the shade. It was expected that this would be the best turnout since pre-war days due to the dresses to be shown off copied from designs in Maria Cabritas' French fashion magazine.

In the Sa Cova promenade the females, the more important element in the procedure, were segregated from the males. For the line-up the female members of the D'Escorreu family, who had provided this year's 'chosen one', were placed in the front, the nine-year-old Marta, still in white, in the centre of the line, flanked by her mother, a pair of aunts and sundry girl cousins. Immediately behind came the Alcalde's wife, as tall almost as if on stilts, accompanied by her two sisters. Next in line was the Grandmother, an ill-favoured daughter on each side, the older daughter Maria tugged at by a spoilt little girl of three who cried and whined incessantly. After that it was the turn of the shopkeepers, the butcher's wife at their head, with her pair of pink-skinned simpering girls. Juan's smart wife Francesca walked with Maria Cabritas, now confirmed in her semi-official function and dressed for Longchamps of the previous year. A line of girls in mourning offered a sombre counterpart at the roadside. They were allowed to look on, but not join in, debarred from any expression of joy by the uncleanness of grief. Some of them had a backlog of fathers, mothers, brothers and sisters to be mourned that would keep them in black until middle age. The Grandmother, only out of mourning that month, had wrapped herself in something resembling a grey curtain for the ceremony, mentioning that she would be happy to get back to her familiar black when it was all over. It was the custom that visitors to the village would fall in immediately after the women, to be followed by the fishermen, each wearing a new pair of pale blue alpargatas and a black hat. The reason for placing them in this position was that when the head of the promenade reached a point some twenty yards from the church the fishermen would fall out without disrupting the proceedings in any way, and wait until the women and the visitors had gone in to pay their respects at the church's open door before turning back. They then joined in again. All this marching and counter-marching was conducted at a funeral pace. Marta, the chosen one, was supposed to keep an unwavering smile on her face for the half-hour or more required to walk from one end to the other of the village and back. Nobody was allowed to utter a word from the moment the parade started until its end, although the men made a low groaning sound, almost a grunt of exhaustion, with each step they took.

It was the moment of grateful surrender to unreason, and people had come to Farol from faraway places for just this. Three women and two men who had been born in Farol, but had spent most of their lives elsewhere, had made the effort to return to the place of their birth for this great moment. One woman had spent twenty years in near-poverty in Argentina, and for the last three of them had been saving up for this trip. She told me that she had never looked forward to anything in all her life as much as this half-hour walk up and down the street of Farol on the day of Sa Cova. It was all meaningless, as Sebastian had objected. No one knew or could even hazard a guess as to what it was all about, and yet a meaningless custom was observed stubbornly, almost with passion, as if the participants craved the opportunity it offered to cast off the responsibility of explaining their actions.

Problems had arisen with the visitors from Sort who had only come in the first case as a favour to Don Alberto and, perhaps somewhat reluctantly, to set the seal on the renewal of normal diplomatic relations between the two communities. Seven of them arrived wearing leather shoes. All the Sort contingent was thoroughly disgruntled to have been told at the last moment by Don Alberto that the fireworks had turned out to be damp, there was to be no circus as promised, no fancy-dress parade, no prizes, no free wine – not even a band, for the bandsmen had trundled their instruments as far as the first village house only to be stopped and warned off. 'Sorry, no music here, if you don't mind. Any other time, but not just now.' It was useless for Don Alberto to try to explain how wholly taboo the wearing of shoes was in Farol, and much as they might be tolerated when worn by an outsider paying a casual visit, or just passing through no one could walk in the Sa Cova promenade wearing anything else but rope-soled alpargatas.

Exclusion was taken as a gross insult. The fishermen were overbrimming with anxiety to make a show of hospitality, offering the local alpargatas to the seven shoe-wearers to allow them to walk in the parade, but the people from Sort had had enough and after a brief petulant discussion among themselves decided to leave.

With this final outraged clicking of tongues and waving of arms

Don Alberto's ham-fisted attempts to impose a pacific solution upon the two peoples came to an end. Witnessing the confrontation between the stolid, striving and calculating peasants produced by the arid landscape of Sort, and the mercurial yet fatalistic fishermen, it was hard to see that they would ever come together. The dog people went home, and the cat people got on with their fiesta. I walked on the promenade with the ecstatic and tearful women who – although treated now as strangers – had at last returned to their village. After dark the whole thing was repeated at the double – a speeded-up version of the evening promenade with plenty of excitement and noise, and a little horseplay.

There was no more to it than that. My fishermen friends said that it had been a successful Sa Cova, auguring well for the prospects of the coming year. The events of the next few days proved them to be wrong.

10

Sharp variations exist in the climatic patterns of the Mediterranean area. Unlike Italy, when October provides a succession of faultless days, this is the month along the Spanish coast when a prolonged summer suddenly collapses, and the year is gone. What follows for the fishermen when the winds calm, the rain ceases and the sun shines once more, is a lifeless parody of the lost summer. The sea's currents change direction and turn cold, and the big shoals of fish, like migrating birds, move away southwards. The fellowship, the shared excitements and frustrations of men working together in the big boats, is at an end. In the dead season a man takes a boat out on his own, or squats alone to fish from the rocks. For the fishermen there are only six months to the year, which fades into a kind of timeless limbo in October, not to be reborn until March. Towards the end of the first week in October the big boats are put on the rollers and dragged to the top of the beach, where from time to time men do a little desultory work on them to make them ready for the next season. For the rest the fishermen sleep what they can of the time away, or spend long periods sitting in bars, staring into empty glasses. The passing of summer is felt even more keenly here than in the north. As my next-door neighbour Juan, with his aptitude for the telling phrase put it, 'In winter, this is the cemetery of the living.'

This year autumn's attack took Farol by surprise. Small shoals of sardines were still reported in the offing as late as Sa Cova, and fishermen working alone were still taking a few in their nets. It had been an erratic season, leading to the belief that a delay in the migration of the fish had happened and that larger shoals might reappear. For this reason, the weather remaining fine, the big boats were kept in readiness instead of being winched up to their winter positions after the first few days of the month.

The only warning given by the calm morning of 8 October of what was to come was the purplish, depressed colour of the sky, and the growth out of the horizon of shapeless yellow clouds. At about nine o'clock a wind blew up suddenly, gusting from the north, veered round to due east, and increased to a gale. I stood at the window of the Grandmother's house, saw the sea boil and turn white as a great, scalloped wave twenty feet high charged up the beach, with a small boat bobbing on its crest like a ball in a shooting range water-jet at a fair. There was only time to winch two of the five big boats to safety before great paws of water grabbed up the remaining three, hurled them against each other, and stove their planks in. The smashed boats seemed irreparable, and the fishermen understood that even if the sardines came in March, most of the harvest would be lost.

On 10 October the news was that Marta D'Escorreu, the chosen one, had been taken ill. The village clubbed together for a taxi to rush her to hospital in Gerona, where she was pronounced to be suffering from tuberculosis, and where she was to be kept for at least three months. The more superstitious of the fisherfolk linked this happening to their other misfortunes, and viewed the future with extreme pessimism.

Don Alberto invited me to his sombre house where we mulled over the prospects for Sort, which seemed if possible worse than those that confronted Farol. 'Make no mistake,' he said, 'we are about to witness a calamity.' He handed me a letter he had just received making it clear that, as foreseen, Puig de Mont would not be coming back. Not only that, said Don Alberto, but what was almost worse, he had sold the family house to the most notorious black-market operator in the province, who would soon move in.

The aged crone who had once been the toast of Madrid came at us out of the gloom with two smeary glasses of *rancio*. 'The situation of these people is tragic,' Don Alberto said. 'They're left with nothing.'

'So it's confirmed that none of the trees will survive?'

'None at all.'

'But surely they have other resources?'

Don Alberto explained that apart from the sale of the bark, which didn't amount to much, but was still something, the villagers had an income from the rabbits trapped or caught by their dogs, from a great variety of mushrooms, berries and nuts collected in autumn, and many birds, large and small, taken in snares at all times of the year. But all of these could only exist in an environment provided by the living trees.

'What about the crops they grow? Can't they fall back on that?'

The land, Don Alberto said, was extremely bad. All the best of it had fallen into the hands of five or six families. 'You can blame it on the inheritance system,' he said. 'People end up with a patch of brambles and having to use a rope ladder to get into their room. Those fat men you see about the place own everything worth having. What you have here is the feudal system in operation.'

'I'm sorry, I may be mistaken, but aren't you a feudalist, Don Alberto?'

'At heart, absolutely not. At heart I subscribe to the noble philosophy of anarchism. I'm a victim of the system just as anyone else is. Let me tell you what anarchism is about. We anarchists are opposed to state interference. We can look after ourselves, build our own houses, make our roads, teach our children all they need to know. What do we need from the state? Take those two policemen who are supposed to keep an eye on us. Anyone can buy them off for the price of a cigar a month.'

I asked him if it might be a good thing to divide up some of the estates.

'It wouldn't make a scrap of difference,' he said. In fact it would only make things worse. Let's suppose I decided to let any of my land go. Who would get their hands on it in one way or another? Guess who? You'd have even worse irregularities than you have now.'

'Yes, I suppose you would,' I said.

'Let me explain. I regard myself as holding this land in trust for the generations to come. Look at me. What do I eat? What do I drink? What do I wear? What do I take away from these people? To each according to his needs, and mine are very small.' Don Alberto was said to give away money in secret, and to let his tenants off payment of their rent in times of crisis, but he would no more part with his land than he would his flesh.

I drained my glass, wincing at the decayed tartness of the *rancio*. This was a setting from a peasant interior by Zurbarán, a room stained by the years and ancient smoke, furniture built like siege-engines, a trough sunk into a corner for visitors to wash their feet, old swallows' nests on the beams, with little white piles of droppings to mark their positions on the flags beneath. The prehistoric odour of smouldering charcoal came through the opening to the kitchen and with it a drift of sad-sweet music from times long past. I could see Don Alberto's crone, backed by a witch's cauldron, bent over a gramophone. She wound it up and put the record on again and for a moment we listened to a quavering soprano rendering of the aria 'The Violet Seller' from the old Spanish opera *La Violetera*.

Spring shines on us shyly, and now once again
the Violetera is here with flowers and hope —

Don Alberto accompanied me to the door.

'So you'll be leaving us soon?'

'In a matter of days. But all being well I'll be back next year.'

'*Si Dios quiere.*'

'*Si Dios quiere.*'

My path crossed his estate on the way back to Sort. The bleached litter of autumn lay on his fields which were the colour of tin plate, and studded with the sabre-toothed calyxes of enormous thistles. Wind ripped and rattled through the foliage of patches of Indian corn, which was the last crop of the season. A dog crossed the path ahead dragging a log yard by yard, stopping after each effort to fall back on its haunches and pant. At the entrance to the village a man was ploughing with a nail-plough of the kind one sees in Roman mosaics. It was a placid and amiable scene.

Sebastian and I walked down to the sea together. It would be the last we should see of each other until I came back in the spring, for his work in the village was at an end now that the Puig de Mont mansion was finished, and he would be obliged to take work as a builder's labourer in Gerona until such time as any new project started up in this area.

We followed a path sloping eventually to a low cliff for a better view of what we were leaving behind. The morning had fallen to a flat calm, full of marine herb scents and the flinty twitterings of finches. The storm had drawn a firm new line of wrack beneath us all along the beach, marking out the new winter boundary of territory claimed by the sea, and children were scrabbling in the coarse sand for the coloured glass pebbles turned up by the storm. We watched a man called Pedro paddle his boat to within feet of a patch of sea that twitched with the movement of fish feeding on a barely submerged rock. His *raï* opened a perfect coronet of splashes where a shoal should have been but he caught nothing. The Grandmother, back in mourning now that the fiesta was past, made a distant black pyramid as she squatted by a boat just beached, to pick through a meagre catch. It was a sign of the times that the widows waiting for the boats to come in limited themselves now to a fish or two per boat rather than the handfuls that nobody missed in summer.

Maria Cabritas, inscrutably smiling and as elegant as ever, passed with her goats down a lower path, and we caught a brief glimpse among the houses of Don Ignacio, a longish parcel certain to contain a shovel under his arm, on his way to catch the twice-weekly bus that would take him to his archaeological dig.

What really engaged our attention in this marine panorama as we took an offshoot of our path leading to the beach was the sight of three stocky young peasants from Sort fishing with rods from the rocks. Several Farol fishermen had spotted them, too, and from time to time a man's curiosity would get the better of him and he would make a pretence of going on some errand that would take him close enough to them to study the details of what was going on. Sebastian and I walked across and asked them what luck they had had, and they made a face, and said none at all. They had baited their hooks with winkles collected from the rocks, and Sebastian suggested they should try sonsos or pieces of octopus. The information was well-meant, but they went on fishing with the bait they had because there was nothing else they could do, and by this time I knew enough about fishing to know that that day they would never catch a fish.

But what of the future? – because even peasants could turn themselves into fishermen of a kind if they were serious about it, and tried hard enough. The competition of three, thirty or three hundred such amateurs would not worry the professionals of Farol in the slightest, but this was a sight, when we discussed it further, which whispered to us both of possibilities undreamed of until this moment.

Season Two

1

I kept in touch with Sebastian during the winter, receiving one letter to say that he had been called back unexpectedly from Gerona to start work on the renovation of the two other abandoned cork mansions. In a second letter he said that he needed a holiday, and knowing that I expected to be heading south again in the near future, suggested that we should meet at Port Bou, just across the Spanish frontier, and go on a lobster-fishing trip together.

His arguments seemed convincing. Nobody bothered, he said, about lobsters along the Spanish coast where they abounded in the cold water at this time of the year. The French, however – and this I knew – were devoted to them, an addiction resulting in their near-extermination along the French Mediterranean seaboard. His plan was that we should catch the fish by hand, using diving masks. He said that a friend of his, using the box with a glass bottom through which the fishermen scan the sea-bed, had seen them everywhere. As far as I was concerned there was nothing to be lost as I proposed in any case to enter Spain by Port Bou. A couple more letters were exchanged fixing a date and place, and at the end of March, exactly as in the previous year, a taxi took me to the frontier from the railway station at Cerbère, I carried my baggage across the theoretically still-closed border into Spain, and took a Spanish taxi down to Port Bou.

Sebastian was waiting for me in the Café de la Marina, where some of the first French tourists of the post-war had gathered, ready for adventure in a country once again mysterious after its years of isolation ('*Parole d'honneur. Ils sont comme les Arabes. Ils ne laissent pas les femmes sortir*'). He was even thinner than when I had last seen him. His face seemed graven with ineradicable anxiety, and heavy labour in Gerona where he had worked nine hours daily for a wage of 21 pesetas had left callouses on his hands. They had gone as far as they could with the reconstruction of the cork mansions, and now, while they awaited the arrival of such things as bathroom fittings, he had been given a month's unpaid holiday.

He was desperately anxious to find some way of raising cash during this period due to a domestic crisis resulting from an ultimatum he had just received from the Grandmother. She had ordered him to procreate a child by the end of May and had already decided on a preferred name, Timburlán (Tamerlane) in the case of a boy, Cleopatra if a girl. In the years of his married life Sebastian had never until this moment stood up to the old woman, and felt only able to do so now if in a position to argue from strength – threatening in fact to move out. But half the furniture in the rooms they occupied belonged to the Grandmother, and Sebastian's savings to date, amounting to seven hundred pesetas, were not enough even to buy a second-hand bed. His hope was to be able to raise a thousand pesetas on the lobster-fishing trip, a hope that to me seemed of the stuff that dreams were made of.

To protect his tiny capital I agreed to pay for the hire of a car, and we found an aged Simca, literally held together by string, with one door missing and wheels of uneven size, and in this we began a cautious reconaissance of the coast, round to the south. We made a first stop at Grilén, hired a boat and made a start with the fishing at Punta Cap Ras. To my immense surprise, and to Sebastian's relief the fish were actually there as reported. They were not lobsters, but escarmalans – a large crayfish of a kind I had never seen before, resembling a lobster, but clawless, and with a minute head. This was clearly a fish of the winter season. To our delight they were to be seen in numbers in stealthy movement among the fronds, the ribbons and the rosettes of weed in water as shallow as ten feet. Sebastian had learned to swim in the interim and had brought with him the old speargun he had inherited from me at the end of the last season, while I had taken the opportunity to pick up a more powerful speargun in France. It would have been possible to spear the escarmalans by the hundred, but to be saleable they had to be taken alive. This was a tricky and precarious business for which gloves were an essential protection. You had to dive on an escarmalan and grab it quickly before it darted into thick weed, or under a rock, and when caught it would attempt to free itself by snapping vigorously with its tail. As the underside edges of the shell were provided with razor-sharp serrations cut fingers were not at first to be avoided.

The real problem was the cold, bad enough on the surface, but increasing with every foot of a dive. Moreover the visibility was bad. The fish were always there, but we lost time in having to dive and search for them among the weeds. After fifteen minutes of this it became impossible to stay in the water any longer. We hauled ourselves back into the boat, pulled on our sweaters, gulped down coffee mixed with brandy from the thermos, and waited for the

76

circulation to return. The sun shone brilliantly on the mirror of the sea, and the great buttresses and pinnacles of rock floated in mist over the water. Below us the escarmalans awaited our return in the murky and frigid depths. Sebastian was calculating now that with every dive, occupying less than one minute, he made a day's wages. We dropped back, groaning, into the water again and began to clutch at the escarmalans with bleeding, freezing fingers and toss them into the boat. In the end we reached a point, numbness spreading from our bodies to our brains, when we began to wonder whether we had done some permanent damage to ourselves. When I pinched my thighs I could feel nothing, but both of us were suffering from pain in the extremities of the limbs, and intense headaches. Watching Sebastian swaying and staggering among the escarmalans, three or four deep, crawling over each other in the bottom of the boat, I saw the pink shadowy outline of his skeleton marked in his skin which seemed transparent.

We rowed to the nearest beach, lit a driftwood fire and huddled round it until our brains began to work again. Sebastian, unable even to express himself in Castellano, kept mumbling, '*Puta, son mort de fred*' in his local dialect which was closer to Italian than Spanish. He told me that only the thought of the furniture he was going to buy had kept him going. Ten escarmalans, half a second-hand bed. Ten more, a bedside table and perhaps a re-conditioned chair. Fifteen, some sort of a chest of drawers, in need of repair in all probability, so allow two more escarmalans for the local joiner's work on them.

On that first day we caught sixty-four fish. The fishermen in Llansá let us keep them in a cage in their vivéro, and we showed our gratitude by giving them a few fish. They pointed out a fonda where we got a room each for two pesetas a head, and the innkeeper, who was one of those brooding, introspective men who seem often to follow this profession, gave us beans soaked in oil with some local sausage, so hard you practically had to break it up with a hammer. Sebastian fell asleep after the second or third mouthful. He knocked over his *rancio*, his head fell on the table and he began to snore. The innkeeper took his food away, sat down at the next table and ate it himself.

We stayed in this fonda, pulling ourselves together slowly, all the next day and the next night and then, the day after, with half the male population of the street pushing the Simca to get it to start, we moved on to Puerta de La Selva where we hired another boat and ventured out after some hesitation along the wild and dangerous north-facing coast to Cabo Creus. There were no weather forecasts to be had then but the fishermen told us that by their experience the good weather should hold up for at least a day. However, they said, one never knew along the coast, and that should a storm blow up there was nowhere to run for shelter. With this possibility at the back of our minds it was hard to settle comfortably to fishing. We moved along at the base of sheer cliffs that would have impressed me with their grandeur at any other time, but, as the fishermen had said, there was not a cover or inlet anywhere. The water here was not only foggy and cold, but too deep in the places where we found suitable weed for us to fish. We carried on for a few hours, looking over our shoulders as we worked, and in the end took twenty-eight escarmalans before being chased by a few wisps of cloud back to Puerto de La Selva again, chilled to the bone and utterly exhausted.

Next day we decided to play for safety and moved back into the more protected area round Cabo D'en Poch where we spent three days, and put up in a fonda almost indistinguishable – even to the beans and hard sausage – from the one at Llansá. By this time, counting the ones they were keeping for us in the vivéro at Llansá, we had 244 fish, so we moved back to Llansá, where our fishermen friends helped us to box up all our escarmalans in seaweed in professional style before taking them on to Port Bou.

There was no market in Spain, but as predicted, the French were eager to buy, and the skipper of a boat from Banyuls took one look at what we had to offer, and paid cash for them on the spot.

After that we tried to repeat the trip but with poor success. The water was still cold and turbid as it had been before, but the escarmalans had become hard to find and were moving into deeper water. We caught some thirty odd fish, and decided to get rid of them locally at whatever price we could get, then call it a day. We had each of us lost a half-stone in weight, and Sebastian was developing a cough. Our profit on the trip was 1,380 pesetas each, a sum equivalent to Sebastian's earnings as a mason in nearly two and a half months. He would now return to Farol better prepared for the coming confrontation with the Grandmother.

2

Sebastian had a request to make that came as a surprise. He asked me if I had any objection to a short excursion to the town of Besalu in the foothills of the Pyrenees before moving on to Farol. The story was that an old friend was living there in a state of dire need, and several of the fishermen who had also known and admired this man had subscribed to raise 3,000 pesetas in the hope of being able to tide him over. Sebastian was carrying this money with him. He would quite understand if I didn't feel like making the journey, he said, and would get there somehow or other by bus.

What struck me as a little remarkable about this proposition was that no mention should have been made of it until this moment. The impression I had was that this was a matter that he had put off bringing up until it could be put off no longer. When I probed for further details about the friendship he said that he had served in the same infantry unit as this man in the defeated Republican Army. Later in the conversation it developed that he had served *under* him and that, while Sebastian had remained a private throughout his short army career, the friend had been a brilliant young officer who had commanded the devotion of all his men.

This latter amplification began to arouse certain doubts. Officers by my experience rarely made lifelong friendships among the ranks. However this mission was clearly of great importance to Sebastian, and it seemed ungenerous to object, so I agreed to make the trip. Besalu was quite close. The map showed some fifteen miles of winding and almost certainly diabolical road across country to the town of Figueras, and thereafter another fifteen miles of dead straight main road to Besalu. There was a shortage of petrol at that time, and all the pumps were empty, but we were able to beg enough from our fishermen friends in Port Bou to fill up the Simca's tank, and after coaxing it once more into a semblance of life, we set off.

The journey of thirty miles took rather more than three hours, and while we bumped and crashed over some of the worst roads in Europe more details of the life and personality of Sebastian's friend began to come out. He had been a battalion commander, aged twenty-five when Sebastian had last seen him, had disappeared after the great

Republican débâcle, been arrested and spent several years in prison. It was a story that had been repeated a thousand times in the history of those fateful days, but in the telling of it there were areas of silence and reserve and missing fragments from the mosaic of the picture as presented. Most of our friends in Farol – enlisted in the Republican Army purely as a result of the village being in government-controlled territory – had spent periods in prison camps, but there was a whiff of mystery about the man who awaited us at Besalu. Had he been among the tens of thousands finally released, or had he in fact escaped? In the latter case I was running some risk by associating myself with any act designed to give shelter or aid to an escaped prisoner. It was flattering in one sense to have been admitted – as far as I had been – into Sebastian's confidence, but a little disturbing in another.

Besalu was an unattractive town, built round a hundred yards of third-class highway, with strangely suburban houses reflecting a pretentious poverty, raw red bricks outlined in white paint like the interior of a butcher's shop, barn-like double doors to admit carts, curtains of chains hanging over shop entrances, and groups of blue-jowled priests in black velours hats and black alpargatas. A cold wind whined round every corner, and this and the full-speed passage of buses with open exhausts down the dirt road kept the town full of swirling dust.

Everything about this town was extraordinary and alien. It belonged to a frontier, full of restless furtive people, who had just arrived – illegally or otherwise – or were planning to escape to another country. Even the name, Besalu, was a strange one, belonging to Tartary or Turkey rather than Spain. Sebastian admitted, with a touch of caution, that it was the smuggler's capital. Two or three miles down the road a side-turning branched off to follow the River Llierca north through the villages of Montagut and Sardenas, and where it ended tracks led to a half a dozen mountain refuges that were virtually on the frontier, within two miles of the French road leading to Arles, Amélie and Céret.

We found something to eat in the Bar Piat, at the back of the town by the church: a pig's trotter stew of the kind they make in these Pyrenean towns, and the first fresh meat we had tasted for a week. The place was like a cave, and smelt as the whole town did whenever the wind dropped, of leather and rope and sweat. There were three or four men sitting at different tables with their hats on, sucking at the trotters, and occasionally glancing sideways as a dog does in fear of a challenge arising as to its ownership of a bone.

The impression Sebastian gave me was one of great nervousness. When replying to a question he seemed to find it hard to concentrate. I asked him how he proposed to find his friend, and he replied, 'I don't know. That's something I have to go into.' The view through the window's grubby glass was of a small square with scraps of paper being blown about, men standing in little groups, face to face with their jacket collars turned up, and two stunted-looking soldiers patrolling with sub-machine guns.

We finished the stew. The men at the other tables had gone, leaving the place empty, and we could find nothing to say to each other. After a while Sebastian got up. He said he would be back in a moment, and asked me to wait. He went out of the door and I watched him through the window cross the square, go up to a taxi parked on the other side, talk to the driver, then get in. About an hour later, when I was beginning to be nervous myself, I saw him coming down the street with a man with a scarf like a bath towel wrapped round his head, and wearing a suit so thin I could see his knees and his elbows sticking through the cloth. They came in and sat down. 'This is Enrique,' Sebastian said. We shook hands and Enrique said something in a soft, practically inaudible voice, speaking like a ventriloquist, without moving his very thin lips. According to Sebastian he should have been in his early thirties, two or three years younger than Sebastian himself, but in so far as it was possible to put an age on this man at all I would have placed him as forty-five. The skin was drawn tightly in numerous shallow creases over the bones of his skull, and his forehead was covered with a rash which he sometimes rubbed with the back of his hand. Sebastian ordered a pig's trotter and bread for him, and I noticed that when he chewed it was with the side of his jaw, the reason being that nothing was left of his front teeth but black stumps. He neither looked at us nor the food on his plate, which he put away with a kind of methodical thoroughness. He spoke a few words to Sebastian in a slurred undertone, but I understood nothing of what he said.

Sebastian had placed himself and Enrique with their backs to the door, and when the bar owner came over and asked us if we wanted any more he stared down at his plate and waved him away. Enrique finished chewing at the bread and drained his glass, and we got up and Sebastian pushed me ahead and we went out into the street. The men

81

were still there with their jacket collars turned up, letting the sun fall on their faces, but the soldiers had gone. We walked down the street, Enrique between us, and the little suburban houses with their painted fronts came to an end and Besalu turned into a shanty town on the river bank, backed by the great green landslides of the foothills of the Pyrenees. Here we stood together for a moment.

I could feel that all Sebastian wanted to do was get away, but somehow we were all the prisoners of a kind of desperate politeness. '*Pues . . . pues . . .*' ('well then, well then . . .') Enrique was hissing through his gums. My feeling was that he too was longing to be gone. 'So make sure that we hear from you, eh?' Sebastian said. 'That's understood, isn't it? Don't leave us in suspense.'

Finally we brought ourselves to shake hands and the small ordeal was at an end. Enrique revealed a little blackness at the core of his parting smile, turned away and went shuffling off towards the shacks.

Sebastian and I made for the car. We were almost running. Five minutes later we were on the road heading east.

'In a bad way, isn't he?' I said.

'He lived on oranges for two years.'

'So he's on the run?'

'Well, I told you, didn't I?'

'Not in so many words,' I said.

It had been a depressing, and in a way disappointing experience. From Sebastian's description the picture I had formed – faceless though it was – was of a hero in defeat stripped of all but defiance, but not wholly divested of tragic grandeur. Yet all the fire in Enrique had long since burned out and I was ashamed in his presence to feel nothing more than embarrassment, even revulsion, and then shame for being unable to experience anything but these feelings.

'Happy with the money, was he?'

'He must have been.'

'But he didn't show it?'

'No, he didn't show it.'

Sebastian settled himself more comfortably as the last of the mean houses of Besalu fell away below the skyline behind us. 'I feel better,' he said. 'Something that had to be done. It's all over now and I can breathe again.'

Now that the thing was finished with I could relax and enjoy the view, which seemed in every way more remarkable than when we had passed down this road only two hours before. This was a Spain as I never thought of it, and had never seen it before, one of immense green prairies under the soft sun of spring. Hares were streaking in all directions, only their heads showing, leaving little comets' tails of waving grass, and we passed a white horse, hooves out of sight, poised absolutely motionless, as if about to rock. Miles away these green pastures met an horizon of toy villages with windmills, each surmounted with a church.

'Are you allowed to tell me what he's doing in Besalu?' I asked.

'Waiting to cross over. As soon as the snows clear they go across. By the dozen. It's a regular business. A guide will take you for 5,000 pesetas. No problem. They split with the police.'

'Is he sure to get across?'

'Most of them do. Once in a while someone doesn't. Every so often the police have to pretend to clamp down. It's a matter of luck.'

3

Re-established in the Grandmother's house, I found little change. In a place remarkably devoid of green things the fig tree in Juan's garden next door proclaimed the arrival of spring, putting on a spurt of growth and reaching with its webbed and perfumed hands towards me over the wall. The beach glistened all over with coloured glass turned up by the winter's tides, Juan was fishing with the palangres, and the two remaining big boats had already made a modest catch of sardines. A woodpecker had arrived to nest in a hole in the ancient tree at the entrance to the village, the bird and its offspring being glutted with offerings of grubs and protected from cats by a fence made from the last of the Grandmother's barbed wire, and from the peregrines by fishing nets hung in the trees' branches. My cat had somehow survived the winter and continued to inhabit the shed, receiving me with indifference tinged with hostility. Following the Grandmother's instructions I gave it a glass of milk (but no more) to re-cement the relationship. It then followed me into the house and was immediately seized upon by Carmela, scrubbing out my room with strong disinfectant, and thrown into the street. Within an hour I was at table. ('This could be off-putting, sir. Take your courage in both hands and pitch in. You won't object to the flavour').

The Grandmother herself seemed depressed over besetting family problems, telling me of Sebastian's refusal to beget a child that year, and of the way her elder daughter Maria and her husband continued to reward her for all she had done for them with nothing but neglect.

The small windfall of sardines had put a few unexpected pesetas in people's pockets, although they were certain to be empty again soon enough. Early spring beans were being sold at cut prices by the impoverished growers of Sort, and the villagers of Farol bought them while they could. Wine from Sort was cheap, too, although as sour as ever, and the bar's trade revived with rarely less than a half-dozen fishermen seated under the mermaid talking to each other in blank verse. Simon described for the hundredth time his adventures lost at sea after the 1922 storm. The stupid boy who helped in the bar giggled over a comic paper, and the Alcalde who had been good at maths at school busied himself with the problems of perpetual motion.

Maria Cabritas' discreetly managed love-life now involved her with a dozen suitors, most of whom had presented her with umbrellas, the best of which she always carried when herding her goats, using it to prod the soft rear parts of any animal that lagged behind. Don Ignacio, as threatened, had turned the principal room of his gloomy house into a museum displaying numerous Roman nails, fragments of pottery and glass, a cracked rib or two, and the celebrated inkwell from his excavations. He was astonished and at first gratified when a number of fishermen turned up, but soon noticed that they were more interested in the flags covering the floor than the antiques. On making enquiries he found out that what attracted them was a rumour that a priest in the last century poisoned the husbands of women with whom he was having a liaison and disposed of their bodies down a hole in this very room.

Outwardly, only one obvious change had taken place in Farol's centre, which was to the fonda. The façade had been scrubbed up, the windows cleared of cobwebs, the dangerous step built across the wide doorway to prevent visitors driving in their carts removed. The old brothers were no longer to be seen, and two sackfuls of cats captured in the cellars had been duly carried away to be dumped in what remained of the forest.

What perturbed the villagers was the possibility that a coat of bright paint might be applied to the fonda's woodwork, and they were unhappy about a board that went up on the day of my return, on which a sign writer from Figueras had sketched in the outlines of the letters making up a notice that read, 'Guests admitted. Salubrious accommodation, and meals served at all hours.'

Within days of my return I had the satisfaction of being allowed to overhear a reference to myself in one of the fishermen's blank-verse sessions in the bar. This was an accolade indeed. That morning a fisherman called Arturo had seemed mildly startled when I surfaced from a dive close to his boat while he was pulling in his net, and he described this episode in the usual form at the evening get-together before the general exodus to sea.

De noche fuí a calar las redes
By night I went to put down the nets,

Pesqué delfines, campañas* ahogadas, luna gastada. [Murmurs of *'sigue, sigue'.*]

I caught dolphins, sound of drowned bells, shred of a moon.

Por la mañana el hambre daba voces,

By the morning hunger gave tongue,

Y volví a la lucha . . . pa' confrontar la suerte.

And I went back to the struggle . . . the battle with luck.

Esta vez saben que pesqué?

This time can you imagine what I caught?

Pesqué el buzo nuestro,

None other than our diver,

Hombre del rostro palido, socio de Neptuno, escarabajo del destino.

Pale-faced partner of Neptune, scarab of destiny.

El que busca en las entrañas del mar,

He who searches in the bowels of the sea,

Para descubrir qué? – quien sabe?

To discover who know what?

The speaker throws up his hands, *'Basta! Tengo sed.'* Someone calls to the Alcalde for a glass of the good wine, and another voice adds:

Que al leñador alienta y engaña al pordiosero.

That refreshes the wood-cutter and deceives the beggar.

I called on Don Alberto and found him busy with a pile of newspapers recently arrived from Barcelona and Madrid, cutting out a back-log of obituary notices which his old black crone, seated with her back to us in a corner of the vast, dank room, was pasting in a book. 'We spent most of the winter in bed,' he said. 'There didn't seem much point in getting up.' He poked his finger into the flesh of the old woman's forearm. 'Look how flabby the poor thing is,' he said. 'I've put on weight myself, but I'll soon sweat it away now the sun's come out.' I could see no difference at all in Don Alberto's skeletal appearance.

His report was a dismal one. The poorer families of Sort had been reduced to eating acorns during the winter. This was mentioned in passing. What really shocked him was that the Puig de Mont mansion had been sold to a man called Jaime Muga, one of the country's most notorious and audacious black marketeers.

Muga's legendary coup, discussed with much admiration by the fishermen in the previous year, had been the buying-up of the whole

---

*A reference to the bells of a submerged church, still to be faintly heard, the fishermen believed, in the solitude of the sea.

of the police force of the sizeable port of Palamos, from their commanding officer down to the unimportant private who polished the horses' harnesses, before unloading a cargo of contraband in broad daylight, and in the busiest area of the port. The only thing he left out, the fishermen said, was the police band.

This was a feat to command even Don Alberto's grudging admiration, but what horrified him was Muga's treatment of the Catalan baroque Puig de Mont mansion, a part of the national heritage, as Don Alberto said, on which – as Sebastian had reported – a small army of workmen had been kept busy throughout the winter, modifying it to conform to his tastes. Muga, a local boy who had married the richest woman in Cuba, proposed to have thirty members of his family live with him, a fact which – bearing in mind the number of servants required to look after them – meant trebling the number of rooms. He therefore built on wings in Californian-Mexican style and, disliking the honey-coloured sandstone of the original structure, covered all the walls with white stucco with inserts of patterns of red brick to defeat any possibility of boredom. Having a taste for church architecture, he next added cloisters and a bell tower. Finally, as a tribute to the environment, as it had once been, he personally designed chimneys to resemble tree-trunks, with projecting stumps where branches had been lopped off, and cork-oak's bark imitated in concrete. Sebastian mentioned that he had stripped a Pyrenean church of its statuary, and set up the neon-lit virgins and saints in niches in the interior walls, and that there was a Roman bust in the garden with a rather stupid smile.

Muga's appetite was a matter of local legend. The peasant and fishing communities of Catalonia prided themselves on their frugality, and status depended rather on an absence of conspicuous consumption than the reverse. The rich sat down to table five times a day, but Muga added a sixth meal, the *resupón*, an informal dip into a pot just before bedtime into which tasty left-overs from earlier repasts had been thrown to reheat. Although only thirty-five Muga was already fat, with a massive torso and pendulous stomach underpinned by insignificant hips and bowed legs. He had no neck to speak of and was balding in such a way as to leave a widow's peak of dense black hair, plus a tuft over each ear. When I first saw him standing arms akimbo, a genial though potentially ferocious smile on his face, watching the decorators at work on the front of the fonda, he reminded me of a Japanese samurai on the lookout for someone to pick a fight with. The rumour was he had bought the place.

4

In late March the sardines had returned after an absence of five years to the Bahia de Rosas and the waters of Farol, but the sardine nets could be carried only in the two remaining big boats, so that 65 cases fetching 73 pesetas a case were all that had been landed. Marriages provisionally fixed for the spring had been put off until the autumn.

The economic situations of both Farol and Sort, interwoven as they were, continued together on their downhill slide. A dry summer plus the loss of cork revenue had brought the dog people, as reported by Don Alberto, to the point of eating acorns, but repercussions from the defunction of the trees were beginning to be felt in Farol in unexpected ways.

As a second line of defence against the possibility of meagre catches, the cat people had done their best to lessen their dependence upon the sea by raising chickens. This was left to the women who were supposed to retain whatever income was made from them, including the sale of the eggs. As no food was ever bought for them they lived by foraging, and it was quite extraordinary to see a fisherman's wife or daughter steering a small flock of hens and chicks along the street and actually controlling them with high-pitched clucking cries on the way from one feeding ground to another. In the summer and autumn of the preceding year more eggs had been put under broody hens, and in the winter the villagers had roused themselves from their normal torpor to get down to the job of constructing pens to protect the chickens from the nocturnal attacks of the local cats or the occasional famished dog from Sort.

Now the loss of the forest, viewed at first in Farol with utter impassiveness, gave rise to a new peril. Hundreds of peregrines nested on the cliffs all along the coast, preying on pigeons that flew too close to the spurs on which they awaited them, and on the cork forest rabbits. By this spring, food shortages had meant that there were fewer pigeons, and there were no rabbits left in the forest. For the first time the peregrines appeared circling on the watch over Farol itself, so emboldened by hunger that they would drop out of the sky and snatch up a chick or a pullet from a flock in the village street, with perhaps a half-dozen villagers in sight going about their business.

The fishermen's retaliation was based upon a principle found effective in dealing with their worst enemy, the dolphin. Whenever a dolphin was taken in their nets, saleable as it was for its flesh, it was not killed, but wounded and then let go, as an example to its fellows of what their fate would be if they continued to damage their nets. The keen-eyed, intelligent and suspicious falcons were almost impossible to trap, but once in a while one got itself tangled up in a hen coop, and when this happened the fishermen would wire up its beak and release it. They claimed that both the dolphins and the peregrines suspended their attacks when one of their number had been treated in this way. For all that, an increasing percentage of chickens were lost to predators of one kind or another who had lost their hunting grounds in the forest. Stoats and weasels were to be seen running about in a demented fashion in the lanes, great noiseless owls came flapping down the village street at dusk, and once the appearance in broad daylight of a fox with a cat in its mouth produced great alarm, as even to dream of a fox – most fateful and sinister of all animals – was considered a dangerous omen.

There was a great increase of amateurs from Sort trying their hand at fishing. In the autumn the men had come down and fished with rods using the wrong bait, at the wrong time of day, in the wrong sea, and usually in places where everyone in Farol knew there were no fish to be caught anyway. Now the fashion was for family parties, and it was a little sad to see how the women tried to make a picnic of this desperate business, putting on flowered frocks to drench themselves in seawater and graze and cut themselves on the rocks, whereas the fishermen's wives, when called upon in winter to drag in the big sonsera nets, took care never to wear anything but black. The amateur fishers had made up enormous nets, unsuitable in any number of ways. These they carried down to the sea, and there was a pretence at good-natured laughter and horseplay, as a half-dozen or more men and women clinging to the circumference of the net lowered it like an immense pocket handkerchief into the sea then pulled it up again. Once in a while they caught a finger-sized fish.

5

Sebastian had tied up his boat in a cove near the spot where we had seen the big fish, and we walked there together along a cliff path with changing vistas of the sea. After the furrowed grey wastes of water surrounding our islands the huge vivacity of the Mediterranean never ceased to astonish. Here it was splashed all over with plum-coloured stains of weed-beds among which bald rocks just beneath the surface were brilliant uncut emeralds. Light-scaled water thrashing about in the deep coves rose and fell, uncovering and submerging great shining boulders like wallowing buffalos. Wherever there was a beach it was spread with the black membranes of drying nets, and here and there a small wedge of colour showed where a woman was at work closing up the holes left by the dolphins.

All Sebastian's expressions seemed accentuated by the thin pencilling of moustaches that rose or fell in sympathy with the elation or depression of a sensitive mouth, and on this occasion he was in low spirits. Open warfare had broken out between him and the Grandmother that morning and she had told him that she objected to his remaining under her roof while denying her daughter a child. The rumour was going round, she told him, that he was sterile. Sebastian knew fishermen feared the malefic contagion of sterility almost as much they did cuckoldry, and men supposed to be suffering from either of these disabilities were not invited to join fishing crews or go on pilgrimages. The Grandmother went on to say that this rumour was bound to affect her trade if something was not done to scotch it. Sebastian had offered to move out, then, having gone from house to house in the village, had found no one with a couple of rooms to spare.

In this subdued frame of mind we threw our gear into the boat, untied it, and rowed out to our chosen fishing ground. Sebastian was still using my old gun from the previous season, only effective with the smallest of fish, and he took the first turn in the water while I managed the boat, shooting a dozen or so wrasse in a matter of minutes, after which I loaded the more powerful gun and dropped into the water. I was beginning at last to appreciate the fact underlying all the fishermen's lore that there are seas of many kinds, all of them having their special problems, and offering their different rewards.

There were 'old' seas, rising and falling seas, full seas and swells and there were hybrid oceanic states in which two or more of these factors could be involved. There were also variables like currents, water temperatures, and above all the time of day that governed the presence or the absence of fish. One thing I could be certain about was that whatever awaited me as I swam out over the shelving sea bed into deep water it would be quite different from what I had seen in my first visit to this place.

I found hundreds of tiny black swallow-tailed wrasse, spaced in geometrical equidistance in the void, and these barely flinched as I passed through them. On the bottom, thirty or forty feet down, I picked out the wavering track of grebias – these tasted of mud and weed, and the Grandmother would not so much as look at them – through the soft new growths of marine grass. There was nothing here to test the quality of the new gun. The mullet – as I was later to learn – were away curing themselves of winter infections and infestations at the mouth of rivers still discharging a little fresh water into the sea. This water was too warm for escarmalans and crabs, and too cold for the magnificent dentols which would follow the warm currents in about a month's time to renew their cautious exploration of their summer feeding grounds. The silver-striped saupas I had watched back in the autumn feeding on the close weed at the top of the rocks were elsewhere because the sun had not yet ripened the new season's growth of weed. The water was too clear, too transparent here for sea bass, which would have to contain their hunger until they could swoop on their prey through the murk stirred up by a storm. I dawdled about in this near emptiness hoping that a family of ciervias might come drifting in from the open sea and be tempted to encircle me at close range to satisfy their curiosity. In this lay the excitement of spear-fishing. One could be taken by surprise. There was no way of knowing what lay in wait round the next corner in this wholly mysterious landscape.

On our first visit to this spot I had seen huge meros with great goggling eyes and dejected mouths watching at the openings of the caves in which they spent their lives when not out foraging for food. What I did not yet realize was that the time to see and hunt meros was in the early hours of the morning – the time when we had made our first trip – or the evening, when they themselves came out to lurk and hunt among the shadows.

To be a competent undersea fisherman the indispensable qualities are those of any other hunter: patience, powers of observation, and the ability to keep still, to merge into the background on the alert for the small irregularity of shape, colour, or movement that betrays the presence of the quarry. By chance it was this that I was suddenly aware of in the moment of giving up and turning back to make for the boat. There was something in the mouth of a cave in perhaps ten feet of water that was in some way not as it should have been. The sun slanted a solid mote-filled shaft across the opening, and behind it I could make out a misted profile that was too regular, too boldly curved for the haphazard patterns of the sea; a veiled shape, half imagined, half seen.

I dived and found myself within a few feet of the largest escorvai I had so far seen. It had placed itself almost as though on guard across the entrance and perhaps a foot inside the cave, and behind it, against the dim architecture of the cave's interior up to a dozen slightly smaller, but still large fish were arranged like so many overlapping metal plates. The big escorvai spread a dorsal fin like a junk's sail, edged forward with a flexing of the body that released soft reflections of copper, pewter and pinchbeck, and the iridescent patch over the neck deepened from purple to violet, then faded again. I levelled the gun and pressed the trigger and with the harpoon's impact the fish seemed to emit sparks of green and yellow light. It carried the harpoon with it in a series of flashing parabolas into the depths of the cave and the metallic wall of fish that had backed it shattered itself, hurling its shining parts into dim recesses out of view. I tugged on the harpoon and it came out with the impaled fish, and my first reaction was one of surprise that it had been unable to escape.

I surfaced and swam to the boat, and lifted in the fish, still on the harpoon. Sebastian was tying his catch of wrasse on a line and when he saw it he swore.

'Beautiful isn't it?' I said, but it was already smaller and duller than it had been less than five minutes before. The colour seemed to be draining away with the small trickle of blood from the hole just behind the head. Sebastian threw a sack over it and emptied a half-bucket of sea water on the sack.

'Any more out there?' Sebastian asked.

'Quite a few in a cave.'

'Going back again?'

'I'm frozen. I've had enough for today.'

Sebastian lifted back a corner of the sack and prodded at the hole left by the harpoon. 'Wonder what they're going to say about that?'

We carried the fish with pride up the beach and several fishermen, generous in their praise and encouragement as in every other way, stopped to admire it. Escorvais, like meros, hardly ever emerged from their caves and were therefore in the main beyond the reach of line or net.

The Grandmother was engaged in a business deal with the schoolmaster provided by the government this year to replace the nuns who had hitherto given some basic instruction in the converted slaughterhouse that served as a cinema at the weekends. In this community only the schoolmaster was paid less than Sebastian, receiving 18 pesetas for working a five-hour day. Being quite unable to live on this sum, he had turned his hand to fishing and had actually devised a system of his own that produced a tiny supplementary income. The schoolmaster had observed something that the fishermen chose to ignore – that mullet, which were scavengers by nature, congregated at the point where the village sewage was discharged through a pipe into the sea. He fitted a most ingenious trap to the end of this pipe which had no adverse effect on the disposal of the sewage, but actually caught the mullet. These he brought live to the Grandmother who, while expressing her abhorrence for the whole business, and uttering shocked cries at the indecency of fish frequenting sewers, was still prepared to pay an exceedingly small sum – in this case 9 pesetas – for the fish. The deal done, the mullet were then thrown into a tank of fresh water and left there for a day after which – since no one would have dreamed of eating them locally – they were passed on to a boy with a tricycle and carrier to be hawked round the farms.

This, said the Grandmother, was what she proposed to do in the case of our escorvai. Fish for local sale commanded a price that varied to some extent according to the method of its catching, those taken by line being in less demand than fish of the same variety caught by net. The local belief was that the suffering experienced by a fish that might have spent several hours on a hook caused a detectable bitterness in its flesh. People, said the Grandmother, were reluctant also to pay the prevailing market price for fish speared by the *fitora* – the illegal trident in clandestine use – and she had no doubt at all that the principle would apply in the case of our escorvai. Her price for an unspoiled fish of this size would have been 70 pesetas, but as it was, 30 pesetas was the highest she was prepared to go to. Sebastian got 15 pesetas for his wrasse. Apart from our success with the escarmalan fishing in the north, it was the best day we had had.

6

It soon became evident that there were certain advantages to be derived from living within the zone of influence of a prince of the black market. Dearth left Muga untouched, but there were also small unstoppable leakages from his abundance, and all those across whom his shadow fell benefited to some degree, however slight.

Meat, hardly to be seen in Farol for years, began to reappear. Somewhere in secret a steer was slaughtered, and although the best of it, for roasting and stewing purposes, would have been delivered to the Muga mansion by discreet men at the dead of night, not even the numerous members of the Muga family and their many hangers-on could eat a whole beast in a matter of days when refrigerators were not to be had, so large amounts of perfectly acceptable offal found its way into the butcher's shop.

When the news got round of this first windfall of tripe, liver, lights, brain, of knuckles, tail and hooves, of glandular sacs, arterial conduits and membraneous messes, there was a stampede to the shop, and Carmela soon returned with a grim smile of triumph and a prize in its bloody package. I was ordered from the kitchenette while the cooking got under way. 'Don't look, sir, whatever you do. Just leave it to me. Appearances don't count. It's all in the mind.'

The meal, reflecting ingenuity and resource based on a great culinary tradition, was a memorable one. ('Pardon me, but don't stare at your food like that, sir. Everything is good. If there's something you don't fancy the look of, just pass it over to me.') As usual Carmela shovelled the remains into a bag, hid it away in the party frock she had worn for so many years, and was off.

Another benefit of Muga's presence took the form of real coffee made from once-used grounds from a reserve Muga kept at the bar. Most nights the black-marketeer would drop in to exchange frowns with the mermaid and drink a cup of coffee before going to bed, and what remained in the pot was carefully preserved, sometimes adulterated with a little substitute made from acorns, and rationed by the Alcalde to his friends.

I strolled over to the bar, and seated myself at an outside table, being found a moment later by Don Alberto who came puttering up on his motorcycle. The Levis had been off the road for the best part of a week because petrol supplies in Farol had run out, and the fact that Don Alberto was mobile again lent substance to the rumour that Muga, who had five cars, had diverted petrol supplied as a priority to the lighthouse, and that a hundred-litre drum had found its way down to the village.

This being a somewhat special occasion, the Alcalde brought out the coffee himself, then threw himself into a chair, groaned and covered his face with his hands. We sipped the infusion from Muga's used coffee grounds, raised our eyes in ecstasy and then the Alcalde told us his troubles. Someone had chalked 'lambs' wool sucked here' across the bar in the night. The allusion was unjust. 'Suckers of lambs' wool' was the derisive title imposed by all those who suffered from the Fascist bureaucracy on the officials who sucked their blood, but the Alcalde, although an official, had become one with reluctance, and was well-known for pulling whatever strings he could in official circles to make life easier for the people of his village.

'I don't know what I'm doing here,' he said. 'All I get is ingratitude.'

The weekly messenger just in from Gerona spotted us and came over to offer Don Alberto a month's collection of obituaries from *Vanguardia*.

'How much?'

'Forty pesetas.'

'But that's all the papers cost.'

'I know, but nobody reads the papers. This is all they buy them for.'

Don Alberto bought the collection, and read the first of them. *Pray to God in Charity for the soul of Dra. Concepción Barber Nogués who passed away on April 14th after receiving the holy sacrament and the apostolic blessing. Mourned by her afflicted family.* Don Alberto shook his head. 'Afflicted is overdone. Disconsolate is better. We suffer from a constant erosion of good taste.'

Don Ignacio, drawn out of his house towards the bar as if some instinct had warned him that real coffee was to be had, joined our little group. The fishermen raised no objection to his sitting outside the bar where any unfavourable influences he generated would be rapidly dispersed in the atmosphere, but out of respect of their prejudices he took care never to go inside. He was eager to tell someone about the remarkable latrine of a Roman villa recently unearthed in Ampurias, but nobody was interested in this subject and Don Alberto made it an opportunity to tackle him on the matter of a woman who had just committed suicide in Sort. Despite his personal intervention the priest there had refused to bury her in consecrated ground.

'Send her over here,' Don Ignacio said. 'I'll find room for her in our cemetery.'

'Won't the locals kick up a fuss?'

'They won't know what's going on,' Don Ignacio said. 'We'll present them with a *fait accompli*.'

'Thank God there are a few Christians left alive,' Don Alberto said.

The story was that the woman, having been deserted by her husband, had put on her white wedding dress, walked up the hill to an abandoned chapel behind the village, bandaged the eyes of the Virgin who still presided there, swallowed an ergot pill of the kind given to cows, and then died.

'She was a mere object for her husband,' Don Alberto said. 'A political necessity. He acquired her along with property. No more than that.'

'It's all you expect of peasants,' Don Ignacio said.

'They've suffered from generations of bad government,' the Alcalde put in. He was on the look-out for an excuse to grumble about the deficiencies of the regime he served. 'I don't see much difference now.'

'They suffer from property,' Don Alberto said. 'Having spent most of my life there I can tell you love doesn't exist in Sort, or if it exists at all it comes second to the love of material things. What does a peasant want to do – cherish his wife and children? No, he wants to add another field to the land he's already got. In the end perhaps he'll get rich, and then he's a peasant multiplied by ten. What is a hereditary land owner? A peasant multiplied by a hundred. That duke you hear so much about who can travel from one end of Spain to the other without leaving his estates – what's he but a peasant multiplied by a thousand?'

'This country's swung too far in the other direction,' the Alcalde said. 'I fought against the Reds, and would again, but when you hear about this duke of yours you begin to think.'

'He's a victim of tradition like all the rest of them,' Don Alberto said. 'In reality what does all this power and prestige of his amount to? He's just adding field to field. I could tell you of tenants of mine who got married to a girl with a bit of land, took the first boat to America and didn't show up in the village again for ten to fifteen years. They come back rich, a pocketful of fields you might say. But what sort of wealth is that?'

'We have a proverb,' Don Ignacio said, ready with his quotation from Barras. 'God never strangles, but property does.'

A party of fishermen passed, laden down with nets that had been dipped in preserving liquid and would now be spread out on the beach to dry. Each man, seeing Don Ignacio, fumbled quickly to touch iron, or failing that, his testicles. 'Nobody can own the sea,' Don Alberto said, 'therefore no court cases, no political marriages, no fuss over inheritances, and plenty of love to go round. They don't know how lucky they are.'

'Going back to this poor woman,' Don Ignacio said. 'Was there any indication as to the state of her mind? I'm putting her in the cemetery whatever anybody likes to say, but I'd like to be able to produce an argument if necessary.'

'She wrote something on the wall of the chapel that didn't make much sense,' Don Alberto said. '"I shall never come back again to this place." That's all.'

'And what did you make of that?'

'What *can* you make of it?'

'If you ask me she was crazy,' the Alcalde said. 'That's not a rational thing to write.'

'I agree with you,' Don Ignacio said. 'She'd clearly taken leave of her senses. I suppose she didn't have a father? Were there any brothers?'

'Only one. Collecting a few fields in Argentina. There are a couple of sisters.'

'To give this some sort of an appearance,' Don Ignacio said. 'we really need a male chief mourner. I suppose there wouldn't be any chance – ?'

'Certainly I'll be chief mourner,' Don Alberto said. 'I barely knew the girl by sight, but I can at least mourn for humanity.'

7

I had been invited with Don Alberto to lunch that day at the house of a rich tenant of his, Pablo Fons, a reactionary as Don Alberto described him of the old school, and here I was hoping for the opportunity to listen to the peasant viewpoint. In Farol most of the real power seemed to lie in the hands of the women. Sort, according to Don Alberto, followed a patriarchal system although this was rapidly breaking up, and the Fons family was one of the remaining few where the father was the centre of all authority, and no decision or action could be taken, even by his grown-up sons, without consultation with him and his assent.

Don Alberto took me to the Fons fortified farmhouse on the back of his Levis. The whole area surrounding this grim-looking building smelt intensely of cattle and their dung, and bluebottles by the thousand buzzed over the puddles of cows' urine, and round women as black as witches washing clothes at a domed-over well. The farm itself was a miniature fortress with small barred windows rimmed with white paint, like sleepless eyes, and it would have taken a battering ram to knock down the door behind which Fons awaited us dressed in a new, blue shirt fastened very tightly at the neck, and grey trousers with black cummerbund. My immediate impression after many months spent in the company of fishermen who had expressions of extreme innocence, even gullibility, was of a highly complicated face and a sceptical smile. At Fons' back stood one of his grown-up sons holding a bowl of water, soap and a towel. We were invited to wash our feet, but declined. A long table had been set in the entrance hall or porch as it was locally known, and we were asked to take our seats. 'Cover yourselves, gentlemen,' Fons said. Don Alberto had provided a scratchy straw hat in preparation for this ceremony, and I clamped it on my head and sat down. 'Pick up your eating utensils, gentlemen,' was the next order and Don Alberto and I raised the knives and spoons provided. Fons followed suit, and only then was it in order for the rest of those at table – Fons' two sons, and a pair of overseers – to prepare to eat. The food – goat's flesh with saffron- flavoured rice – was served by two cowed-looking females in black, one of whom I supposed to be Fons' wife, who then made themselves scarce.

Don Alberto drew Fons out, explaining that I was a foreigner interested in local customs, that I was staying in Farol and had been surprised to hear of the antipathy displayed towards each other by the people of the two villages.

Fons then asked me what I personally thought of the fishermen, and I told him I got on very well with them.

'Do you really want to know what I think of them?' Fons asked.

'That's why he's here,' Don Alberto said. 'You're supposed to be a man who doesn't pull his punches. Let's hear you speak your own mind.'

'Very well, then, objection number one. We here at Sort have a close and devoted family life.'

'At this point perhaps I ought to point out that two of Pablo's sons haven't spoken to him for a couple of years,' Don Alberto said.

'You're talking of tiffs. These things pass,' Fons said. 'I repeat that we have indissoluble family bonds, and we respect our ancestors. My great-grandfather, or maybe my great-great-grandfather fought against Napoleon. We have a history. Nothing of what I've said to you applies in Farol. They don't worship Almighty God, most husbands don't sleep with their wives but practise self-abuse, which is proved by the fact that half of them don't have children. Moreover, they monopolise the sea.'

'Nobody can do that,' Don Alberto said. 'The sea's yours for the taking.'

'The Bible tells us we should earn our bread by the sweat of our brow. What do our friends at Farol do? They carry a net to the water, put it down, and wait for it to fill with fish. Half the time they're asleep.'

'Forgive me,' Don Alberto said. 'I know of no men who work harder. Try not to talk nonsense in front of my friend, who will get a bad impression of us.'

Fons took a spoonful of rice, and his sons and farmhands who had ceased out of respect to eat while he was talking hastily pitched into their food. A dog came through the door dragging a log inch by inch on its chain. Fons threw it a gobbet of gristle, and began again, waving his spoon reproachfully.

'My respect for you is enormous, Don Alberto. After all you're one of us, but for the life of me I can't see how you can take these people's part. Excuse me but I feel it as a kind of betrayal. Doesn't an obsession with cats offend you, for instance? It's something that makes my flesh creep.'

'You're just as bad with dogs. The fact is I'm in a position to see both sides, and there's a lot to criticise in Sort, where I happen to have been born. Take the case of that poor unfortunate girl. Something must be wrong with any kind of community where a thing like that can happen.'

A small splutter of protest decorated the front of Fons' blue shirt with golden grains of rice.

'A tragedy can happen anywhere. How you can blame us for what took place at the chapel I can't imagine. We're Christians, respecters of the passion of Our Lord. What are you going to say about people who tolerate prostitutes in their midst? I'm referring to the woman who used to herd goats in this village. I'm told she's been seen in the Sunday promenade walking at the side of the Alcalde's wife.'

'I wouldn't describe the young lady in question as a prostitute,' Don Alberto said.

'And how would you describe her, your honour?'

'An attractive and popular young woman with a number of suitors.'

Fons appealed to his sons. 'What do you think of that, boys? We're referring to Maria Cabritas?'

The sons put down their spoons to laugh scornfully.

'With due respect, Don Alberto,' Fons said, 'let me remind you of our customs. A girl is entitled to entertain any number of suitors providing the intentions of all parties are serious.'

'Quite right,' Don Alberto said. 'I remember a girl in my young days who had fifteen, of whom I was one. Naturally I was rejected.'

'Tuesdays, Thursdays and Saturdays were and still are the days on which courting takes place. Suitors are received starting at 8 p.m., and each may remain for a period of fifteen minutes. Normally the mother of the girl or her aunt is present.'

'I know all these things so well,' Don Alberto said. 'Usually it was the aunt, and sometimes it was possible to bribe her. As a nation we are disposed to corruption.'

'But everything must be kept within reason,' Fons said. 'This is Spain, not the Congo. Nobody's going to object to a young person getting a bit more than their due once in a while if they can, but every girl that has young men round to the house is expected to take one of them to church within a reasonable time. If this doesn't happen people cease to take her seriously, and in the end she's likely to be stoned.'

'Symbolically,' Don Alberto said.

'As in the case of the girl under discussion. A couple of responsible women went to the house and threw a few pebbles at the door. She and her mother had the good sense to get out. If they hadn't they'd have run into something more than a symbol. It was made clear that they wanted her to go and she went.'

'Why do you leave this kind of job to old women?' Don Alberto asked. 'It's the only time you ever take any notice of them. In any case Sort's loss is Farol's gain.'

'I wish it were our loss,' Fons said. 'The point is it's not. She cleared out of the village itself, but she's still living within the limits of our community.'

'How can you say that?'

'Look at the map and you'll see the house is at least twenty metres over our boundary'.

'All she has to do is to put up a shack at the bottom of the garden, and she'd be in Farol.'

'It would please me to see her do that,' Fons said. 'We'd be clear of the responsibility.'

'Don't be childish, Pablo,' Don Alberto told him.

We left, puttering back across the fields on the asthmatic Levis for a coffee outside the bar in Farol. This time it was a straightforward substitute made from acorns and locust beans with a strong flavour of tar. 'That man,' said Don Alberto, 'is dangerous, not just stupid as you would assume. Notice the craving for status? Now he's got himself an ancestor who fought against Napoleon. His great-great-grandfather was a peon on the finca. A slave if you like. They used to tether them like horses at night.'

'Why's he dangerous?' I asked.

'Because something is building up between these two villages. A *lío*. What you call a vendetta. And this man is a moving spirit. I think these people are plotting something. There's no way of saying what it is, but we'll soon know.'

8

That evening I was surprised to see a new face in the normally unchanging human vista of the evening promenade. An extremely fat, though pretty girl was walking arm in arm with the Grandmother, and she was clearly well known and respected, as any man who happened to be wearing a hat made a bee-line for them to raise it as he passed. There was something familiar about this girl, but seconds passed before I realised that it was Sa Cordovesa who was almost unrecognisable.

Sebastian was full of excitement about what had happened when we met in the bar a little later, and the story passed on by his wife was a remarkable one. The admiral who had fallen in love with her, proposed marriage, been accepted, and had whisked her away supposedly to Madrid, turned out to be an assistant purser in a ship of a minor coastal line operating between Barcelona and Vigo. Sa Cordovesa had found herself shut away in a three-room walk-up apartment in the dreary little industrial town of Prat del Llobregat awaiting a wedding which, as the admiral said, had had to be postponed to await the formal assent of the ministry of the Marine. She had been placed in the care of an old woman who took away her shoes, never let her out of her sight and constantly served her enormous meals. This was explained by the admiral's concern for her health after a doctor he had called in to give her a check-up told her she was suffering from tuberculosis. The doctor had prescribed medicines and also a régime designed to build up her resistance to the disease. She was obliged to eat several pounds of potatoes a day, plus an immense amount of oily stews, fatty meats, cream cakes and pastries of all kinds. The doctor also instructed her to spend twelve hours out of the twenty-four in bed, to walk slowly, and avoid taking undue exercise.

The lover, never out of his admiral's uniform, with a chestful of decorations, came to see her and announce a new date for the wedding at fortnightly intervals when his ship got in from Vigo. The true facts came out when he was taking an afternoon nap and she went through his pockets and found not only his identity papers but an affectionate letter from another sufferer from tuberculosis who was undergoing the same treatment as she, and who proudly announced in it that she now topped the scale at 196 pounds. This convinced Sa Cordovesa that the admiral was just a man who collected fat girls and, having cleaned out his wallet, which contained barely enough to pay her fare back to Farol and buy a pair of shoes, she left him and the old woman to their siestas and departed.

The problem that arose now was – what to do with her? Sa Cordovesa had enjoyed life in Farol where she had been admired by all and loved by quite a few. The discreet service she had performed for the community had been taken over by Maria Cabritas and carried out by her with equal efficiency and discretion. Sebastian said that the feeling among the fishermen was that whatever the sacrifices involved a place would have to be found for her in the life of Farol, the difficulty being that few if any fishermen shared the admiral's passion for obesity.

I was invited by the Grandmother to discuss with her the medical aspects of the problem. Sort and Farol shared a doctor, a brisk and cheerful mannikin of four feet ten inches or so, whose real name was Churrimina, meaning 'Bonfire' in the Basque tongue, but who had earned the nickname of Dr Seduction following allegations that he had had unlawful intercourse with a fisherman's statuesque wife after administering a whiff of ether to remove a splinter from her toe. For this reason, and the fact that he was not properly qualified but allowed to practise after three years' experience as a medical orderly purely as a result of the national shortage of medical men, he was rarely consulted; and anyone like myself from the outside world was constantly approached to give an opinion on minor problems of health.

The interview, with Sa Cordovesa present, took place in the Grandmother's kitchen, after the Grandmother had scrutinised the contents of two 'Pride of the Onion' pickle jars that Sa Cordovesa had been asked to bring with her, and clearly remained baffled. The patient was seated with some difficulty in a chair of the kind favoured in Farol, having nine-inch legs and therefore more suited to the use of dwarves than people of normal proportions.

Sa Cordovesa came as a pleasant surprise. She was uncomplaining, full of humour and grace. Her corpulence was uneven, adipose tissue having taken over here and been resisted there; a great benign spread of breast, a rosebud mouth compressed by softly cushioned cheeks, trim ankles, and small feet thrust into the new over-showy shoes. One sensed the reality of finely chiselled Andalusian bone under the puffy amiability of her face. She was ready, almost eager to discuss her misadventures, doing so in a voice full of self-mockery lilting up and down the scale to the accompaniment of the soft bass rumblings of the Grandmother's counsels and consolations.

The thing was, what was to be done about this mountain of fat she had suddenly been encumbered with? Could it be massaged away? Could it be charmed away? Was it a fact that pills existed to remedy the situation? How long, if all else failed, would she have to live on a diet of bread and water before the nimble girl she had once been could step forth from this prison of flesh?

The Grandmother could not answer any of these questions because Sa Cordovesa's problem was one that had not arisen in Farol before, where with her own exception, and that of the butcher's wife, the tendency was to be slender. It was inevitable that the talk should be of the Curandero, who had a cure for almost all ills, but the Curandero would not return until the end of the summer, heralding the arrival of the tunny. I was sorry to disappoint, but there was nothing I could do, for although I had heard of slimming pills, I thought it unlikely that they were available in Spain. All I could promise was to bring back a supply from England in the following year.

They went off together, and I watched them go down the street into the sallow evening with all the light and colour drained away into the sunflowers flagging over the grey walls. A last sliver of moon was encircled by black, screaming swifts. Cats and a pig called Mercedes that lived on seaweed were racing across the beach to meet an incoming boga boat, and the man with the pack-mule who had finished work in Farol for the day was on his way back to Sort to pay for his glass of wine in the usual way. As he passed the slow-moving and stately ladies he swept off his hat. I heard Don Alberto's motorcycle come puttering into the village from the opposite direction making for the bar and his evening *rancio*, and I went to join him, planning on the way a fishing trip for the next day.

The responsibility of looking after Sa Cordovesa in her hour of need was shared among the fishing community, and she stayed two days with one family and three days with the next while people looked round with solicitude for a place she could call home. I brought up the problem with Carmela, who said. 'Send her to me. I may be able to fix her up.'

Carmela remained a mystery. She kept apart from the life of the village, and after her morning stint spent in washing out my room and cooking the midday meal, I hardly ever set eyes on her. At eight o'clock she would be suddenly there, to announce in her flinty voice, as if reading out a legal sentence, what the shop or the butcher's offered in the way of food for that day. At about one, after the completion of the daily miracle of the transmutation of whatever repellent raw materials she had come by into a delectable dish, she would suddenly and soundlessly be gone. On the rare occasions when I had sighted her outside these morning hours she had been slipping through the shadows in the uncertain light just before nightfall.

She was imbued with the aroma of clandestinity, of small-scale secrecies and unobtrusive operations concerned with survival. Her shape under the party frock was bulky at one moment and inexplicably deflated the next, as if divested of mysterious contraband. Once, taking a short cut at twilight through the edge of the cork-oak forest I had glimpsed her flitting from tree trunk to tree trunk on her way homewards, and I asked myself if this obvious desire to escape attention did not suggest an illicit adventure among the hen-houses of Sort. Sometimes after her morning arrival I noticed a large bag in my cupboard, and opening it one day I found it to be crammed with a kind of chickweed the dog people grew to feed their animals, from which I gathered that Carmela's rabbits were fattened for market at Sort's expense. In a way I was reminded of Muga, prince of the black market. They were both of them professionals, practising the arts of self-defence and self-advancement on different scales but – since scandal was largely avoided, and their victims hardly realised what was happening to them – with equal skill.

Carmela's old father had dropped dead during the winter and, reporting this, Sebastian told me more of her story. This, when I tackled her, she neither confirmed nor denied, warning me off the subject with an unwelcoming glance of a misted, basilisk eye. The story was that she had been saddled with the care and upbringing of a grossly handicapped child, a girl left in infancy with her by a prostitute who had paid the regular sums agreed upon for a year or so, and then suddenly gone off to South America to be heard from no more. Few people in Farol had seen this little girl, Rosa, now believed to be about twelve years of age, and there were wild rumours about her, one being that she was exceptionally beautiful, and another that she was covered with hair like a monkey.

When I saw her for myself, it was by accident on the day after Sa Cordovesa went to live in the shack Carmela had put up on the village's outskirts. On the afternoon of this day the Civil Guards called on the Grandmother with a stern rebuke for having failed to comply with regulations by not reporting to them Sa Cordovesa's presence in her house. There was no other male about so the Grandmother asked me to go to the shack and warn Sa Cordovesa and Carmela of what had happened, and let them know that a routine visit by the police was to be expected.

The fishermen liked to be soothed when on shore by a calm environment, with grey stone, whitewashed walls, and clear, unclattered spaces. No fishermen lived at Carmela's end of the village and there was a great deal of unpremeditated colour in the scene. The shack had been carpentered together by Carmela and her old father from an assortment of wreckage collected along the shore, braced and smartened up with partitions and doors filched – as I had heard – from the old cork mansions. Nobody in Farol liked the colour yellow – possibly because it was associated with magic practices, this being the colour of the eyes painted on the boats. But the shopkeeper had had a can of yellow paint on his shelves for years, so Carmela bought this for next to nothing, and painted the sea-bleached wood to protect it from the weather. The shack had been put up on the deepest of red earth, and a violent rain-storm on the morning of my visit had splashed the soil with dramatic, even sanguinary effect over the lower parts of the canary-yellow wood. Finally, this was a neglected area where rampant convolvulus had taken hold, and although the villagers regarded it as a stubborn weed and rooted it out wherever they could it poured like an irresistible vegetable flood over Carmela's shack covering much of the paintwork with its great shallow trumpets of the most intense blue.

Carmela had made do without windows. A door hung askew on a single hinge, but the view of the interior was screened off by a curtain of sacking. Bantam chickens scampered in and out of the building and dashed about in all directions in the open, chasing after ants. I rattled at the door and called out, but there were no signs either of Carmela or Sa Cordovesa and I was going away when I heard the sound of a child blubbering. I lifted back the sack and went in, finding myself in a dim little cell of a room with an earth floor, a chair and a bed and a chest of the kind into which such as Carmela are obliged to stuff the often strange miscellany of their worldly goods.

Beyond a second aperture, also screened with sacking, was a yard, and it was from this that the sound of blubbering, now subsided, had been coming. I went out to investigate, knowing that this would involve me in a single-handed encounter with Carmela's subnormal child, and when for the first time I saw Rosa I was not shocked because

I had been prepared for worse (there had been rumours of hereditary syphilis and blindness).

I understood at first glance that she was a spastic who could not straighten one leg, held from the knee down almost at right angles to the thigh. Despite this extreme disability, and the fact that she appeared to be on the point of toppling over sideways through one leg being in effect shorter than the other, she was able to move – as she did now – in a grotesque, bounding fashion, flailing her arms in helicopter fashion in order to keep her balance. At the moment of my appearance she had burst again into shrieking, babbling incoherence, and was advancing in a series of leaps and bounds on a goat, tied to a stake that was doing its desperate best to avoid her. The goat raced round and round the stake, backed away straining on its rope and scuttering with its hoofs and Rosa went after it, howling and hooting and brandishing her arms. The possibility occurred to me at that moment that this could be the sort of desperate game to appeal to the imagination of a totally isolated child – perhaps her only game.

She bore down on the goat like a tiny grey witch, and now perhaps the game – if game it were – had reached its normal climax, because the goat, having retreated as far as its rope would allow, put down its head and charged.

I rushed to pick the child up, do what I could to console her, wipe the grimed tears from under the fine, sensitive eyes. The top half of her face was that of an angel, and the bottom half of a monkey. She gave me what I later came to know was a smile of gratitude and affection, but which the monkey mouth had translated into a simian leer.

At that moment Carmela arrived, put the girl on her feet and sent her hobbling and flopping away. 'Don't bother yourself, sir. It's absolutely nothing to worry about. This is the kind of thing she gets up as as soon as my back is turned. She likes to tease the goat, but really they're the best of friends.'

9

The rumour that Muga had bought the fonda proved true. In a matter of weeks while the villagers hardly noticed what was going on, the builders from Figueras had torn out the labyrinth of odd-shaped rooms and replaced them with fourteen bedrooms built to a standardised low-priced hotel design. Three bathrooms were incorporated, an exotic extravagance in local eyes, where De Barros' counsel, '*De las cuarenta pa' arriba, no te mojas la barriga*' ('From forty on, don't wet your guts') was scrupulously observed.

Muga built a large verandah at the back of the fonda – now upgraded officially to the status of an hotel. Dances would be held on this, he let it be known, later in the year when the tourists came. The view from the verandah would have been a romantic one had it not been spoiled by an L-shaped wall in the corner of which horses were taken to be castrated, and an exceedingly ugly building which an expatriate from Sort had put up brick by brick, working single-handed, in exactly twenty-nine years.

Hardly anyone outside Farol and Sort had ever heard of the old fonda, and the few casual travellers who had stayed there had done their best to forget the experience, but the energetic Muga was determined to put the Hotel Brisas del Mar, as the fonda had been renamed, on the tourist map. He therefore joined the hoteliers' association and, by guaranteeing to provide a few basic facilities, was accorded C Category registration on their list. The all-in price of 8 pesetas charged by the two silent brothers for a gloomy and malodorous cell, and hard-boiled eggs and sardines twice a day, was summarily increased to 50 pesetas a day, causing the locals to burst into peals of disbelieving laughter.

Muga called on Don Ignacio, eased his belly into as comfortable a position as the low chair he was offered would permit and outlined his plans for the village's development and eventual prosperity. Don Ignacio repeated to me what he could remember of his remarks on the subject of religious observance, which the priest had found funny.

Muga mentioned that he had already been to the shop and given them a list of the things they ought to stock, such as souvenir fans,

Sevillian dolls, and carvings of Don Quixote, if they wanted to derive any benefit from the tourist trade, and he had had a word with the Alcalde about the terrible quality of the wine sold in his bar. Now he turned his attention to church arrangements. 'Who goes to Mass in a place like this?' he had asked. 'The grocer, the town clerk, and the police?'

'That about sums it up,' Don Ignacio said. 'No one would call our people devout.'

'I notice that there was no Mass at all last Sunday. Don't think that it matters to me one way or the other, but I'm running an hotel and the law obliges me to put up a notice for the benefit of visitors, giving the hours of Mass.'

'Choose your own time,' Don Ignacio said. 'Would 8 a.m. on Sunday be convenient?'

'As long as we can depend upon it.'

'You may put up your notice,' Don Ignacio said. 'Mass will be celebrated at the time announced.'

So, he told me, his archaeological researches at Ampurias had come to an end, because there was no public transport to take him to the dig in the middle of the week.

The first guests at the Brisas del Mar arrived in some style in a chauffeur-driven Isotta-Fraschini at the end of May, providing instant and final confirmation of the villagers' belief that all outsiders were basically irrational, when not actually mad. Apart from the chauffeur, the party consisted of an absolutely genuine forty-six-year-old Marquesa with enormous estates in the impoverished south, and her lover, a bullfighter aged twenty-three who appeared in fights at such places as Medina del Campo, the Spanish equivalent of Stockton-on-Tees, where the best ringside seats cost 18 pesetas. The bullfighter, who was much smaller than the Marquesa and who only wanted to go for long walks, did so to local amazement holding an iron bar in his outstretched arm to strengthen the muscles employed in his profession. When he became tired the Marquesa picked him up and carried him on her shoulders, passing him over to the chauffeur when she herself weakened. Like many of the very rich and powerful, she cared little for the good opinion of others, and was quite ready to discuss the details, mostly scabrous, of her private life with the chambermaid, who duly passed them on. She had just been hauled before the court in Madrid for 'public scandal'. As she told the chambermaid, she was crazy about footballers, and had entertained three forwards and two half-backs of Real Madrid at a party in her flat where they had been induced to remove their clothes to give a demonstration of dribbling, passing, and shooting, just before the police broke in. She appeared before the judge in her widow's weeds, wearing the many medals won by her defunct husband fighting in the Nationalist cause, and was fined five pesetas. She blamed two unsuccessful facelifts for the fact that she was unable to close her mouth, and travelled, as the chambermaid reported, with her own black bed-sheets, which she had personally had edged with exceptionally fine lace.

After aristocratic dissolution, bourgeois sobriety. Within a few days the Marquesa and entourage were replaced by Julio Letrell, a member of the City Council of Barcelona, and his wife, and the second or third day after his arrival Letrell came up and introduced himself while I was sipping a glass from the barrel of wine the Alcalde had felt obliged to import from Alicante. Letrell said he had chosen Farol for a holiday because, from the map, it looked like the most off-the-beaten-track place within a hundred miles of his office. He said he couldn't get the sound of tramcars out his ears, and to see our shopkeeper take a couple of minutes to walk from one end of his counter to another and up to a half-hour to serve a customer induced in him a profound sensation of peace.

Letrell said that he was keen on fishing, but had found the local fishermen hard to approach. He had been led to believe that I did a good deal of fishing myself, and wondered if I could put him in touch with anyone who had a boat who could be persuaded to take him out on a trip.

He seemed a pleasant enough man, so I mentioned this to my neighbour Juan, who agreed to take a couple of hours off next day from his afternoon stint of preparing his palangres to be put down in the evening, and take Letrell out. It was an excursion that we both understood could be nothing more than a complete waste of time. We warned Letrell that for a number of reasons he would almost certainly catch nothing, our only hope being the slight possibility of running into mackerel. But there were no mackerel and Letrell sat there quite contentedly dangling his line in the watery wastes, and trying to involve Juan, who resisted all such overtures, in conversational topics about village affairs. After two hours we gave up and went back, having caught nothing. I formed the opinion that Letrell knew nothing whatever about sea fishing, and that he hardly knew one fish from another. Juan, sorry to see any man lose his time in this way, offered by way of compensation to take him out at night with the palangres, or at dawn to put down the boga nets, both of which offers he declined.

Letrell seemed to want to talk to people, and frustration in this direction was inevitable, given the inbred suspicion with which the people of Farol viewed outsiders of all kinds. Next day I found him at my table outside the bar again. I asked him if he planned any more fishing trips, and he said he did not. He wanted to know how long I'd lived in Farol, and I told him. Did I find the people reserved, difficult to reach? Yes, very. They were also non-materialistic, generous, poetic and superstitious in the extreme. But I'd got to know them? he asked, and I told him that I had not, but that I had made progress in that direction.

Letrell then said that he wanted to talk to me on a highly confidential matter. He was making enquiries, he said, on behalf of certain friends into the fate of Mariano Oliver who had disappeared from Farol in 1939, at the end of the Civil War.

I told him that a police captain had been here investigating the case in the previous year, beginning to wonder if Letrell could have been one of the innumerable plain-clothes agents one saw so much of in those years.

Letrell said that his interest in the case was a purely humanitarian one. Mariano Oliver's family wanted to know if he was still alive. That, and no more.

Oliver, he told me, was not the missing man's real name. He was the son of a noble family, immature, irresponsible and spoiled, who in the early thirties had been found guilty of an apparently motiveless impulse murder, inspired by a highly publicised killing for thrills that had taken place in the US. In this case publicity had been suppressed by the family, who had '*mucha influencia*'. Oliver spent a nominal two years in a criminal lunatic asylum looked after by his own servant, thereafter being sent to Farol to be kept out of the public eye. Nothing whatever could be learned, as I knew, of his life in the village, except that he had built a strange folly of a house set in a complicated garden of his own design. All trace of the house except the visible foundations had long since been removed, and only the outlines of the garden, the raised beds and the little irrigation channels, showed under the weeds. The villagers seemed determined to do their best to forget that this man known to them only as Mariano des Horts (Mariano the Gardener) had ever existed.

This, said Letrell, was a classic mystery, and the more he had heard from his friends of the facts of the case, the more intrigued he had become. Throughout the war Mariano Oliver's family had heard from their son with fair regularity and they had found ways of getting money to him despite the fact that he had been cut off from them in territory held by the Republicans until the final stages of the conflict. After the débâcle of the first week of February 1939 they had heard no more for several months until a series of letters began to arrive from France. There was no reason to suppose that these letters could be in any way suspect. They were signed, as ever, 'Pep' – a pet name only used among members of the family. Pep told his parents that he had joined the flow of refugees crossing the frontier into France where he suspected he would be obliged to stay for some time. The inference was that he had compromised himself with the Republican régime.

The letters continued to arrive for two years, but very slowly doubt took hold. Mariano Oliver's family were sufficiently powerful to obtain a pardon for their son, whatever he might have done, and they assured him of this, but he continued to show himself averse to the idea of returning. In France he kept on the move, constantly changing accommodation addresses to which mail and money were sent. His father wanted to go to France to meet him, but he made weak and unconvincing excuses to avoid the meeting.

The family then went to a private investigator who studied all the letters from Mariano – those dating from the Farol period, and those sent them from France. His conclusion was that the latter series was probably fake. He based this not on comparison of the handwriting and signatures – which a handwriting expert had pronounced identical – but upon tell-tale differences in the style of the writing. Pep writing from Farol had shown a liking for jokes, and clearly enjoyed puns and plays on words. The letters from France were spiritless and flat. Whoever wrote them, said the expert, had no sense of humour.

By this time, with the advent of the Vichy régime in France, relations were settling down between the two countries, and the assistance of the French Sureté could be sought. A trap was set for the letter-writer, but it caught nothing, although the letters came to an abrupt end. The private investigator's theory was that Mariano Oliver had been kidnapped, and forced by the kidnapper to write the letters. Some news of the affair leaked into the Spanish press, since when the family had been victimised, Letrell said, by hoaxers. Purported sightings of the lost Mariano were eagerly and unquestioningly accepted by the mother who, like so many mothers in the aftermath of the great Spanish tragedy, refused to believe that a missing son would not one day reappear.

The years had passed, the hoaxers had ceased to trouble, and slowly the maternal obsession calmed down and the wounds began to heal. Then, in the previous year, a mysterious telephone call to the father had opened up the whole issue again. The caller, impelled he claimed by motives of conscience, said that Mariano had been murdered in Farol on the day before the Nationalists had occupied the village. From the evidence the man had offered, both the father and Letrell had come to the conclusion that this was what really had happened. The police had been called in, but had got nowhere with their investigation. Hence, said Letrell, his presence in Farol, where he had to admit, after a week of talking to anyone he could find to say a word to him on the subject of Mariano Oliver, he was no wiser than on the day he arrived.

Was there, he asked of me, any point in going on? To which my reply was, there was no way of saying, but I doubted it. The people of such villages, who hardly believed in the existence of justice, and who had inherited an unshakeable ancestral belief in the corruption of all rulers, defended themselves traditionally by silence and forgetfulness. Whatever had happened here that might be seen as damaging to the community was in the process of being forgotten, and the memory of it would eventually be as wholly and utterly consumed as a corpse committed to the worms.

On second thoughts, I told Letrell, it was truer perhaps to say that they destroyed memory, when it became necessary to do so, stripping it of its malefic power by transmuting it into poetry and myth. In the years to come these fishermen's grandsons might recall in their blank verse the tragic events of these years, but they would by then have slipped into legend, depersonified in the human epic, mingled with all the other ancient tragedies the Spanish peninsula had suffered.

Yet within days of Letrell's return to Barcelona mention of Mariano Oliver was made in my presence. It was in illustration of the inexplicable power that certain human beings have over animals.

'There was a man who used to live here,' Juan my neighbour said, 'who could whistle in a way he had and bring the birds down out of the trees. He had them flying in and out of his house. There was even a jackdaw he taught to talk – in a fundamental fashion, understand me, but still understandable, using a bit of imagination. He was good with dogs, too. He built a little water-wheel in his garden, and a couple of dogs used to take turns to work it.'

'Would that have been Mariano des Horts?'

'That's right. The Gardener.'

'What did you think of him?' I asked.

'Well, put it this way, I admired him. You have to admire anyone who can train animals by kindness the way he did. But I was never quite sure that he was right in the head.'

The people of Farol showed little interest in the goings on of the outside world, but lively commentaries on village happenings relieved the monotony of net-mending to which many women were obliged to devote the major part of the daylight hours. Net-mending was a wholly mechanical procedure, leaving the brain free to create its own fancies, and to work on the raw material of speculation and known fact from which the tissue of gossip was woven. The men, absorbed in more creative and demanding labours, had little to say to one another outside workaday topics. They talked to their wives, who passed on whatever was regarded as newsworthy, picked up while patching up the rents left by the dolphins in the nets. This was not quite a closed circuit of information, due to marriages contracted by village people with outsiders such as Sebastian, who remained alien to village traditions, including that of silence. About a year was to pass before the facts of the Oliver case, as passed on to Sebastian by his wife, were leaked to me.

A fisherman called Vicente Ferrer had just been drowned. Ferrer was casting his *raï* from a foothold on a not quite submerged rock when he slipped and drowned in six feet of water. He was forty-five years of age, having thus precisely completed the life expectancy of a Farol male, roughly matching that of the English labouring classes in the early nineteenth century. Ferrer dominated one of the big boats, for which he was held in great respect, and had been an anarchist in his youth, a member of the FAI, consequently serving two years in prison at the war's end. He left an only son, and a widow who could be expected to survive him for about eighteen years. Don Ignacio made an excellent impression on this occasion by agreeing that he should be buried in hallowed ground although his family refused to allow the burial service to be read.

Passing on this information Sebastian said that Ferrer was the last of a trio involved in the Oliver case. Of these, one had disappeared in

France and another had been drowned some years before in practically identical circumstances in which Ferrer had met his death.

Sebastian had only seen Oliver once, briefly, and remembered little of him; he had been away caught up in the aftermath of defeat in some other part of the country when the Nationalists occupied Barcelona and begun their final drive to the French border. Oliver had been conscripted into the Republican army, and then discharged on health grounds, after which he had been in trouble with the FAI and suffered the kind of harassment that anyone with his family connections had to expect. The opinion in Farol was that he had taken these experiences to heart and become, at least passively, a Nationalist supporter.

In war as in peace not a great deal had happened in Farol. Soldiers marching to battle had on the whole stayed on the main roads, and the only fighting in that part of the country had been between discordant factions of the Left who did as much damage to each other as they did to the Fascists. In November 1938, with the long foreseen collapse of the Ebro front, several fishermen from Farol joined the number of those who found the excuse and the means of making their way home where, as soon as they arrived, they got rid of their uniforms and started fishing again. And with this unobtrusive communal surrender Farol returned to a kind of normality, although most people preferred not to think too much about the future.

The bar was still functioning, and after netting a few bogas, which was all that was to be expected at that time of the year, the fishermen used to go down there and drink the last of the wine and wonder when whatever was about to happen, would finally happen.

On the evening of 27 January 1939, Mariano Oliver came into the bar. It seemed to have become part of the mythology of those last few days of waiting that Oliver went everywhere with the famous jackdaw perched on his shoulder, and that on this particular occasion it had croaked something that sounded like an oath in the direction of the fishermen huddled at their tables. Oliver stood in the centre of the car and announced in his high-pitched voice, 'Barcelona has fallen.' He then went up to Vicente Ferrer, smiled at him, according to the tenth-hand account given by Sebastian's wife, and said. 'I have my little list all ready.'

He then went out again, without drinking, and the first thing everybody wanted to know was, was this terrible piece of news true, and if so, how did Oliver came to be the first person in the village to hear of it? Within the hour, Barcelona radio, which had gone off the air, came through again, and it was playing the Nationalist hymn.

Since at the present rate of their advance the Fascists could confidently be expected in Farol within the week, the question now was what to do about Oliver who seemed to have made it clear that he was preparing to avenge himself on anyone regarded – for real or fancied reasons – as an enemy, as soon as they arrived.

Despite the traditional aversion of the fishermen for any but pacific solutions, the belief was that he was jeopardising the safety of the whole village, and that the only remedy was to kill him without delay. At that time a curandero was living in the neighbourhood, keeping out of sight of left-wing fanatics who would have shot him at the drop of a hat. The fishermen went to this man for his advice but he poured cold water on the idea of killing Oliver unless absolutely necessary, and to decide whether or not this was so he proposed to enter Oliver's house at night and go over his personal papers for any evidence to show he was a Fascist spy.

This he did, but next day after the nocturnal visit, he had changed his mind and said that Oliver would have to be put out of the way. He had consulted the Book of St Cyprian – the illicit witches' bible used by most curanderos – and set the date of the execution for three days ahead.

By this time, with Nationalist patrols only thirty miles away, panic had begun to set in and the roads were overflowing with refugees on their way to France. In some mysterious fashion the Curandero had established his influence over Oliver, appearing to have robbed him of his willpower, to produce a kind of drugged acquiescence in whatever lay in store for him. One of the women had told Sebastian's wife that she personally had seen the two men walking together, and that Oliver's jackdaw had sworn at the Curandero who had snatched it from Oliver's shoulder and twisted its neck. How much truth there was in this story is anyone's guess. Even an eyewitness finds it difficult to describe a happening without some slight variation of the story with each retelling, and the transformation of hearsay into fable is rapid. Did the Curandero really wring the jackdaw's neck? Did Oliver even own a jackdaw that he had taught to say 'I shit on God'? Was there even a curandero involved in the events of 1 February in Farol – or could he have been invented in an attempt to rid the fishermen of the spectre of guilt? But if it is accepted that Oliver was murdered without leaving the village, only a competent forger – as the Curandero might have been – who had had access to Oliver's personal papers can explain the letters from France.

It was shortly after dark when the Curandero called on two

fishermen called Julian and Pals, told them to wash, put on clean shirts. and go with him. The three then went to Ferrer's house, and the Curandero told him to clean himself up because everything was ready. Julian was the man who had died in the first drowning accident, and his wife, Carmen, described this meeting to Sebastian's Elvira. Ferrer showed himself highly agitated, and said he wanted to drop the whole thing, and the Curandero laughed, clapped him on the shoulder and said, 'let's go.' Oliver was waiting at his door when they got there and they all shook hands with him. The Curandero lit a cigarette and put it in Oliver's mouth, and he took two or three puffs. The Curandero said, 'We've come to take you for a little walk by the sea.' Oliver showed no surprise or objection, and they walked through the village, which was quite empty at the time, and went up along the cliffs.

The Curandero made Oliver walk close to the cliff's edge, and told Ferrer to walk next to him. Ferrer shook his head and said, 'No,' but he did as he was told, and the others followed close behind. When they reached a certain point the Curandero said to Ferrer, 'Push him over.' Ferrer said, 'I can't do that,' and he turned round and began to walk back to the village and the others followed him. Carmen told Elvira that what had so much surprised her husband was the fact that Oliver seemed quite unable to understand that he was in any danger, and that he took the incident on the cliff top as a joke. By this time Julian too was getting cold feet about the whole operation, and was hoping that the Curandero had given up any idea of killing Oliver. He felt very relieved when they returned to the village, and the atmosphere was a friendly one. Somebody suggested they might as well have a drink, so they went to the bar, which they found shut. The Curandero picked the lock and let them in.

They went down to the cellar and found a barrel with some wine in it. There was a table and chairs down there and they sat down and began to drink the wine, then the Curandero excused himself to go to the toilet which was at the back. Julian noticed that he took a glass with him, and when he came back he put in in front of Oliver. He also noticed that Ferrer who had calmed down again by this time started shaking and sweating. He got up and said he was going and ran up the steps, but then he found he couldn't get the door open so he came down again, and the Curandero told him to sit down. He asked Ferrer what he was afraid of and Ferrer told him he was afraid of what was in the glass. The Curandero laughed at this. He took out a box of matches struck one and held his finger in the flame, showing no sign of pain. Julian told his wife that the sight of it made his hair stand on end.

After he'd held his finger in the flame, the Curandero said that any of us could do the same thing, and he passed the matches to Ferrer and told him to try and Ferrer scorched himself. The Curandero then put the matches away, picked up Oliver's glass gulped down half the wine in it and put his own glass in front of Oliver. They all drank a number of toasts including one to the death of all traitors, informers and spies.

Julian said that despite the fact that everybody's nerves were on edge, there was a lot of laughter and foolery going on. Someone switched on the radio in the cellar and they listened to a Fascist general in Barcelona telling them about the bloodcurdling fate in store from them all. The Curandero ordered Oliver to get up and give the Fascist salute which he did, and they all found this very funny. Then Oliver suddenly decided to go home and invited them all to his house. He made the excuse that he had to go back to feed all his animals. Ferrer and Julian agreed to go with him but the Curandero said that nobody would leave the bar, because it was too late and what had been done couldn't be undone.

Oliver was then very sick, and Julian realised that the Curandero must have been able to distract their attention with his trick with the matches so as to switch glasses and ensure that Oliver got the almost certainly poisoned wine. Julian recognised the symptoms of acute ergot poisoning, for Oliver was vomiting repeatedly, weeping and clutching at his stomach. He and Ferrer decided to make a run for it and they went up the steps with the Curandero, a strong man, after them, grabbing at their legs and hanging on to them until they were able to kick themselves free. The lock on the street door had jammed in some way, and while they were wrestling with it Oliver began to scream. Going back to the top of the steps they saw Oliver lying on his back on the floor, and the Curandero and Pals bending over him. Julian thought that the Curandero was trying to strangle Oliver with a belt. At that point Pals ran to turn out the cellar lamp, and the shrieking stopped. A moment later the two men came up from the cellar to say that Oliver was dead. Julian's story was that someone went for a spade and they took up the flagstones in the cellar and buried him on the spot.

Later, my neighbour Juan added a suggestive detail by way of a postscript to this story, mentioning when some discussion about the bar came up that the Alcalde's predecessor had surprised everybody by putting himself to the expense of covering the cellar floor under three inches of concrete.

10

It was becoming clear that Muga's influence in the area was in the ascendant, and inevitably to some extent a consequence of this, Don Alberto's was on the wane. The fishermen found it amazing that a man who appeared so childish to them should wield so much power. Muga could decide that a road which had been hardly better than a cart-track must be widened and properly surfaced, and that a dangerous bridge carrying it should be rebuilt at the national cost. He provided running water piped from a distant spring for his own house, but raised no objection to any villager whose rain-water cistern ran dry in summer bringing any number of receptacles to be filled at his tap. A word in the ear of a well-placed friend was enough to bring an extension telephone line some twenty miles to Muga. Not more than three people in Farol had ever used a telephone, but there was nothing mean-spirited about Muga, and he let it be known that anyone could come to his house in an emergency, and make use of his, at any hour of the night or day.

So far, so good. What astonished the fishermen, who were realists, was Muga's enthusiasm for make-believe and for toys. Sebastian, helping to fit an Andalusian-style fountain into one of the rooms, had been fascinated to see Muga take a telephone call while seated at his desk. No bell had rung, but a sound like the shriek of a railway engine's whistle in a Pyrenean tunnel had been followed by the appearance of a miniature locomotive through gates that had sprung open in the wall, and this had come chugging over ten feet of miniature viaduct to pull up, carrying the telephone on its single carriage, to within inches of Muga's hand. The call conducted, Muga had replaced the receiver, and the engine whistled its departure, let out a couple of puffs of smoke and backed away out of sight into the wall.

Don Alberto, detesting everything that Muga stood for, conceded that he was a force to be reckoned with, and clung to the delusion that it might be possible to tame the black marketeer, to civilise him, and head him off from the direction of barbarous change. He was beginning to see that the ideal human society – as he remembered it – of responsible landlords and devoted tenants was breaking up before his eyes under assault of natural calamities and disruptive ideas.

Both peasants and fisherfolk were at the end of their tethers. In Sort, after the acorns of the winter, the spring rains had failed, so that every inch of the land had to be watered by hastily dug irrigation channels. The situation of Farol was an ironic one. For once both the spring tunny and spring sardines had arrived on time and in plenty, but with only two big boats able to put to sea the catch had fallen short of normal, and there had been no spring marriages. Don Alberto pocketed his pride and called on Muga, being received, as he reported, in surroundings of asphyxiating vulgarity. Their conversation, which was about the possibility of raising credits to revive the local economy, was interrupted by the incursion of the telephone-bearing locomotive and Don Alberto found himself obliged to listen to one end of a conversation with a man in Madrid who was afraid that the bottom was about to fall out of pigs, and had 100,000 to unload.

After Muga had bought 50,000 pigs and put through another call to resell them, he was ready to listen with sympathy while Don Alberto tried to make out his case. Muga showed himself full of concern, but in the end shook his head. The past was dead and done with, he said, and now they had to look to a future of a different kind. What was the point of putting modern irrigation systems into land used to grow wholly unmarketable crops? 'It's growing for the market that brings in the cash, and you can't sell beans any more!' Why also delude oneself about inshore fishing? It was at an end, so investing in new boats in Farol would only be throwing good money after bad.

'I want to help people,' Muga said to Don Alberto, 'because that's the kind of man I am, but subsidising them to go on living in the way they do now is only perpetuating their misery. Of course I'll help if I can but I'd want to be sure that any credit that had my support was directed towards bringing about change. If you've any concrete proposals along those lines, I'm your man.'

Don Alberto got up to go. 'I'm not sure we're talking about the same thing,' he said.

Muga now started a campaign to tidy up Farol, in the course of which he ran into a number of obstacles. In addition to his own house he had bought the two other old cork mansions, one of which he renovated, covering its austere façade with fanciful Portuguese tiles. The other he was obliged for the time to leave untouched owing to the presence of sitting tenants, Maria Cabritas and her mother, who occupied the two inhabitable rooms in what was otherwise a near ruin. They had found some way of paying a peppercorn rent and there were legal difficulties in getting rid of them that Muga might have been able to get round if he had not been anxious to do nothing likely to tarnish his image in the vicinity.

He had also taken note of Carmela's garishly-painted shack. This time the law was on his side. The thing had been put up without consent, and it could have been just as easily pulled down. Muga preferred the soft approach. He said that one way or another the shack would have to go, but that he wanted to come to an amicable arrangement with her, and he offered to find her proper accommodation in the village, for which she would pay nothing in exchange. Carmela's reply was that she chose to live where she did well outside the village because the sight of other children playing made Rosa unhappy and unmanageable. Muga asked to see Rosa, and said he would pay for her to be brought up in a home. This offer was turned down with indignation, but his next suggestion was more to Carmela's liking. Muga agreed to foot the bill for a visit by the two of them to a Barcelona specialist and for any treatment he might recommend. It was a proposal, she told me, she was seriously thinking about, one indeed she felt she had to accept.

The stiffest problem confronting Muga was what to do about the house that spoiled the view of the sea from his hotel. Cabezas, the man who had built it single-handed, showed him over it with pride. It was a single-storey building with six rooms in line without ceilings, going straight up to the naked tiles of the enormously high roof. For the sake of appearances Cabeza had built windows to non-existent bedrooms on a non-existent first floor, and an outside staircase that pretended to give access to these. One of the rooms in which the animals would be kept in winter had a sloping concrete floor down which the urine would drain to a channel. A stall-like enclosure provided with a bucket and having a three-feet high fence was for human use. The door was designed to resist assault by corsairs who had frequently operated along this coast a century and a half before, and Cabezas had to lean all his weight against it to push it open.

Muga asked Cabezas why he had decided to devote the active years of his life to building this house, being content until now to live in a cave in the forest, just as his ancestors had done ten thousand years or more ago? Cabezas replied that he had done it for the sake of his family. Question: where were they? Answer: his wife and two children were dead, leaving him with one son. Question: and was the son proud and happy at his father's achievement? Answer: he didn't seem to care much one way or another.

Every man, according to Muga's philosophy, had his price. He asked Cabezas how much he thought he'd invested in this project over twenty-nine years, and Cabezas said, very little but love. He'd quarried the stones himself, wheelbarrowed them to the site and raised one on to the other, day after day, week after week and year after year and he and his family had lived, somewhat abstemiously, he agreed, on a minute legacy that brought in 50 pesetas a week. He thanked God for the miracle that had allowed him to finish the work just as his strength ran out. Cabezas quoted Barros: 'We've built the house. Let's make a start on the grave.'

And what was he going to do with it, now that he was finished? Muga asked, and Cabezas said, live in it. He and his son, now aged twenty, would live in style, and forget the hard past. Muga offered him one million, two million, three million pesetas for it – the final price being more than he'd paid for the three cork mansions put together – and Cabezas laughed and shook his head.

Frustrated by Cabezas' obduracy, Muga next turned his attention to a well-publicised crisis facing the once prosperous and powerful Pablo Fons.

A single bad year was enough to convert Fons from a rich man by peasant standards into a poor one, and poverty stripped him of his self-confidence and some of his spirit. His early crops failed, a number of cows were found to be suffering from mouth ulcers and had to be sold to a discreet butcher at ruinous prices. A law suit that had been running up costs for several years failed, and finally his eldest son was in trouble with the police for exposing himself to a French girl who had risked sun-bathing on a beach near Farol. For this he was thoroughly beaten up, and Fons had to pay a stiff bribe to keep him out of prison.

These facts were passed on to me by Don Alberto who said that the local view was that Fons' son had been harshly treated. It was pointed out that the Civil Guard would normally never have bothered about a case of self-exposure, regarded rather as a family affair within the village, and it seemed hard that young Fons should have been punished for what was almost a traditional reaction of wonder and admiration just because this had been directed at a foreign woman. The grave news that followed these misfortunes was that, having heard of Fons' losses, Muga had offered to buy part of his farm. For a peasant to sell land was quite unheard of, but Fons had no choice in the matter. Don Alberto said that by the terms of an old contract Fons was obliged to offer any land he had for sale to him first, but he had decided to waive any claim on it, having no wish to extend the boundaries of the semi-desert he already owned. I asked, of what use was the land to Muga if nobody else could do anything with it? Don Alberto said, in the slightly shocked tone of a man describing malefic practises, that he was prepared to use fertilisers. It was something he said that no local man would dream of doing. Not only because of the costs involved, but because it called into question the value of something given into his keeping by Almighty God.

A few days later the deal went through. Muga became a landowner, and let it be known that he expected to be addressed by the village underlings as Don Jaime in future. He was frequently to be seen clumping across his new acres accompanied by a man with a kind of enormous auger who from time to time drilled a hole in the iron-hard surface to take out a core of earth and drop it into one of a number of small labelled bags.

Fons and Muga got on well together. Fons could not have carried on without Muga's money, and Muga found it valuable to draw on Fons' experience as to how things were best arranged in an environment where the force of custom could be stronger than that of law. It seems probable that Muga had asked Fons' advice as to how best to deal with the sitting tenants in the third cork mansion, and that Fons suggested a plan by which the easily provoked fury of the witch-hunters of Sort could be harnessed to Muga's expansionist ambitions.

On the night of 7 June someone broke into the corral Maria Cabritas had put up in the garden of the house, released her seven goats and drove them into the fields where they wrought havoc among the meagre crops. The sight of Maria next morning in her silk stockings and modish dress careering about their land in chase of her goats provoked the explosion of wrath that was to be expected, and the Alcalde of Sort, admirer of goats though he was, and predisposed until this to favour Maria's cause, was obliged under pressure of village opinion to issue what was known as a solemn warning.

The next night there was no moon, the most favourable condition for fishing with the lights at this time of the year, and almost every boat put to sea immediately after dark, leaving Farol nearly denuded of its able-bodied population. It was a circumstance that seemed to Don Alberto to tie in with the fact that on the evening of this day the two Farol Civil Guards had been called to their headquarters in Figueras. Such overnight absences were rare indeed, and in this case, he thought, in the light of what took place of exceptional significance. Don Alberto supposed that if Muga had been able to buy up the whole of the police force of the port of Palamos, there was really nothing to stop him giving orders to the major in Figueras if he felt he needed to.

At about eleven o'clock a party from Sort surrounded the house in which Maria Cabritas and her mother were sleeping and began to beat on the tin trays, the kettles, the pots and the drums they were carrying and to scream obscenities at the couple they were determined to drive out of the neighbourhood. The *encerrada*, an ancient and now illegal custom, was the traditional method of ridding a village of the contamination of a man or woman who had flouted public opinion by remarrying after the death of a spouse, or more rarely of an adulteress. Those who took part in it were expected to be above moral reproach, yet the *encerrada* not only licensed but encouraged the grossest public indecencies. When, after two hours of trying to sleep through the racket I went to see what was going on, I found a red-eyed lynch mob of men and women who had been rescued by hate from the chrysalises of little lives. Banging on their tin trays, blowing their horns, neighing the filthiest god-sullying oaths their imaginations could create, they whirled and slobbered like dervishes. Ugliness and obscenity were demanded of them, and they gave lavishly and with all their hearts. The place stank of sweat and excrement. Men lined up to piss against the wall of the house and women mouthing and screaming squatted by the roadside to relieve themselves under their skirts. Someone was throwing dung at the windows.

Two lords of misrule drove up in a cart, their faces inflated with a hideous piety. They rushed into the corral at the back and began to bring out the goats, legs tied, one after another and flung them into the cart. Then one of them kicked open the door and went in. A few minutes later he came out with the two women, hustling from behind as they struggled with their bundled-up possessions. Maria and her mother settled themselves among their bundles. The girl had dressed herself as carefully as ever for this moment. Her mother held a cloth to her eyes but Maria looked straight ahead, and her expression, as usual, was one of indifference.

The cart was driven away. The mob howled after it and gesticulated fornication with their arms. Then the hate began to run out, the screams quieted to a low grumbling murmur of satiety. Anticlimax was upon them as they began to wander away.

The episode, Don Alberto said, marked in a clear-cut fashion the end of an epoch, as well as showing how easy it was for a vulgar gangster like Muga to manipulate simple peasants into destroying themselves eventually, along with the delicately adjusted balance of village life that had produced them. Don Ignacio, chained now to a routine of Masses that no one attended, was all for an end to all forms of outside interference, and agreed with him that Muga would have to be stopped somehow. The stand against him might as well be made now when there seemed to be a chance of cobbling together an accusation of conspiracy to break the law. Disorderly gatherings for any purpose were taken seriously by the régime which could usually be counted on to act against them, or in punishment of them with exemplary promptitude and severity.

Don Alberto said he had questioned two of his tenants who not only admitted having been persuaded by Fons to join the *encerrada*, but claimed that he had paid them a small sum to do so. These men, according to Don Alberto, were so alarmed at the possibility of their involvement in any action that might displease their landlord they practically begged his permission before sleeping with their wives, so naturally they told Fons they ought to get Don Alberto's approval before committing themselves to the *encerrada*, however much they might enjoy the excitement. To this Fons had replied that no one had anything to fear from Don Alberto any longer, and that if any problem arose Muga, who was the richest man in the province, would look after it.

Sebastian supplied a small piece of information that Don Alberto eagerly jotted down, to the effect that shortly before the *encerrada* Muga had stopped him in the street and told him that the hold-up over the third cork mansion had been settled, and he would be starting work there within the week.

The most telling piece of evidence was offered by the leader of the female contingent at the *encerrada*, an old fanatic who headed the Christ the King movement in the region. This woman I had once seen carrying a banner in a procession which said, 'I promise the Sacred Heart of Jesus to read no novels, newspapers or magazines, and never to wear makeup as long as I live,' told Don Alberto that Muga had recently given her a crucifix. 'For a service,' she added, smiling bitterly.

There seemed to be enough substance in the evidence he had gathered to warrant going ahead, and Don Alberto asked Don Ignacio to help him with the composition of a letter to be sent to the commandant of the Civil Guard in Figueras. To this enormously long document they received a considered reply. Reading it, Don Alberto decided that all hope was lost.

The commandant said that he had ordered a full investigation of the matter reported to him by his man on the spot, and his conclusions were as followed:

> One: The nature and importance of the incidents referred to seemed to have been much exaggerated. There had been public criticism of a woman alleged to have been engaged in immoral acts, but there had been no acts of violence or damage to property.
>
> Two: Contrary to assertions contained in the letter no coercion had been used to induce this woman and her mother to leave the village, and they had signed a statement to that effect.
>
> Three: The commandant did not find that the public criticism of which Don Alberto and Don Ignacio complained constituted an unlawful gathering, a plot or incitement to plot, and was to some extent a regional and traditional expression of disapproval and accepted as such. The commandant understood that one of the signatories of the letter was a well-known student of folkloric themes, and should appreciate this.
>
> Four: The couple in question had been formally invited by the Alcalde of Sort to return to the village and take up residence again in the house they had vacated. This they had declined to do.

In conclusion the commandant said that he had decided that he was not justified in taking action in this instance.

11

With the departure of Maria Cabritas it was a matter of urgency to find someone to take her place, and an underground movement sprang up in Farol having as its aim the restitution of Sa Cordovesa to her original role in the life of the community.

She had naturally been recommended to slim down as fast as she could, and she applied to a number of persons for advice as to how this was to be best done.

Dr Seduction prescribed a diet based mainly on a sludge made from ground-up locust beans mixed with lemon juice. Don Alberto's aged ex-mistress resurrected several remedies from the far past, urging Sa Cordovesa to drink nothing but Bulgarian ambrosia, available in all the spas in Europe before the first World War. The women of the village suggested that she should expose her limbs for as long periods as possible to the light of the waning moon, and Don Ignacio, when approached, could only offer prayer, which he did without conviction.

The female leading lights of the village, led by the Grandmother and the butcher's wife, began to concoct little stratagems and conspiracies by which, at the end of a month's seclusion after the slimming processes had taken effect, Sa Cordovesa would be formally re-launched into village life.

The occasion chosen for this was naturally the Sunday evening promenade. This, the women agreed, should be a theatrical moment, and when the day came they prepared Sa Cordovesa for it like a kabuki actress for her entrance on stage. Spanish women kept a close eye on the girl tourists beginning to arrive from France for pointers on matters of style, and whatever appealed to them was slavishly copied. It was a year when the French had taken to the use of stark-white face-powder so when the Grandmother and the butcher's wife had finished with Sa Cordovesa's makeup in preparation for the promenade, the great black eyes stared out from a chalk-white mask on which the first post-war lipstick to arrive in Farol had painted a somewhat uneven mouth. This was the colour of the dark gore so abundantly splashed about the butcher's shop.

The visitors from France wore heavy costume jewellery this year, so Sa Cordovesa's arms were ringed with many glass bangles, and she wore a necklace made from sea-shells, and earrings like miniature chandeliers that actually tinkled in the gusts of wind. Her two sponsors were disappointed to find that the weight loss brought about by exposure to the moon's rays, a starvation diet, and prayer, was less than expected; however they forced her into one of the Grandmother's corsets, and then into a blue dress of the kind no French girl would have been seen dead in by reason of its old-fashioned frilled skirt. The Grandmother and the butcher's wife added the final touches, then clapped their hands in delight. They put a pink fan in Sa Cordovesa's hand to signify that she was neither married nor promised in marriage, then they all climbed into a cart and were driven round the back of the town to be deposited at the top of the street, by the church door.

The further report on chic Parisiennes was that, when not frolicking on the beach, they moved stiffly, taking small steps, arms hanging at their sides and palms raised as if to pat the heads of large, invisible dogs. This was the style in which Sa Cordovesa took her place in the promenade and, flanked by the Grandmother and the butcher's wife, began her slow geisha totter towards the end of the village in the alpargatas lent her that were a size and a half too small.

It was a spectacle that filled the women with wonder and admiration, although the menfolk seemed doubtful. Fifty or more persons had joined the promenade, strolling in groups of threes and fours, stopping frequently to exchange gossip with elderly folk excluded by custom at roughly the same time in life when they gave up taking baths. The function of the Sunday promenade was that of a marriage market. Parents placed their eligible young on display and the young eyed potential partners with hope prepared for long deferment.

Ideally in the composition of the promenade both sexes should have been equally represented, but I noticed on this occasion a remarkable preponderance of females. It was – or it could have been – a subtle affair full of innuendo and cautious sexual signalling, most of which would have been lost on the outsider. A young man would display his attitude towards a girl, rather than expressing any intention, by the manner in which he inserted himself into the promenade, overtook her, passed her, and turned back for a ritual second look. This procedure was known as 'signing on', it committed nobody to anything, and further intricate movements would be performed in the ceremonial spider's dance of love before an engagement would be presumed to exist.

The young males of Farol were conservative, ill-at-ease in the presence of novelty or change of any kind, inclined – I would have said – to be frightened off by the would-be sophistication of Sa Cordovesa in her new image, whatever they might have felt about her excessive weight.

Sa Cordovesa and her sponsors progressed slowly up to the end of the street and turned back, but no young men overtook her party, and the gap of twenty yards between the three women and the first of the promenading males never showed signs of closing. Smiles stiffened, the interchange of courtesies became spiritless, Sa Cordovesa brought up the hand holding the pink fan to swipe at the flies attracted by her makeup. Most of the young males were now beginning to trail away from the promenade in the direction of the bar.

When they reached the church again the Grandmother put her hand on Sa Cordovesa's shoulder and said something in her ear, perhaps by way of commiseration. At that Sa Cordovesa burst out laughing. She had a strong voice, and people in the vicinity looked startled and embarrassed.

Later it was reported to me that she had used a disgusting oath, of a kind tolerated in a man, but unthinkable in the mouth of a woman. The cart came rattling round the corner, and Sa Cordovesa threw away her fan, hitched up her skirts and climbed into it like a man. She then spat over the tailboard in the direction of nothing in particular, and was driven off.

Two days later Carmela left with Rosa for consultation with the specialist in Barcalona, and Sa Cordovesa went with her.

12

Don Alberto saw his world threatened by rapid and irreversible decline. He thought of himself, he told me, as the least superstitious of men, admitting that had he been inclined to be influenced by such things as presages and omens, he might have linked the abandonment of the fiestas of Sort and Farol with this premonition he had of change and decay. The boring Sort fiesta, tied to the well-being of the trees, had automatically been extinguished with them. In Farol the mysterious Sa Cova, central to the village's metaphysical existence, had been suspended indefinitely following the news of the death in hospital of Marta D'Escorreu, the last chosen one. No family had been found ready to put forward their child as candidate for this year.

Muga, striding through the village, arms akimbo, and terrifying the children with his ferocious samurai's smile, tightened his grip. Within days of Carmela vacating her shack it was pulled down and burned, to the enormous regret of Don Alberto, an artist of limited talent who had sat there at his easel for many hours struggling to explain in paint the great conflict of colour and light to be observed as the rampant blue flowers struck out like serpents across the chrome walls.

It was Muga's intention next to improve the sea-front, a goal which he approached in an extremely subtle fashion, having understood by this time that embellishments of any kind would arouse the fishermen's tooth and nail resistance.

A meeting took place between Muga, the Alcalde and the fishermen who dominated the principal boats, at which Muga reminded his listeners of the storms of the past autumn and winter, telling them that meteorological experts had warned of a change in weather patterns along the Mediterranean seaboard, and said that they were entering a cycle of bad winters. There was general agreement about this. The fishermen had already gone through three bad winters in a row, and the general belief was that there were four more to come.

Muga told them that he had now come to regard Farol as his home, and that he wanted to do what he could for it. The storm of last October had sent waves across the beach as far as the fishermen's houses, not only smashing the boats but carrying away a number of outbuildings, chicken pens, rabbit hutches and the like. Muga thought, and the others agreed, that this could happen again.

What Muga had come to tell them was that he was prepared to build at his own cost a sea wall that would banish this threat for ever. He went on to say that in order to give access to vehicles carrying the stone to build the wall, a strip of land would have to be cleared of obstacles and levelled between their houses and the top of the beach. This would in effect be a narrow road.

At this point Muga noticed stirrings of ill-ease and there were muttered objections. 'No tarting up, eh? No trees.' Muga put down this threatened insurrection. He guaranteed to plant no trees, nor to attempt to prettify the area in any way, but apart from that insisted on being able to do whatever was to be done in his own way, and without interference.

The fishermen remained uneasy about the suggested road, largely because if it came to be built, people would be likely to stand on it, looking out to sea, thereby in some cases – however innocent their intentions – bringing bad luck to the fishing.

In the end it was agreed in principle that the wall and the road should be built. The problems concerned with undertaking such new constructional work were less complex in Farol than elsewhere due to the fact that it was rare for anyone to lay claim to the ownership of unoccupied land. Moreover all land covered at any time by the highest tide fell within the public domain.

Don Alberto, threatened with this calamity, put his hope in the office of the *Aparejador*, the provincial planning authority, famous for procrastination, indecision and general sloth. Plans would have to be drawn up and submitted for consideration at a meeting held at three-monthly intervals, and Don Alberto had learned that it was the habit of the inert body of men who formed the committee to play for safety by the almost automatic rejection of five applications out of six.

The Alcalde had provided Don Alberto with a preliminary sketch of the planned alterations and we visited the area together. It was a place of forlorn, wasted beauty, a marine frontier tinted with delicate washed-out colour, striped with the bluish foliage of oleanders that put down roots to any depth where water was to be found, although in this case they grew in the coarse sand of the shore, which they puddled with their fallen blossom. The boats leaned over in line at the bottom of the beach, freshly painted the lemon yellow of exorcism, with a green stripe round their middles, and purple bottoms. This was a place where the cats came to chase after land-crabs that had learned never to stray more than a foot or two from their holes, competing for their prey with a small population of pale-furred, distinguished-looking rats which amused the fishermen endlessly with their mating rituals, and were therefore regarded, if not with affection, with some respect. There was no mess on this beach. Everything but the rusted anchors was made of wood, and the sea and the sun had gradually shaped and chamfered and endowed every such wooden object – an old windlass, a gallows on which fish were hung to dry or an ancient tree trunk – with a soft grey patina of salt. 'We're losing it,' Don Alberto said. 'It's slipping away before our very eyes.'

The original plan, the Alcalde had told Don Alberto, provided for a four-foot wall with castellations, to which the fishermen had instantly objected. 'Why the castle effect?' they asked. 'What's the point?'

Muga gave way to the protest, but asked for the road to be edged with a narrow garden planted with Livingstone daisies, which were notorious for the fact that they grew and spread in all directions producing an unending multiplication of their tin-foil blooms without the slightest care or attention.

The Livingstone daisies were out. The fishermen had insisted from the start: no trees, no tarting-up, no seats.

What Muga was determined to put through was a lighting scheme, embodying a dozen standard lamps, and this, after much argument, the fishermen were persuaded to accept. 'We shall see,' Don Alberto said. 'We shall see. I have friends at court, too. Even I can pull strings if they force me to.'

Next day, even before the final plans had been submitted, the alterations began. A gang of men arrived to grub out all the oleanders and clean up the beach. A tractor dragged a harrow backwards and forwards over the part colonised by land-crabs, and on the following day shortly after dawn a marksman with a .22 rifle arrived to deal with the rats. He had picked off two of them before a fisherman came out of the nearest house and asked him to go away. The man was bewildered. 'Everybody knows rats are a health risk,' he said. 'They carry the plague.'

'As soon as anyone gets the plague we'll get rid of them,' he was told. 'We don't like to kill things here unless we have to.'

The Alcalde told me that Muga had been to see him to ask him if he couldn't do something about the bar.

'In what direction?' the Alcalde asked.

As it was it lacked any romantic appeal, Muga said. He expected an influx of tourists from France at any moment, and from his knowledge these people had an exaggerated idea of what Spain had to offer. They thought of it, for example, as a land of music and song. Muga suspected that with preconceived ideas of that kind Farol might come as a let-down.

The Alcalde told him he knew of an old man in Sort who played a pipe with five notes. He personally didn't regard it as an inspiring performance, and moreover the old man wasn't very presentable owing to a permanent infection of the eyes. Muga said what he had in mind was not so much a primitive pipe but a guitar, and the Alcalde told him that if he was thinking of introducing guitar music to Farol he faced an uphill struggle with the natives, who by his experience didn't go much for music of any kind.

'Tourists want to go somewhere and listen to music,' Muga said. 'Whether we like it or not. The location of this place makes it ideal. Couldn't it be fitted up if necessary with a gramophone and an amplifier?'

The Alcalde said he was trying all the time to stall him off. 'I'm always ready to listen to new ideas,' he told Muga. 'Provided I don't lose my customers.'

During this conversation the boy who helped in the bar sat there giggling, reading a comic paper, and picking his nose. He was a nephew of the Alcalde's, who had felt obliged to give him the job. 'I'm not too happy about that fellow you employ,' Muga told him.

'He's harmless,' the Alcalde said. 'I wouldn't like to get rid of him.'

'Someone should tell him to stop grinning about nothing, not to breathe on glasses before polishing them up, not to sit down at a customer's table and pour himself a drink, and to keep his farts quiet.'

'I'll mention all these things to him,' the Alcalde said.

'And where by the way did you get that mermaid object?' Muga asked, jerking his cheroot in the dugong's direction.

'A man who used to own the place bought it from an exhibition that closed down in Barcelona,' the Alcalde told him. 'It's unique. It possesses a real vagina. The police made him stitch on a flap to cover it up, but you can pull it back and look for yourself if you like.'

'It's the ugliest thing I've ever seen,' Muga said. 'I can't bear to look at it. It gives me the creeps and I imagine it would have the same effect on most people.'

'You soon get used to it,' the Alcalde said. 'They say here you can tell the weather by the way it looks.'

'It would frighten any foreigner who came in here out his wits. If you don't want to take it away, couldn't you cover it up? Couldn't you put a curtain in front of it?'

'They don't appreciate changes of any kind in this village. The mermaid's a fixture of the place. For my customers it's practically a human being.'

'One final question,' Muga said. 'Would you sell this place?'

'No.'

'Not even for two or three times what it's worth?'

'There wouldn't be any point,' the Alcalde told him. 'Ask yourself. What would I do with the money? I'd have to go off somewhere and buy another bar, wouldn't I? As this place happens to suit me, I might as well stay as I am.'

Isolation Muga saw as the enemy of progress, guardian of stagnant tradition and the promoter of fears and xenophobic suspicions of every kind. Farol was cut off from the world for six days in the week and the undependable bus operating on the seventh day served, as it seemed, the sole function of carrying Don Ignacio away from his priestly duties to his archaeological dig in Ampurias, from which he was obliged to return as best he could. Muga pulled strings to organise a daily bus service to Figueras, but after a week the driver called at his house to appeal to him. He was dying of boredom, he said. How long was he expected to go on driving the bus when to date he had not had a single fare?

It was only at this point that Muga realised that the people of the village he proposed to take over did not travel, not because there was no transport but because they had absolutely no desire to do so. He next learned that half the population both of Farol and of Sort had never left their villages except to go on picnic excursions along the coast. Of the rest only about one in ten had travelled as far as Figueras, villagers who had driven there for medical reasons to avoid treatment by Dr Seduction – treatment, in the case of all external injury, with blue unction (an ointment recommended for the softening of venereal chancres) or, in the case of internal disorder, by drastic purging with epsom salts. The public sentiment of Farol was that those who were obliged to leave the village were instantly exposed to evil influences which increased almost mile by mile until Figueras – seen as a huge, bewildering and utterly immoral metropolis – was reached. On returning from such a journey it was normal to take a purifying bath, to which certain herbal distillates were added, and if the traveller had passed his fortieth year, and baths had become taboo, he put up with whatever he might have been suffering from, and declined to stir abroad.

A permanent fair went on in Figueras with popgun ranges, swings and a handcranked roundabout, and Muga had handbills printed describing its excitements printed and distributed round the village, accompanying them with an offer of a free outing for the children. This the children accepted with enthusiasm and all parental objections were instantly overcome. Muga paid the bus fares, gave each child a packet of chewing gum, an aniseed ball, a paper hat and a balloon, as well as footing the bill for the swings and the roundabouts, and for sniping ineffectively with the popguns at ginger bread and kewpie dolls suspended on strings. The children were entranced, and Muga watched them full of satisfaction. They were the raw material of the future, and it was a future, as Muga had repeatedly proclaimed, that he proposed to shape. The parents who had come along remained on the defensive, huddled together nervously in a corner of the fairground, on the lookout for pickpockets and city slickers who might approach them with immoral propositions, but the children had adapted instantly to the temptations and pleasure of the outside world, and would never be quite the same again.

13

It was not only in Farol and Sort that brusque changes were taking place, Don Alberto said. They were happening at a breakneck pace all over Spain. Good communications were the great leveller of customs, and military necessity during the war had compelled the building of roads into many isolated places that had hitherto resisted change. Roads, the radio, the telephone, and now the arrival of tourists, whose appearance and behaviour Spaniards were so eager to emulate, were putting an end to the Spain of old, Don Alberto said. And for those who wanted to see it as it had been, there was not a moment to be lost.

He had just read a gloomy report in the journal of the Sociedad Española de Antropología of which he was a member, noting the demise of about half the popular festivals of Spain in a period of forty years, a few discouraged by the authorities on the grounds that they perpetuated barbarous attitudes unacceptable in our days, but the vast majority quietly abandoned because people had lost interest.

It was this piece of information that prompted his suggestion that I should accompany him on an expedition to San Pedro Manrique in the province of Soria, where he had ascertained by writing to the Alcalde that one of the country's most remarkable customs, the fire-walking ritual practised on St John's Eve, the twenty-third of June, still took place. Don Alberto said that we could be certain that this ceremony, practised according to the anthropologists since Celto-Iberian times, would not survive many more years.

It seemed an opportunity not to be missed. Don Alberto had warned me that the journey would be atrocious, and so it was. When we met at the crossroads where the taxi for Figueras was to pick us up I could see that he was ready for anything in his chamois-leather jacket, polished by age, over a Cuban shirt with numerous pockets and breeches tied with tapes below the knees to exclude crawling insects, nankeen boots and a *sombrero de exploración* having a sort of rail round the rim to which, if required, a shallow mosquito net could be attached.

At Figueras we took third-class seats in the *tranvía*, the slow train which rattled through the heat of an airless afternoon to Barcelona.

Here there was a five-hour wait before we boarded a train for Burgos, once again occupying hard, narrow third-class seats. The Spanish railway system was generally supposed to be owned by the Church, and for this reason Spaniards claimed that the trains were slower, less accountable to time-tables, more inefficient and uncomfortable in every way than those anywhere else in Europe. Our train was diverted for major line repairs to one-way tracks, and some hours were used up waiting in sidings in provincial towns for trains coming in the other direction to pass. At every station peasants clawed their way in to reduce our living space with their innumerable parcels and their baskets of livestock. We sat jammed together, our knees almost touching those of the passengers we faced, swaddled in air like wool, through a night full of snores and groans, of the wailing of children and the sleepless clucking of hens.

There was no way of getting along the corridor, sealed as it was by bodies and baggage, to the lavatory, which in any case was certain to be blocked. The train swayed, rattled and bounced through opaque gorges and round invisible sierras, and the passengers struggled to form sad little queues to vomit through the windows into the black cavern of the Aragonese night. To all this, Don Alberto, eyes screwed up over a volume of Seneca in the dim and flickering light, showed a noble indifference. The peasants untied their food packets and thrust on us thick *bocadillos* dripping with onion, oil and tomato, and I learned from him how to decline these, and the jugs of goat's whey, without giving offence. When he spoke he was full of good cheer and repressed excitement. 'We are going to a great adventure,' he said. 'I believe that we shall return from it spiritually refreshed.'

At Zaragoza where it was two in the morning, we escaped to the platform to be besieged by bootblacks, sellers of lottery tickets and tripe pies, by beggars with appalling deformities, and by an urgent and insistent man who guaranteed to fit us on the spot with perfectly-fitting sets of new false teeth.

Next stop was Calatayud, where we should never have been, carried there through one more major diversion for track repairs. The faces had changed, but the odours and discomforts remained as before. Our travelling companions included a honeymoon couple, a red-eyed unhappy looking girl with a drunken groom who had sagged over her knees and gone to sleep. Two nursing mothers suckled their babies with great slurping and slobbering of milk within inches of Don Alberto's face as he strained forward with his book to catch what he could of the feeble light. An unshaven, cigar-smoking priest outlined a scheme by which we could subscribe through him for regular prayers for our souls. Then it was dawn and the cocks crammed into wickerwork baskets thrust their heads through what apertures they could find, and began to crow. Two hours later we chugged into Soria.

A bus took us to San Pedro through a sun-flayed, calcinated landscape strewn with the bones of ancient rock. The grey villages looked as though they had been ravaged by earthquakes. Troglodytes lived in holes in the walls of a dried-up river, and there were cave dwellings in the plain, with chimneys sticking up through the ground. Men rode like Arabs on the rumps of tiny donkeys, with turbaned heads, blanketed against the heat. We disturbed hooded crows hollowing out a sheep that lifted themselves with a scuffle of wing beats into the air and dropped back again as soon as we passed.

It surprised us that about half of our fellow passengers should have been what is known in Spain as *gente formál*, who commented on what they saw with curiosity and sometimes amusement. There were more of them in the meagre street of San Pedro Manrique – women in flowered dresses, with elaborate hairstyles and wearing white shoes; men carrying cameras, in well-cut flannels and ties with clips. Don Alberto found out later that they were a party of business executives and their wives who had come from Madrid to see the fire walking. They had been joined by several doctors who hoped in due course to offer an explanation for the phenomenon by which the human body could be exposed for a few seconds to extreme heat without causing visible damage.

One glance at San Pedro Manrique was enough to convince me that true poverty in Farol did not exist. The sea provided the fisherfolk with the certainty of survival, but here such a fundamental guarantee had never existed. Tudela was the capital of this stricken region. In bad years before the Civil War people died of starvation in the streets of this town, their bodies sometimes nibbled at by the famished dogs before they were discovered and removed by the police.

Few people had heard of the town's wretched little satellite, San Pedro, and fewer outsiders still had ever visited it. It had nothing to offer, produced nothing but bitter olives and goats that had learned to climb trees. For this reason the villagers were left in peace – if peace it could be called – to live much as their ancestors had 3,000 years before, and carry on such practices, forgotten elsewhere, as that of purifying themselves at the time of the summer solstice by passing through the fire.

The isolation that preserved fire-walking favoured that other Spanish speciality of the remote sierras – banditry – and in the Tudela region the two could be linked in a kind of ritual significance. When on a St John's Eve back in the nineties, Zolico, the last of the *bandidos generosos*, suddenly appeared in San Pedro, passed his gun to a follower, removed his boots, muttered a prayer, then 'taking eight slow paces' crossed the fire, he was able to do so, he explained, because his trade had taught him how to repress fear. There were other bandits who performed the same feat but with less style. Don Alberto and I spoke to the aged local doctor who had been present at this performance as a young boy, and had joined the rush to kiss the bandit's hand. He was a tiny man, almost a dwarf, Dr Villalobos said, who may have wished to look like a gnome, as he had grown a white beard and wore a pointed red hat. He thanked his many well-wishers, recommending them not to offend God by blasphemy, was lifted to his horse and galloped away.

Fame came suddenly to San Pedro Manrique after a visit in 1939 by a Madrid journalist who saw the fire-walking and wrote an account of it in the weekly *Domingo* full of crafty injections of anthropological lore lifted from a study of fire-walking in the Far East. This took the eye of two academics who went there next year, joined the fire-walkers and were taken to hospital with second-degree burns. These proto-martyrs were followed by a flow of investigators, several of whom allowed themselves to be more or less severely damaged. Their sufferings provided excellent publicity for San Pedro, but in the end the authorities thought it better to lay a ban on attempts by outsiders to cross the fire, which inevitably came to grief.

San Pedro, as we discovered, made no concessions to the comfort of the visitor, but prided itself in keeping up with the times in other ways. We called on the Alcalde who was guarded against intruders by a pretty secretary, engaged when we arrived in typing a letter in reply to one of the many received that week – in this case from a scientific body in Copenhagen. The Alcalde, darkly suited, impassive and a little aloof as befitted his position, took Don Alberto's card on which he was described as *Proprietario* and asked him how much land he owned; when Don Alberto told him, using the grand old-fashioned unit of measurement, *cabellerías* – denoting the area a horse could be ridden round at a brisk walking pace in one hour – he unbent. He handed us a leaflet he had written entitled *El Rito en San Pedro Manrique de la Purificación Por el Fuego*, quoting the comments of a number of men of science who had witnessed the ceremony, prefixed by a lengthy disquisition by an Indian mystic, Khuda Bux, described as 'the King of Fire', who had performed similar feats to the satisfaction of the 'London University for Psychical Research'. All the experts cited favoured a para-normal, or psychological explanation to the phenomenon, and it was clear that the Alcalde agreed with them. No space was given to one or two investigators who had published opinions suggesting that the apparent immunity of fire-walkers is explicable in physical terms.

The Alcalde implored us to put our hats on, clamped his own, by way of encouragement, firmly down over his ears, and clapped for sherry to be brought. He then launched into a short lecture, delivered in a somewhat premeditated fashion, as if often repeated. All that was needed to cross the fire unscathed (he claimed that the surface temperature of the bed of embers was 700°C) was the inner certainty that one would not be burned. This psychological precondition was only present in the case of persons born in San Pedro. Outsiders who attempted to emulate them did so in a state of real or subconscious terror, and thus inevitably failed. They failed, too, because their motives were impure. San Pedreños approached the rite in a mood of religious fervour. Others did so from motives of curiosity, because they saw what they were doing as an experiment, or simply to show off. The Alcalde reeled off a list of casualties suffered in recent years, adding with a trace of proprietorial satisfaction that in 1922 an overbold foreigner had died as the result of his burns.

We strolled down to the space in front of the church where municipal employees were busy with brooms, helped by children who were picking up every stone, matchstick or leaf in sight. It was about eight in the evening. A sparse crowd had gathered, and shortly four carts stacked with olive-wood faggots drove up, and the men with the brooms put them away and unloaded the carts. Then, in a precise and deliberate fashion, they built the faggots, criss-crossing them one above the other, into a pyre. A man identified by Don Alberto as mayordomo next arrived. Municipal employees stood at each corner of the pyre like recruits at kit inspection, while the mayordomo, in a big old-fashioned hat, white ruffled shirt worn with an artist's bow tie, and carrying a long iron ruler nodded his approval of the finished work, measured the height of the piled-up wood and declared it to be exactly one and a half metres. The crowd had now thickened to about five or six hundred, and at a signal from the mayordomo, a dozen or so fire-walkers pushed their way through to the front. They were all men in their early twenties. By order of the Alcalde they had been required to boost the village's image in visiting eyes by wearing white shirts with dark ties, and their trouser legs had been cut off above the knees. They were received with a small outbreak of applause which the mayordomo instantly stifled with a loud cry of '*silencio*!'

At ten o'clock, with the extreme punctuality displayed in Spain on such public occasions, the mayordomo was handed a torch which he applied to the four corners of the pyre, from which the flames crackled up instantly. We were standing with the Alcalde at the front, and within seconds we were driven back several feet by the intense heat. Excited as a child, and encouraged by the metaphysics of Khuda Bux (fire sought out impurity and was to be resisted by purifying oneself), Don Alberto had begun a conversation with a group of fire-walkers.

He was looking for reassurance, and wanted to know if it was a fact that the fire-walkers were animated by religious fervour.

The answer may have seemed depressingly matter-of-fact. 'Not in my case. I'm here because my friends will be watching . . . well, yes, I suppose it helps to believe in God and the saints.'

A spiritual driving force was also disclaimed by the second young man who said that the verbena was the one time in the year everybody relaxed and enjoyed themselves. Being chosen to walk across the fire was like being picked for a football team. He enjoyed the prestige. Who wouldn't?

Don Alberto refused to give up. But surely a good deal of self-preparation must be involved?

Reply: 'None at all. Whoever spread that story made it up. Care to look at my feet? They're no different from yours. They talk of mental exaltation, whatever that means, but when I cross the fire I feel the same as I do at any other time.'

'But if I did it, I'd get burned,' Don Alberto insisted.

'Yes, of course you'd get burned.'

'Why should that be?'

'Frankly I don't know. You can read about it in the newspapers. They make up a lot of things.'

The old account in *Domingo* had spoken of secret and prolonged rites of self-purification. Don Alberto saw his miracle slipping away and clutched at a straw. At the least he demanded to be told that fire-walking was more than any other acquired skill. 'You wouldn't say that it's no more than a matter of technique, would you? The way you place your feet?'

'It must come into it. You'll see for yourself. Our method is to press down hard with the heels, take short steps and lift the feet as high as we can.'

'A thing that anybody should be able to do.'

'They ought to, but they can't.'

Crestfallen, Don Alberto broke off battle.

Shortly before eleven the fire had burned down to leave a low mound of embers and ash. The man from the municipality raked this over to form a bed two metres in length by one wide, and the mayordomo was ready with his rule to measure the depth, which he found to be nine centimetres. These figures were passed on by the Alcalde who had joined us again, now wearing his chain of office. The levelled bed was fanned by blankets into an incandescent glow, sparks snapped and crackled, then the glow faded to leave the embers whitening to ash, crested all over with small blue flames. The first of the fire-walkers pulled off his boots, walked to the edge of the fire and stubbed at it with his toe like a bather testing the water. It was a solemn moment, acknowledged by the crowd's hush. A number of women crossed themselves, and the Alcalde put out his cheroot and threw it down.

The young man walked into the fire, lifting his feet as if from deep snow and raising small flurries of powder and smoke as he crossed in six short paces. A doctor was waiting at the far end with a torch and a cloth to examine his feet, and his announcement that there were no burns was greeted with applause. The ceremony was to be carried out at high speed, for by this time the second man was already on his way, and six more waited in line, smiling and waving to their friends, to follow.

All the crossings were successful and, with the basic requirements of the ritual completed, several visitors agreed to be carried piggy-back by the fire-walkers through the embers. Don Alberto declined an offer of the experience, saying that he found it frivolous.

At a quarter to twelve they doused the fire and we walked back to the inn where a traditional Verbena de San Juan meal was to be served immediately after midnight to the celebrants, some of whom had kept fast throughout the day. We were invited to inspect the mess bubbling in an appropriate cauldron in the kitchen, and trapped by our respect for custom we allowed ourselves to be served a ladleful of dark anonymous gobbets.

The food, followed by a flagon of wine, seemed to possess extraordinary restorative virtues. Don Alberto cheered up and told me that he had come to the conclusion that the young fire-walkers he had questioned had not wished to disclose their true feelings to him. It was a sign of the times that the young were afraid to admit that they believed in anything. They were no more atheists than he was, but they were nervous of being laughed at. What did I think of it all?

I told him that I had been unable to share the emotions of the distinguished anthropologist Mariano Iñiguez, quoted in the Alcalde's paper as saying that the sight of a man walking on fire had provoked 'a holy shudder, an instant of veneration, as if a solemn ancestral memory had stirred deep in my subconscious'. On the other hand I was inclined to the belief that self-hypnotism had been added to the knowledge of the right way to place the feet, and that had Don Alberto or I followed the fire-walkers for a single pace into the fire we should have spent Midsummer's Day in Tudela hospital.

Don Alberto agreed. 'For me,' he said, 'our pilgrimage to San Pedro has been a great spiritual experience.' He leaned against the hard back of the bench. The cavernous room, lit by a single lamp, was draped in shadows, and from all round came the soft drone of voices of men who had experienced the fulfilment of a successful fiesta. Don Alberto's eyes began to close. 'It has affected me,' he said. 'I feel more hopeful than I did.' A moment later he was asleep.

14

'Sir, I warn you to look away and not turn your head. Better to breathe through the mouth. Of course, it's pure prejudice, but why have doubts? As Barros puts it, "Only the cook needs to know what's in the pot."'

It was the beginning of August, Carmela was back, and she had returned from her first shopping expedition for my midday meal. She had appeared as unexpectedly as ever with a rasp of rope-soled shoes on the tiles and a whiff of green soap, like a genie summoned from the bottle. Her gaze as ever held criticism and, inspecting my quarters,, she emitted a flinty chattering of disgust at the disorder uncovered wherever she looked. The cat that had slipped in behind her was kicked expertly through the narrow door-opening into the street, and she grabbed up a broom. I was told that Muga had kitted her out with a bottle-green jumper and skirt, a handbag and leather shoes for Barcelona, but now she was back in her workaday party dress bulging at the midriff as the result of some quick piratical adventure on her way from her new dwelling to the Grandmother's house.

To Muga's huge irritation she had turned down, as the Grandmother reported, his offer to refurbish for her an old log-cutter's cabin outside the village's limits, seizing for herself, instead, a disused boathouse built into the base of a low cliff within yards of the end of the smartened up sea-front that Muga was in the process of imposing upon the village. From this she let it be known that nothing would ever shift her, and when the Civil Guard, hearing of Muga's displeasure, offered to throw her out, Muga told them that he preferred to handle the thing in his own way.

She put away the broom, clicking her tongue in disgust, sloshed water over the floor, and went down on her knees with a scrubbing brush.

'What news of Rosa?' I asked her.

It was Carmela's habit to ignore two questions out of three as unworthy of reply. She got up, her face twisted at first with habitual scepticism, as if to say, do you care one way or another? 'They performed a miracle,' she said. 'She still limps, as is to be expected, but you'd never recognise her.'

'I'd like to see her.'

'What's to stop you? There'll be a party for her saint's day next week. Come along if you like.'

I remembered then that Sa Cordovesa had accompanied Carmela and Rosa to Barcelona, and there was news of her, too.

'We saw quite a bit of her,' Carmela said. 'She got work carrying trays up and down to a first-floor restaurant in the Barrio Chino. It took five kilos off in the first week.'

'A relief for her,' I said. 'I imagine we'll be seeing her back here before long.'

'That's not likely to happen, sir. She didn't move fast enough for them, so they put her downstairs in the delicatessen. The sight of the food must have been too much for her. She was fatter than ever when we left.'

Carmela had moved into the boathouse only the day before. It was in full view of the Grandmother's house, and watching later from the roof I could see her at work putting the place in order. It had been built in impeccable local taste, a dry-stone construction fitted into a natural cave, with a wooden runway down to a scallop of beach which Carmela had calmly incorporated into her domain. Scuttling frantically hither and thither, like a worker ant, she gathered up all palings and suitable pieces of driftwood to make a fence, almost completed by the end of the day. The boathouse walls were of honey-coloured sandstone from the same quarry as the stone taken to build the cork mansions. Carmela decided to make the place more homelike by slapping her yellow paint over this. She put a row of geraniums in old oilcans on the wonderfully-tiled roof projection from the cliff, and on the third day the goat, which had taken to self-cannibilisation in addition to being hideously afflicted by some sort of skin disease, came into view tied to a stake in the centre of what had become Carmela's private yard. Of Rosa, so far, there was nothing to be seen, and the word went round that she was being kept out of sight with the intention of enhancing the drama of her presentation to the village on the occasion of her fiesta.

Despite the fact that on the whole the villagers disapproved of Carmela, many of them were sorry for her and were happy to do anything they could to create a little interlude of happiness in Rosa's barren and isolated life. The Grandmother was making the little girl a skirt. Juan's wife Francesca had bought her a shell necklace in Figueras, and there was a general rummage round for items of cast-off children's clothing and discarded toys that might make acceptable gifts. Sebastian had a few calamares on ice for the meal to which a number of us were invited, and I hoped to be able to make a substantial contribution of damaged fish.

At that time I was fishing with a man called Pujols whose brother who normally worked with him had had to take to his bed with a poisoned foot. The Pujols brothers used an enormous net 4,000 metres long and 8 metres and a half in depth. This net, set in about 100 metres of water, took about two hours to put down and the same to pick up, the real work being to extricate the fish, most of them very small, from the meshes in which they were sometimes so entangled as to look like cocoons. This process took up to four hours, at the end of which our hands bled freely from many small lacerations inflicted by sharp fins and spines. Through long practice Pujols worked at at least double my speed. He was a thin man suffering from a chest complaint who was credited with extraordinary sexual stamina, generally attributed to the fact that he ate practically nothing but raw crabs. They were taken from the nets in abundance on such excursions, and Pujols, never without a crab's leg hanging from his mouth, coughed, chewed and sucked continually as we struggled to extricate the fish from the net. When the fishing was over at least a quarter of the fish were found to be so damaged in the process of disentangling them as to have no commercial value. Of these I took what I wanted, and they went into the Grandmother's ice-box along with Sebastian's calamares.

The fortnight spent with the nets was not without its risk. It was a period when the Civil Guards had decided to renew their harassment. All the boats had been checked to ensure that their old atheistic names were not showing through the purposely thin coating of paint with which they had been covered, and the occasional stubborn heretic who had repainted eyes or even stars on the bows of his boat was called to the *casa cuartel* for official rebuke. Although I had taken out a fishing licence, the law prohibiting boats from carrying any person apart from their registered crews was still in force. The Pujols boat, owing to its size, was a borderline case, but to be on the safe side Pujols gave the guards a kilo of fish apiece, and from that time on they looked in the other direction.

A half-dozen fishermen and their families attended Rosa's party. They had been hand-picked by the Grandmother. Only those able to bring children with them had been invited, and I suspected that several were there purely because they dare not refuse a request that was in reality a command. Led by the Grandmother, who had put aside her black for the occasion in favour of a curious hooded garment rather resembling the San Benito worn by an Inquisitional victim, we filed into the little enclosure. Nervous glances were exchanged. Some doubts had arisen in people's minds about Rosa's condition, and we were not sure what to expect, but all were determined to do what was possible to make the party a success. Carmela waited to welcome us dressed in her bottle-green jumper and skirt and carrying her handbag, which she immediately flung aside. She had twisted her face into a smile of kinds which made her hardly recognisable.

The trestle table which, with its complement of dwarf's chairs, was a village prop, had been set up. We sat down uncomfortably and Carmela went round handing out mugs of *palo*. An odour of superb cooking leaked from the boathouse and the sweet liverish liquor began to take effect. The men, ill-equipped to talk of other things, were on the subject of fishing. Their wives sipped their *palo*, patting their lips delicately between each sip, and chatting in excited high-pitched voices about the incidents of their confined lives. The children, recovering their confidence, gradually separated themselves from the parents and went off to inspect the collection of oddments – empty bottles, odd slippers, cans of paint, drying corncobs, tortoise shells and peacock's feathers – that Carmela had left lying about. They were careful to keep out of reach of the goat tethered at the back of the enclosure and watching them with inflamed eyes as it chewed over the matted detritus shed from its coat.

The stage was now set for Rosa's entrance. Carmela had slipped quietly back into the smoke and fug of the boathouse from which she and Rosa now made their dramatic appearance. Carmela held Rosa in a kind of arm-lock as they came down the runway. Rosa was staggering dreadfully, her body contorted and writhing under the shapeless cut-down dress. She brandished a free arm, not, as the nervous onlooker might have thought, in a gesture of fury, but simply to help keep her balance. She seemed worse in every way than when I had last seen her and, catching sight of the children, she began to scream with excitement. Threatened by the approach of this apparition, the children dropped whatever they were doing and rushed for the protection of their parents.

Rosa broke free, cavorted and tottered, then crashed down. Carmela pulled her to her feet, and two fishermen went to her. For a moment Rosa faced us, babbling anguish through the lipless mouth while tears splashed from the great, serene eyes. 'She wants to play with the children,' Carmela pleaded. 'Tell them to come and play with her. There's nothing to be afraid of.'

The children edged away, ready to dash for safety, while Rosa was soothed and calmed and finally half-led, half-carried to a contraption like a makeshift invalid chair in which she was fastened by a single strand of home-twisted hemp. Carmela flustered round the guests. 'Put it down to over-excitement. When she's on her own you wouldn't believe the difference. She can speak as well as I can. It's nothing short of a miracle.'

She served up the food which, although much of it was unrecognisable, was exquisite. After a brief guttural outcry Rosa was silent. The guests ate, drank, and relaxed, and the children recovered enough courage to leave the table and start their favour ring-a-ring-of roses game.

This, for Rosa, was the final straw. She watched in sullen silence for several minutes then, with a sudden shriek, she broke free, lunged out with her arms and began her struggle to reach the game. The most direct route brought her across the path of the goat. Carmela, at the far end of the table, was too far away to reach her in time, and the goat's charge lifted her clean off her feet.

The women carried her into the boathouse where the sound of blubbering soon ceased. Shortly afterwards they came back to say she was asleep. The guests finished their wine, and went, and Carmela untied the goat and took it to graze on the ledges of the cliff.

Next day she was full of gratitude for my contributions, thanking me for the first time for anything she had been given. Rosa, she assured me, would not stop talking about the party, which she had enjoyed more than anything in her life.

15

On the eighteenth of August the Civil Guards, full of their usual sinister buffoonery, came to the house to ask if I had bought any meat within the last two days. I assured them that I had not tasted meat for at least a week. After sniffing round the kitchen in a desultory fashion they went off. This performance was repeated at a number of village houses, and when it was reported that they had spent some time poking about in the village shop rumours began to fly.

Next day Don Alberto had a strange story to relate. The butcher, Mayans, an intelligent, scheming illiterate, had turned to him for counsel over a somewhat murky business in which he had been involved. Mayans told him that a man living on a remote farm had offered him a bull for slaughter. All animals were in theory registered and could only be slaughtered by licence, but as Don Alberto well understood, such black-market transactions were commonplace, and he had agreed with Mayans that any other butcher would have done what he did, which was to go and see the bull with the intention, unless it hapened to be spectacularly diseased, of offering a price. Mayans was surprised that his offer should have been accepted without haggling. The farmer then imposed a curious condition, which was that he himself would slaughter the animal, after which Mayans could come in his van to collect the carcase on 16 August, at any time he liked in the afternoon.

Mayans found this a mysterious business. In addition, the short notice he had been given raised problems as to the disposal of the meat. He therefore dropped his price by 600 pesetas, but, a little suspiciously, the man quite cheerfully agreed. Mayans then paid over in advance one third of the purchase price, stipulating that the carcase should be intact and undamaged, and that no offal should be removed. The farmer assured him that as he proposed to kill the bull with a knife-thrust in the vertebrae of the neck, there was no possibility of any meat being spoilt.

On 16 August at four in the afternoon Mayans went to collect the bull and found it lying in the farmyard, tied to a stake. The carcase was still warm, but on examining it he found severe burning of the head;

149

indeed the eyes had been burned out. At this point his two men showed signs of disgust and alarm, and he told them to go back to the van while he questioned the farmer as to what had happened.

The farmer's story was that a stranger had come to the farm and offered him an enormous sum for the privilege of slaughtering his bull, the meat to remain the farmer's to dispose of in any way he thought fit. It was left that if an immediate outlet for the sale of the meat could be found, the slaughtering would be done next day, and precisely at midday on the sixteenth, after the farmer had spoken to Mayans, the man returned, accompanied by a second stranger who was carrying a large, flat object wrapped up in paper. The farmer told them that everything had been fixed up. He then tied the bull to a stake, and the man handed over the promised sum of money, and told him to go for a walk and come back in an hour.

He walked off, but as soon as the men turned their backs, he hid in an irrigation ditch to watch what was going on. A clump of bamboos obstructed his vision, but he could see the bull capering about and smoke was going up, as if a fire had been lit. The bull was bellowing a good deal. When he thought an hour was up he went back, and found the animal on the ground, and one of the men unfastening what looked like an iron mask from its head. There was a smell of burnt hide and hair. He asked the men what they'd done, and the first man said, 'That's the way we kill bulls in my country.' The men gave him some brandy. The impression he got was that they'd both been drinking heavily.

The more Mayans thought about this business, the less he liked it, and he told Don Alberto that his first impulse had been to drop the thing there and then and go away. On second thoughts, he decided that he was already heavily committed. He'd recently quarrelled with one of his men, whom he believed would damage him if he could. So he called them both back, and told them to skin the carcase and cut it up and load it into the van. They delivered the meat to a middle man who would take anything if the price was right, and Mayans threw the head into a ravine. He bribed his two men to keep their mouths shut with gifts of meat but it was clear now, Mayans told Don Alberto, that for all that one or both had gone to the police.

But why should there be any problem with the police? Don Alberto asked. Illegal slaughtering, as everyone knew, went on all the time, and nobody benefited more from it than the police themselves.

Mayans agreed that the local guards had been too often round to his back door for prime cuts on the side to make things difficult for him in that direction.

'What was he worried about, then?'

'Rumours,' Mayans said – the possibility of a story getting round that he'd been involved in witchcaft. Most of his customers were superstitious. It would ruin his trade. It might even get into the newspapers, in which case the Civil Guard in Gerona would be down on him like a ton of bricks.

'I told him I didn't think he had any cause for worry,' Don Alberto said. 'While he'd been telling me all this rigmarole I'd been doing a little thinking and putting two and two together. I asked the man if he could remember anything more the farmer might have told him about the two strangers, and he said that he'd mentioned that they had funny accents, like the Aragonese. That settled it, because I remembered that the sixteenth of August is the feast of San Roque in Aragon and that they hold a quite famous ceremony in Villanueva de Giloca, involving the sacrifice of a bull. At midday. That's where these two fellows must have been from.'

'They burn the bull to death?' I asked.

'That is the time-honoured custom. Our friend managed to remember that one of the two strangers had played the bagpipes while the burning was going on, which also enters into the tradition. They fix balls of pitch between the horns and set light to them so that only the brains are damaged. The iron mask arrangement is intended to slow down the process. The longer it takes the better. I told Mayans that if they didn't go for him for dealing in unlicensed meat he could forget about it.'

'Cruelty to animals is without importance?'

'It wouldn't be seen as cruelty. This is an ancient festival, recognised and approved of by the state and the Church. The bull is blessed by the priest before they put it to death. I can't imagine that anyone would want to make a fuss because two villagers from Villanueva who can't get back for their fiesta hold a little private celebration. The only offence they could be charged with would be an infringement of licensing regulations.'

16

The year went downhill rapidly. A vicious circle was established of boats that became progressively less seaworthy, and equipment that was wearing out because the fishermen could not make enough money with their defective gear to put it in repair. In August the Feast of the Assumption came and went without the appearance of the Curandero, who was rumoured to have died in the end from the after-effects of the great beating he had received. This left the villagers of Sort saddled with the year's crop of legal and family disputes with no one to help them solve them, while the women of Farol, unable to renew their stock of birth-control requisites, and having no faith in products obtainable from other sources, began to refuse cohabitation with their husbands even in the hour of the siesta. The fishing suffered another blow. Deprived of the Curandero's guidance, the fishermen hardly knew how to set about finding the tunny. They blundered largely by accident into a few small shoals, but the catch was less than half that of the year before.

Don Alberto had complained of the monotonous character of local fiestas. This year the fact had to be faced that the fiesta at Sort had come to an end. At Farol the Sa Cova evening promenade would happen as usual but, according to Sebastian's Elvira, the sea pilgrimage, abandoned through lack of a candidate for the central role, was unlikely to take place again. Mentioning this, Sebastian added an item of personal news, which he admitted had left him much depressed. By the purest chance, while sifting through a bundle of old *Vanguardias* left over after the obituary notices had been removed for sale, he had come across an account of the tragic end of Enrique, killed back in April while attempting to escape across the Pyrenees. 'Frontier Guards In Action Against Bandits', the item was headed. Enrique and three companions had attempted the crossing at night, and fallen into an ambush. Once in a while, as Sebastian had said, the police had to pretend to clamp down.

While Farol began its slow loss of identity, Muga went from strength to strength, busied with his plans for the coming of the tourists, determined to create for them here a Spanish dreamland, a gimcrack Carmen setting in which the realities of poverty and work were tolerable so long as they remained picturesque.

Despite Don Alberto's attempts to pull strings in the planning department he had crashed through all bureaucratic obstacles to the development of the sea front, but in carrying these out he had so far stuck to the letter of his word. As promised he made no attempts to plant trees or create flower beds, and the sea wall was built without medieval embellishments. Six bronze lamps in modern rectangular style were suspended from stark-looking cement standards. These, at night, emitted a vibrant bluish light, irresistible to winged insects of all kinds and to night-flying birds, which collided with them in great number, providing manna for the cats waiting below.

The fishermen were quite unable to understand how it could be that a man of Muga's intelligence and wealth should be so devoid of taste. Naturally enough, there had been no mention in the agreement reached between Muga and the village of the *colour* of the road, and the fishermen looked on with incredulous horror as Muga's workmen emptied sackloads of imitation marble chippings of many clashing colours and began to press these into the unset concrete of the road's surface. 'I have to tell you,' said my neighbour Juan, 'that when I look at this road I have the feeling of having eaten something I cannot digest.'

The effect of Muga's tidying up was a deadening one. The ancient handsome litter of the sea-front had possessed its own significance, its vivacity and its charm. A spirited collection of abandoned windlasses, the ribs of forgotten boats, the salt-wasted, almost transluscent gallows and frames on which the fish had once been dried, the sand-polished sculpture of half-buried driftwood that had constituted the stage-scenery against which the rituals of the sea had been performed for so many generations, was now abolished at a stroke. Muga, high priest of the standardisation and monotony that lay in wait, was consumed with a passion for make-believe. Walls with castellations and arrow slits for the archers had been ruled out, but before the villagers knew what was happening to them he had made a start on a Moorish-style café with a dome and horse-shoe arches at the end of his road, within fifty yards of Carmela's boathouse. The fishermen went to the Alcalde who asked Muga for an explanation. Muga wondered what all the fuss was about. The tourists were coming and Moorish cafés were what was expected of Spain. With the intention of cutting the ground from under the Alcalde's feet, he announced his intention of presenting the village with the café. The Alcalde asked him if he had acquired the land upon which the café was being built, and Muga told him that, like the road, it lay in the public domain. Was the café to be run on a profit-making basis? the Alcalde asked. Muga was ready with his answer, and his ferocious smile. All profits, he said, would go to the community. He was about to set up a trust, he explained, with himself as one member, and he hoped that the Alcalde would raise no objection to becoming the second trustee.

The moment clearly seemed right to Muga for a major confrontation, and he asked the Alcalde to convene a meeting with the five senior fishermen at which he would put forward suggestions for saving the village from impending ruin. This meeting was held in the bar with most of the village males present, and nobody saw any objection to my going along.

Muga asked the men if they had given any thought to what they were faced with in the coming winter, and Simon, who did most of the talking for the fishermen – who had warned him not to allow himself to be bullied by Muga – said it was too early to say. They had been at work through much of the year rebuilding one of the boats smashed in the big storm, and hoped to put it into the water in time for the autumn sardine season.

'If there is one,' Muga said. He had dropped his habitual bluff and bluster, and adopted a conciliatory manner. The fishermen had accepted the cheroots he handed round.

Simon told him that the growing belief was that the cycle of bad years was coming to an end. This view, as Muga probably knew, was based on the Curandero's predictions and the Tarot cards, but he forebore to show scepticism. 'You lost the tunny,' he said. 'Suppose the sardines don't come. How long can you carry on?'

'We'll live on our fat,' Simon said. 'We're used to it. We don't need five meals a day. We'll all go to bed for a month or two if we have to. They say if you sleep you don't need to eat.' There was a growl of assent from the other fishermen.

Muga had been studying the economics of fishing, and probably knew as much about it by this time as the fishermen themselves. He asked what an average catch fetched in the market when one of the big boats went out.

The fishermen were vague about this, and a long argument went on before a rough figure of 300 pesetas was agreed.

'Shared between how many men?'

'Five.'

'Sixty pesetas per man in fact?' Muga said.

Well no, not quite that, somebody broke in, because there were small sums to be paid to the one or two widows who had an interest in any boat, and the owner or owners of the nets. In two cases there were engines to be looked after and the men who did this expected a few pesetas.

'Let's strike an all-in figure,' Muga said. 'What does that leave us with? 35 pesetas, would you say?'

There was more argument, but 35 pesetas was thought about right.

'For this,' Muga said, 'you put in eight hours' hard work, two hours to put the nets down, two hours to take them up, and four to get the fish out of the nets and box them up. I don't want to talk about all the time that goes into mending the nets, especially when the dolphins have been at them. At Palamos they take tourists for a two- or three-hour boat trip, and they're paid 1,000 pesetas. Quite a difference, isn't there?'

Blank faces all round. Nobody could find anything to say.

'Can you turn a proposition like that down?' Muga asked them.

'First of all, we're fishermen,' Simon said. 'Secondly we don't have tourists here. Why talk about it?'

Muga then announced that parties of French and German tourists would be arriving on 25 August and had taken every room in his hotel. 'This is your chance,' he said. 'You can charge 1,000 pesetas for taking a party to one of the beaches. Why bother about sardines? Why bother about tunny?'

The fishermen's expressions made it clear that they were horrified, that Muga's proposal seemed to them immoral, almost indecent. They had perhaps an inflated view of their own dignity and that of their profession, feeling themselves immeasurably superior to the parsimonious and cringing peasants and the tasteless and ridiculous bourgeois such as Muga, with whom they were in contact. What Muga now suggested, they complained, was an affront not only to them, but to the sea. They were *gente honrada*, not tourist touts or pimps.

'I don't expect a decision now,' Muga said. 'You need time to think about this.'

'We don't need any time,' Simon told him. 'The thing's out of the question.'

'As you know,' Muga said, 'I'm not the one to argue. I'll talk to you again in three days' time. If you've changed your minds by then, all well and good. Otherwise I'll hire a boat in Palamos and bring it down here. Why should I worry? It doesn't matter to me one way or the other. I'm only trying to help you.'

In his attempts to arrange entertainments for the expected tourists Muga ran into the same difficulties as Don Alberto had encountered in his failed campaign to brighten up the annual fiesta, but Muga was forceful and persistent where Don Alberto had been easily discouraged. He located an itinerant gypsy family with a performing bear. This wretched animal had been trained – as all such bears were – by dragging it a number of times across a bed of heated stones while a certain tune was played, to prance and hobble in a grotesque and afflicted fashion for the benefit of an audience whenever the tune was subsequently played. Muga was not altogether sure of whether or not the bear would be considered an attraction, but it turned out that one of the boys was a guitarist, so he spoke to the Alcalde about allowing him to play in the bar. The Alcalde wanted nothing of this but Muga bribed him with the promise of a supply of good wine from Alicante and he gave in. It was agreed that no music should be played before ten o'clock at night, by which time all the men of the village were either out with the boats or in bed. Muga's next step was to force the Alcalde, by producing the text of a law relating to the suppression of improper spectacles, to cover the mermaid with a curtain. These provisions, he considered, made the bar acceptable to the visitors, twelve of whom were to be lodged in the Brisas del Mar and the remaining nine in California-style chalets on his estate that the builders were working on night and day to get ready.

At this moment a rumpus broke out in the Grandmother's household, as Sebastian's Elvira announced that she had taken a job as a chambermaid in Muga's hotel. Sebastian, cowed by the Grandmother's scorn for a man who would allow his wife to go out and work, dared only support her in secret. His wage now, as agreed by the Government syndicate, was 28 pesetas a day, whereas Muga offered a minimum of 50 pesetas a day to anyone who entered his service. There were stormy scenes in the village when two more women, trembling with nerves and spruced up as if for a christening, went off to take similar jobs. When Simon's wife told him that she had agreed to cook for Muga for the hitherto unheard-of reward of 75 pesetas a day, Simon informed her that he proposed to emigrate, and actually left the house, staying away for twenty-four hours. None of the men of Farol would agree to associate themselves in any way with Muga and his project, so Muga enlisted cleaners, handymen and a gardener in Sort.

The twelve French tourists arrived by bus from Perpignan on the twenty-fifth, and the party of Germans were picked up at the Figueras station next day. In Farol they were objects of intense curiosity. The villagers were surprised, they told me, at the loudness of the foreigners' voices, their emphatic gestures, and the informality of the clothes. They seemed anxious to please, and over-generous with their money. The Alcalde and the stupid boy he employed were startled after serving a party of them with drinks, to be offered tips, and the money was still where they had left it, lying on the table, when the foreigners returned next day. Purely out of politeness the young fishermen lined up to follow the foreign ladies – most of whom were plain – when they appeared in the street, and the ladies giggled in an embarrassed way, but seemed pleased at these attentions.

In preparing his hotel for its inauguration, Muga had shown imagination. Vines had been planted in tubs along the verandah, and the handsome decorative foliage trailed along a species of pergola, from which fairy lights had been suspended. After dinner amplified music was switched on. Most of it was the spiritless stuff of the post-war period when the Spanish had begun to lose their grip as a musical nation, but the whole thing was a huge success with the foreigners. Thumping mechanical paso dobles and the drunken bear-torturing guitarist in the bar was the Spain they had come in search of.

Muga had gauged their mentality and aspirations fairly well but, for all the modern gadgetry of his life, remaining a Spaniard, there were still lessons to be learned. The main view beyond the trailing vines and the twinkle of lights was of the ugly house Cabezas had spent the whole of his life on building single-handedly. At one end of the verandah there was another limited prospect, that of the old wall with its recess in which horses were castrated. The people of Farol had no horses but those of Sort were dealt with here because the castrator had chosen to live where he did in a hutch with a view of the sea. Horse castration was a lengthy and finicky business with trimming-up to be done with a razor after the basic operation, and Muga, looking down from the verandah shortly after the tourists had settled in, and admiring, one supposes, the perfectionism of an acknowledged master of his craft, was suddenly surrounded by horrified and protesting guests. Foreigners, as he later confided to the Alcalde, had to be protected from the unpleasant facts of life. That same day the wall was demolished, and the castrator presented with 5,000 pesetas, and told to go and practise his trade elsewhere.

Muga continued to do all that he could to ensure that his customers had a good time. Within a few days he arranged what he called an open-air gala supper, setting up tables in the street outside the hotel. This went down badly with the villagers who by tradition and temperament were opposed to what in this instance came close to a vulgar display. Muga supplied an over-abundance of food, and champagne flowed like water although it was in reality no more than sweetish white wine pumped full of carbon dioxide. Too much fake champagne followed by too much heavy brandy fostered an uproar that continued deep into the night. Even if there were no desperate shortages in Farol at that time, some people still went hungry, and it upset them to see large quantities of food of the kind they could never in any case afford being surrendered to scrounging cats, and even more tipped into trash cans at the end of the feast.

The Alcalde let Muga know as best he could that the villagers objected to being treated like African tribesmen. Notably, they did not wish to be disturbed while at work or engaged in their private affairs by having cameras thrust into their faces. He passed on the message that they found it insulting to be offered money to allow themselves to be photographed. The matter of beach protocol was more prickly. Muga promised to post notices asking his guests not to attempt to enter boats while wearing leather-soled shoes. He did not feel he could embody any prohibition in such notices against urinating on the beach or in the sea.

Don Alberto lent his services in a rather half-hearted way to provide a touch of folklore by inviting a group from Figueras to dance the sardana. Since Farol wanted nothing of them, the performance took place on a Sunday morning in the little square of Sort. The sardana was recognised as the national dance of Catalonia, but Don Alberto was unenthusiastic because it had only been invented in about 1890, was relatively unknown in the countryside and had become the speciality of typists and shop assistants in the towns. The occasion was not an overwhelming success. The visitors enjoyed the dancing, took numerous photographs, and were happy to be taught a few of the dance's exceedingly simple steps. Some of them, however, showed discomfort at the presence of emaciated dogs dragging themselves about in the last stages of starvation, and there was an unsavory moment when, through lack of planning, the muleteer arrived outside the bar, within yards of them, to allow his animal to discharge the contents of its bowels in the usual place. It was at this moment when a French tourist leaned over to tap Don Alberto, to gesture first in the direction of the dancers and then at the mule and the dogs, and say with a laugh, 'The myth and the reality, eh?'

Carrying out his threat, Muga hired a fishing vessel in Palamos, and its crew sailed it to Farol and took the tourists on their beach picnic. Four members of the party who had booked for the trip got lost in a walk through the devastated cork-oak forest, and found by the time they reached the beach that the boat had already left. Several villagers gathered, full of sympathy, to discuss their predicament. Despite the embargo imposed by the fishermen on carrying them in Farol boats, it was generally agreed that something ought to be done. A young fisherman called Jordans who came on the scene and had absolutely nothing to occupy himself with for the rest of the day was encouraged to make an exception in this case and row the four tourists over to the beach. It was a long haul, and the two French couples showed themselves overwhelmingly grateful. They insisted on sharing their packed lunches with Jordans and, because it would have been impolite to do otherwise, he accepted. Later the matter of a reward had to be considered. Jordans insisted that he did not want to be paid, but the French were equally adamant, and in the end he gave in and accepted 100 pesetas. The fact that he had taken this money caused hard feelings when he reported it to the other fishermen, who talked about the thin end of the wedge. That same evening the Alcalde's young barman was caught by his employer in the act of pocketing a tip of ten pesetas. 'I've been paying him twenty pesetas a day until now,' the Alcalde said. 'What can I expect?'

After dropping the tourists off on the return trip the three men from Palamos called in at the bar for a drink and bought a round for the Farol fishermen they found there. They apologised for their unintentional interference in the dispute, but apart from that defended the ethics of what they were doing. 'It's not as if we've any intention of giving up fishing,' they pointed out. 'We go out at night and put the nets down the same as ever. This makes life a bit harder, but there's more money coming in. You ought to give it a thought.'

The Farol men nodded their polite agreement, returning as soon as the outsiders had left to their private discussions and their versifying.

It seemed that a measure of decadence was to be detected in these later sessions. Of old, every day at sea had produced its adventure. Now experiences were on a smaller scale, and spontaneous interchanges in blank verse satyrical rather than epic in inspiration. The fishermen poked fun at the foreigners who involved them in a succession of ludicrous experiences. Too often the males were undignified and drunken, while as this ungallant fragment suggests, the women on the whole appeared to them overdressed and plain.

> *Chicas nos vienen a visita'*,
> Girls come here to visit us,
> *Ricas son, plata tienen,*
> All of them rich, stuffed with money,
> *(Pero) Aunque la mona se vista de seda,*
> (But) Even if the monkey dresses in silk,
> *Mona es, y mona queda.*
> She's a monkey, and monkey remains.

The time came for the visitors to go home, but to the villagers' surprise it turned out that two of them had decided to stay on. These were a young German couple of whom little had been seen hitherto, and who had absented themselves from beach trips and such entertainments as Muga's gala supper and the sardanas at Sort. They were both in their early twenties and made a strikingly handsome pair. The girl, Mitzi, possessed a kind of pale, withdrawn, pre-Raphaelite beauty that left the fishermen stunned. I shared a table with them at the bar one evening, and we exchanged a few words in Spanish. The girl had little to say, and rarely smiled. She was almost over-endowed with the quality of serenity – something the Spanish much admired. For my personal taste the sparkle and the vivacity both of Sa Cordovesa and Maria Cabritas were to be preferred. The girl ran her fingers through the fine silk of her hair and her eyes roved from side to side, like those of an Indian dancer, to take in her surroundings. Klaus, the husband, or boyfriend – I was never sure which – watched her continually. By this time in the evening the gypsy guitarist had started his strumming, and at the end of each piece Klaus clapped twice. Shortly before midnight the couple got up and slipped away.

It was evident that they had intended to stay on in Spain because they had brought a small tent with them. This they pitched on a triangle of beach wedged in the rocks about two miles from the village, and settled to a life which filled the villagers – who had hardly heard of camping before – with utmost curiosity. By this time most of the young fishermen were deeply in love with Mitzi and consumed with jealous hatred for Klaus, and several of them got into the bad habit of hanging about the shore, or lurking in the woods in the vicinity of the tent, in the hope perhaps of the occasional glimpse of the couple's domestic life. The Alcalde made it quite clear in a discussion with the senior fishermen at which I was present that this was a situation he disapproved of, although he didn't see what could be done about it. In his own words, it put wrong ideas into the lads' heads.

The general opinion was that the couple were short of money. Once in a while they came into the village, sat speechlessly in the bar and drank a *palo* between them. When the fishermen wanted to buy them drinks they shook their heads, but an offer of fish was accepted with gratitude. There were several isolated farmhouses in the vicinity of the beach, and it was learned that they occasionally visited one or other of these to buy food. The farmers, who were always dying of loneliness and boredom, would have been overjoyed to see fresh faces, and people assumed would have charged little or nothing for whatever they were able to supply.

The two Civil Guards, walking side by side, rifles slung, patrolled most of the village and the neighbouring beaches every day, and whenever they passed the Germans' tent they made a habit of stopping to exchange a few words with them, on one occasion warning the girl that her habit of wearing a two-piece swimsuit would have to stop.

About a week after the tent had gone up they decided to check on the Germans' visas. Only the girl was there, and they looked through her passport and told her they'd call back next day to see the man. Next day there was no sign of Klaus. Mitzi, who seemed in no way alarmed, said that he had been away for a day and a half, and that he must have had his passport with him. She invited them into the tent and they went over its contents. They were shown Klaus' rucksack stacked with his gear, a wallet with family photographs and a few pesetas which she said belonged to him. She told them that at some time on the previous night Klaus had got up and gone out, she assumed to pass water. She went back to sleep and awakened in the morning to find him gone. Was she surprised? they asked her. Quite surprised, she said. But not really worried? No, not really worried. Klaus went in for impulses. And did she expect him to come back? He might. Spanish are brave but emotional people. The guards told the Alcalde later they had never before run into such calm. Had they quarrelled? the guards asked. No, she said, they never quarrelled.

They had a tiff once in a while. No more than that. Later she told them she seemed to remember hearing voices in the night after Klaus had gone out, but this she said might have been a dream.

The Civil Guards told Mitzi to pack her things up and move back to the village, which she did, and Muga, who had never been able to keep his eyes off her, put her up free of charge in the hotel. A search was then mounted of the area where the couple had camped, in which the Alcalde and a number of volunteers assisted the guards. No one seemed quite to know what they were looking for. The guards showed interest in the marks indicating that a boat had recently been dragged up on the beach, and a few meaningless rags were found in the fairly dense pine and juniper trees at the back of the beach, but nothing more.

Later in the week a senior Civil Guard NCO was sent down from Figueras to ask Mitzi more questions. They visited the beach together and he made a drawing to illustrate his report. What concerned the police was the possibility of foul play but the sergeant ruled this out. He handed Mitzi her passport back, and next day Muga drove her in to Figueras to take the train home.

Later that week it was Muga's saint's day, in celebration of which he presented the village with a cask of Alicante wine, leaving it to the Alcalde to effect a distribution. The wine was full-bodied and aromatic, with a faint flavour of almonds, and the fishermen, accustomed to thick, cloying *palo* and the near-vinegar produced in Sort, had never tasted anything to equal it. Each family was offered a litre, and free wine was served in the bar to all comers on the great day. The senior fishermen and a few of their resolute followers rejected Muga's gift, but many of the lesser fry allowed themselves to be persuaded, and a number of young men got thoroughly drunk before the evening was out.

A day or two after this, an extraordinary rumour began to circulate in the village to the effect that Mitzi had been the victim of a sexual attack on the night of Klaus' disappearance. Much alarmed, and to pre-empt action by the police, the Alcalde tracked this down to its source – a young man called Tiberio Lara, only notable in any way up till now as the first village boy to have a name imposed upon him by the Grandmother, an admirer at the time of his birth of the Emperor Tiberius.

162

The Alcalde sent for Tiberio and questioned him, and after a threat to call in the Civil Guard, the story was out. Tiberio told the Alcalde that on the evening of Muga's party he had got drunk in the bar with Cabezas' son Pedro, commonly known for his dependence on his father at Hijito de Papa ('daddy's boy'). Pedro, a nineteen-year-old loafer who preferred to do without money rather than work, could not afford in the ordinary way to drink, and two glasses of free wine had been enough to send him staggering. Reeling out into the night together Pedro had boasted to Tiberio of the attack, saying that he had spent three nights in the woods watching the tent, and finally, as he had expected she would, the girl came out with a torch. He had tied a scarf over his face followed and overpowered her. After the first attack he was prepared, as soon as released, for her to get up and run away, but she had not done so, so he had had intercourse with her for the second time, meeting with no resistance. While they were lying there among the juniper scrub, a torch was shone on them, and Pedro jumped up and found himself face to face with Klaus. He drew the knife he was carrying and Klaus said, 'Don't hurt me. You can take her. She's yours.'

At first the Alcalde found this story improbable, describing it as a typical teenage fantasy on Lara's part, based on repression. However, he felt obliged to call Lara senior, a man said to rule his family like a biblical patriarch, who arrived wearing a hat borrowed for the occasion and his son walking two paces to the rear. 'Your honour, if you believe what this fellow tells you, you'll believe anything,' Lara said. 'He's a hysteric and a liar.' The Alcalde sent for a Bible and told Tiberio to take it in his right hand, and testify on oath. Tiberio immediately broke down and retracted, saying that he'd made the story up because he was bored, and enjoyed causing a bit of a stir. His father struck him across the face with the back of his hand, and they went off home.

By this time I was on good terms with the Alcalde. A typically Mediterranean relationship had developed in which we were able to help each other out in small ways, and he frequently took me into his confidence. It transpired that he'd had second thoughts about the case and now suspected that Tiberio might have been telling the truth after all, but had been frightened out of his wits by old Lara. We lived in a strange world, he said, but whatever had happened, the thing was settled as far as he was concerned. Like most men in his position, he asked nothing better than to be left in peace, and he was inclined to let sleeping dogs lie. He saw nothing to be gained in questioning Hijito de

Papa. He had acted to put a stop to the spread of a dangerous rumour and head off the police, and now he hoped to be able to let the thing drop.

He confided in me that he had been able to find out that Hijito de Papa had been one of the numerous lovers both of Sa Cordovesa and Maria Cabritas. Otherwise he was a quiet boy, unobtrusive, fond of his own company. We exchanged glances as the warning shadow of Barros fell across us, and the Alcalde quoted, 'I mistrust men that are silent, and dogs that don't bark.' He poured a glass apiece from what was left of the Alicante wine. 'Let's talk of other things,' he said. 'I've got enough on my plate as it is.'

17

The rest of the year went roughly as foreseen. The large-scale repairs to one of the big boats smashed in the storm of the previous October were completed, but not in time for the autumn sardine fishing, which produced the meagre harvest generally expected. Boga shoals were thinning now, and certain varieties of fish common in the past were no longer seen. The incursions of amateurs from Sort became a regular thing. They caught little but greatly disturbed such fish as red mullet which grazed in a slow and ruminative fashion on minute organisms in shallow water, and were scared away from the vicinity. There were cases, too, of nets being plundered, of fish being unhooked from standing lines, and taken from the *vivéros* in which they were kept alive in the sea. Such incidents led to several affrays, in one of which the Civil Guards had to intervene.

No marriage took place in that year, and there were signs that a dangerous loss of able-bodied males might have begun. One man emigrated to Argentina, another engaged himself on a trawler operating in the Atlantic, and two more moved to Palamos, where it was believed they had joined a gang of cigarette smugglers.

Two more parties of foreign tourists arrived, the second being so large that both the hotel and its annexe were full, and the overflow had to be accommodated in the two cork mansions, hastily adapted to their needs. Each party was submitted to the established pattern of entertainment; the gala supper, the folklore expedition to Sort, the beach trips when in both cases the official boat from Palamos received blackleg assistance from local fishermen, for which they later came under the bitter attack of supporters of the boycott.

A small social problem arose out of the relationship between the tourists and the village, due to the fact that one or two unattached foreign ladies seemed over-willing to cultivate the acquaintance of young fishermen. When Tiberio Lara presented himself in the bar one evening in the company of a French woman probably twice his age, the Alcalde served the woman, but refused to take Tiberio's order.

Very slowly the village was adapting itself to the foreigners' requirements, as my neighbour Juan found to his amazement. Juan fished for preference in deep water and had developed special skills in order to be able to do this. The fish he caught, such as *pollas* and *mollas* – there is no name for them in English – were notable for their firm, exquisitely-flavoured flesh, allied to a somewhat grotesque appearance. In my first season's fishing with Juan we were never able to catch enough of them even to satisfy local demand, but by the end of the second year the Grandmother advised him to change his fishing methods and concentrate on the better-looking fish, dorados, brill and bream, to be taken in shallower waters. All Juan's fish now passed through the Grandmother into Muga's kitchens, and his customers put cosmetic appeal before taste. By the time Muga's third group were installed frozen hake, extremely insipid in flavour by comparison with fresh Mediterranean fish, was being shipped in from the Atlantic coast.

Such changes – mostly for the worse in Farol – were paralleled by a major upheaval in Sort.

Pablo Fons' world had fallen about his ears since his effeminate second son had sneaked off to Figueras where he had worked as a barmaid before his arrest by the police for wearing female attire. The shock had brought on a mild heart attack, following which Fons decided to pass over to Muga what remained of his property, and take up light work involving the use of dynamite – at which he was considered an expert – in the excavation and improvement of wells.

In the meanwhile Muga discovered that few of the small farmers possessed title to the exhausted land from which they scraped a living, and when pressure was brought to bear many were happy to extricate themselves from a legal quagmire by selling out. Muga, always preferring blandishment to force, guaranteed to settle matters with the law, besides paying good prices. Finding his newly-acquired territory criss-crossed by ancient rights of way that could not be upheld in the courts, he coolly drove his tractors across these, thereafter taking over a few more parcels of land belonging to peasants who could no longer cultivate them because they were out of reach. Apart from using fertilisers Muga pumped water down from the hills, thus irrigating land upon which it was normal for not a single drop of rain to fall from March until November. He planted nothing but potatoes, for which there was an urgent and world-wide demand. When they lifted the potatoes, wheat would go in – durum wheat, for export to Italy, to be used in the making of pasta. Many of the dispossessed smallholders now worked for Muga, their diet hitherto having been rice, beans and maize porridge. They asked Muga what would they be eating in future – surely not potatoes? Muga told them they could decide for themselves. He proposed to open a shop in Farol offering an endless choice of food in cans: meat, fish, vegetables, soup, anything they could think of. Gone were the days when a man had to grow his food before he could eat. The future awaiting them was bright.

Don Alberto planned a rearguard action, choosing as allies Don Ignacio and the ultra-conservative senior fishermen of Farol.

Don Ignacio had never forgiven Muga for insisting on rigidity in the matter of the hours set for the celebration of Mass, which deprived him of his weekend archaeological trips. He agreed, too, with Don Alberto that the foreign influence was on the whole pernicious. In a matter of weeks, as he had pointed out to me, money values had become wholly distorted, so that women scrubbing floors and washing bed-linen for Muga gained far more than skilful and dedicated fishermen who had spent their best years at an exacting trade. Don Ignacio believed that the democracy of foreigners was misunderstood by a people who had never encountered it before and were encouraged by it to presumption and lack of respect. A small nucleus of hangers-on of which Tiberio Lara was an example was beginning to form, who treated the visitors with a kind of contemptuous over-familiarity. Don Ignacio had to admit that there was a lack of dignity and restraint on both sides, and that French and German holiday-makers who came to Farol probably behaved in a more subdued fashion on their home-ground.

This viewpoint was strongly supported by the senior fishermen who vowed to do everything in their power to stop the Muga advance and to see to it that he did not get away with more flagrant abuses such as the building of the pseudo-Moorish café, recently inaugurated with a noisy and drunken party for foreigners and a number of Muga's kinsmen, which had gone on half the night. The senior fishermen promised effective sanctions against the increasing number of their juniors who had, on one pretext or another, broken ranks and carried foreigners in their boats. They proposed, also, to order the Palamos boat to stay away in future from Farol.

Don Alberto, who had seemed a little jaded for some days after the arduous journey to San Pedro Manrique, had now recovered and, eager to give battle, kicked his Levis into action and dashed hither and thither in his efforts to drum up new support. The Grandmother, knowing by this time on which side her bread was buttered, could offer nothing better than lukewarm approval, and the Alcalde was favourably disposed to his cause, but prepared to do absolutely nothing. For the first time Don Alberto, who usually settled for his morning drink and a glance at the obituaries outside the bar, saw the curtain over the mermaid, and he was furious. 'Let's face it, this man can make or break me,' the Alcalde said. 'I have to toe the line in certain small ways.'

I visited Don Alberto at his house for the last time that year to say goodbye, and happened by purest chance to be there when the seven peons, who had stuck with him through thick and thin until then, called to discuss a problem.

We were on the roof, savouring the crystalline, razor-edged beauty of a day hovering in the sweet limbo between summer and autumn. The sun had crisped away the last of the stubble from Don Alberto's land, covering the naked earth with a faint patina, like rust, in which sparse details, a horse trough, a stile, a well-head, were engraved with extreme clarity. The atmosphere had an alpine thinness. We could have almost counted the leaves on a tree a half-mile away, and the intensely dry clicking of a water-wheel turned by a donkey, sounded like the solemn tick-tock of a grandfather clock deep in the ears. A hard line drawn clean across the middle distance marked the frontier with the dark and featureless acres of Muga's land, newly turned by the plough.

We saw the seven peons coming like Indians, single-file up the path. The scene was so sharply defined, I could see the grain of the log dragged by the dog they had with them. We went down the steps into the main room. Don Alberto's aged mistress was playing *La Violetera* on the gramophone and he signed to her to go to the door. 'I'm afraid her mental processes are beginning to fail,' Don Alberto said sadly. Although they had long since left their nests on the beams and ledges, swallows were still twittering in and out through a shutter which would be left open until they went. Someone called '*Ave Maria purisima*' at the door, and a moment later the peons were let in.

They stood in a line among the swallows' droppings, twisting their hats in their hands. They had thick, sensitive aboriginal features, and under the shiftiness and ingratiation of their expressions I sensed a closely guarded hostility, and was reminded of Giovanni Verga's

Sicilian peasants, sickle in hand, ready for a *jacquerie*.

'Well, what is it?' Don Alberto asked.

'We've come to talk to you about Don Jaime,' one of the peons said.

'Do you mean Muga? What about him?'

'He's asked us to give him a hand.'

'In other words, work for him. You work for me.'

'There's not much to be done at this time of the year.'

'Surely that's a good thing, when you get paid just the same. What's Muga asking you to do?'

'He'd like us to take down a few trees. So he can get a plough in.'

'My dear friends,' Don Alberto said. 'Don't stand on ceremony.' His smile reminded me of a skull. 'Put on your hats and sit down. In this world every man is ruled by his own interests, and I expect you to be by yours. Just tell me one thing. What do you expect to eat when you sit down to a meal?'

The peons sat awkwardly on the edges of Don Alberto's throne-like chairs. 'Bread and beans. Rice on Sundays,' it was agreed.

'I feed you, don't I?'

'Yes, sir. That's true.'

'If you work for Muga you'll eat cow that was killed ten years ago before it went into the can. I say killed, but it probably died of disease. How do you like the idea of that?'

'Not much, your honour, if that's the truth of the matter.'

'Of course it's the truth of the matter. Tell me another thing. How do you spend most of the winter?'

'We sleep it off, sir.'

'Of course you do, and so do I. We have a proverb, "December, fire and bed." You only get up to eat and relieve yourselves if the truth be known, but I keep forking out money just the same. Work for Muga and you'll find you'll be working up to twelve hours a day spring, summer, autumn and winter. You may have heard he's put a stop to siestas for the people on his payroll. . . . Do you like the idea of your sister or your daughter wearing trousers?'

'It doesn't appeal to us at all, sir.'

'If they work in Muga's hotel they will. It's supposed to stop the men they'll have to work with from looking up their skirts. What the real reason is I'll leave to your imagination. If you take a job with Muga he'll find some way of getting his hands on your womenfolk, too. My advice to you is keep them at home.'

'We certainly intend to do that.'

'I've big things planned for the future. Something it wouldn't be wise to talk about at this stage, but leave it to me. We'll storm new heights together. The law, as you know, doesn't allow me to pay you more than 19 pesetas a day, but I'm going to find some way of getting round it and putting your wages up to 25. Is that all clear then?'

There was an exchange of glances, and a half-hearted muttering of assent. The peons got up, and Don Alberto brushed aside their thanks and shooed them out of the door. It was a victory of a kind, but I could see battles ahead.

Sebastian came with me to Figueras in the taxi to see me off. We did our best to turn it into a jovial occasion, plastering a little foolery over the cracks of the sorrow of leave-taking. It was a time for the hasty mustering of reminiscence, of which our fishing trips offered so rich a supply. We had caught many fish together, and suspected that few people in the years to come would see what the sea had shown us off these remote shores, hardly more troubled, I suspected, by human interference than in the days of the voyages of Odysseus. The high spot had been the great fishing of escarmalans back in the spring, and we promised each other that we would repeat the success in the coming year.

A little fun had gone out of life, Sebastian said, since that memorable episode. The adventure had set too high a standard for the rest of the year. His work had become boring, demanding much patience of him but little skill. He was now building chalets for a contractor that were delivered on site as an assembly kit, so many doors, so many windows, so many lavatory fittings, all of them identical, merely requiring to be put together. It produced a boredom of a rabid kind, entirely different from the benign monotony, the dulcet withdrawl of the mind experienced in calamar fishing, which remained his favourite pastime.

We passed through a salient of forest with the trees sloughing their bark like snakeskin and showing white, leached-out wood beneath. Further on the bad corner round a shallow ravine, once dynamited by the landlords to keep outsiders away, was being widened again for the second time in two years, a danger sign had been put up, and concrete blocks striped with black and white paint marked the edge of the road.

The talk was of change and the future. For all his efforts Sebastian remained as hard-up as ever. Elvira had given up her job at the hotel after a German had slipped into a room behind her as she was making up the bed and waved a 100-peseta note at her, accompanying the offer with unmistakeable gestures. The incident had sparked off a major row with the Grandmother, present when Elvira ran weeping back to the house, who accused him (once again) of impotence and sterility, and of readiness to live off her daughter's immoral earnings.

However there was no way of getting away from her while the prospects remained uncertain. All the construction workers were employed by a contractor who paid the regulation wage. In order to break out of the economic straitjacket, he would have to change his job and this, he hinted, he was prepared to do. It was a big decision to make, and he preferred to say no more about it at this stage. He promised to write and keep me posted.

He was cautiously optimistic, he said. We had put the bad year behind us. Things couldn't get worse, and the general feeling was that they would now improve. Elvira would certainly never go back to the hotel, but he had no objection to her taking in laundry as suggested by the housekeeper. Most of the fishermen held the view that next year would prove to be the first of a cycle of good years, and they awaited it in confidence with the second of the three smashed-up boats now fully repaired and ready for the sardine shoals in March. He suspected that the Grandmother's ill-humour of late had been to some extent the result of falling fish sales, and that any substantial increase in catches might help to make life easier for him. The possibility of the change of job came up again, and he remained evasive. Should something happen in this direction, he said, he would make the change at such a time as to be able to take a week or two off in April. He hoped we might go escarmalan fishing again.

It was on this determinedly cheerful note that we parted for that year. The tranvía, an hour late and glutted with nursing mothers, incontinent children, and countrymen carrying chickens in wickerwork baskets, came crashing over the points in Figueras station. It was instantly stormed by sellers of lottery tickets, stale sandwiches, and soda water the colour of diluted blood. There were twenty or thirty heads at every window of the train, and hands reached out as if to grasp at salvation. Half the people who crowded the platform would not be travelling but were there for the excitement of watching the trains come and go, and anxious to strike up friendships with passengers that would be terminated in a matter of minutes with the departure of the train.

This was Spain as I knew it and had come to terms with it, just as I had grown to know and appreciate Sebastian, who typified in so many ways the country of his birth; this thin man with a bold but melancholic eye and a head full of poetic fancies, this passive but successful resister of despots, living on little more than air, and with no demands upon the future other than that it should show some slight improvement on the present.

The guard, a huge watch in hand, bore down on us. 'Sorry to butt in, gentlemen, but we have to be going. I wouldn't want to leave anyone behind.'

I boarded the train, struggled through to a compartment and then to the window, to wave.

'Till next year, then.'

'If God's willing.'

'Of course he'll be willing.' We had begun to copy the Grandmother's habit of making up God's mind for him.

The peasants waited for me to sit down, ready to thrust their food into my mouth.

Season Three

1

That winter brought a brief note from Sebastian in which he said he had changed his job, but the nature of the new one remained unspecified. No mention was made of the projected escarmalan trip, so I assumed he had dropped the idea, probably through pressure of work.

At the end of the summer I had struck up an acquaintance with a middle-class Spanish visitor to Farol, interested in spear fishing, but more so in underwater archaeological exploration, and I spent some weeks of the opening season with him in the area of Ampurias – within a mile or two of Don Ignacio's hunting ground – where we collected a large quantity of broken Roman pottery, none of it of importance. Later we visited the islands of Espardell and Espalmador, near Ibiza, out of reach at that time of local fishermen, where enormous untroubled meros were still to be seen, mooching through the shallows within yards of the beach.

It was early June before I returned to Farol, where it was instantly obvious that drastic changes had taken place. The Grandmother received me with undiminished affability, but she too had changed with the village. Where she had been slow and stately she was now brisk. The dignified near-widow's weeds had been replaced by a utilitarian jumper and skirt, and the coarse grey hair had been ruthlessly cropped back to reveal more of a scraggy nape of the neck. I was astonished to note that the ultimate village taboo had been ruptured by the black leather shoes she wore, with their gaudy buckles.

She had kept my room for me, but I could count myself lucky, she said, because for the first time Farol was to have what she called a 'high season' comprising the months of July and August, when it had been announced that all prices were to go up, and there would not be a room to be found at any price. An agent carrying a briefcase wherever he went, and wearing the first tinted glasses to be seen in Farol, had established himself in the village and gone from house to house in a search for accommodation, offering to pay 15 pesetas per day on a seasonal basis for a room whether occupied or not. It was an offer people found hard to refuse, especially after the catastrophic failure once again of the sardines to appear in March.

The agent had stipulated that any household wishing to qualify for inclusion would have to fall into line in one essential matter. Toilets providing no more than a hole in the floor and usually ceramic footprints in indication of where the feet should be placed, were out, and pedestals were in. The Grandmother led me into the cubicle in which her artistic floral tiles had been scrapped and the contractual fitment installed in readiness for my successor. She flushed the cistern, peered down at the swirl of water and nodded with calm pride. 'Just the thing,' she said, 'if you want to relax and reflect on life in general. I wouldn't call it hygienic.'

Carmela was still about, she said, but was too busy elsewhere to be able to do much for me. The Grandmother hinted that Carmela had access to sources of prepared food, and was in no doubt that at a push we could come to an arrangement with her. Failing that, a stall had been set up near the church selling *perros calientes*. From this information I understood that the hot dog had begun its conquest of Spain. Also, said the Grandmother, *hamburguesas* – both of them excellent. All in all, there was little fear of starving. My cat, she announced, had mysteriously disappeared, and if I wanted another I should have to feed it, because the village had been cleaned up, leaving not a scrap of edible rubbish to be found anywhere, which was hard on the pig Mercedes.

The Grandmother's own business, she told me, had gone with the fish, so naturally enough she had been obliged to look in other directions. She hoped to receive building permission for another room to be added to the house, and showed me the plans with some diffidence. It was clear that the addition of a breeze-block cube would wreck the natural, unplanned charm of the building and convert it into a blot on the landscape. The agent had been repelled by the austerity of the houses of Farol and hoped to inject a little cosiness by insisting that each room let to a visitor contain at least one framed picture, to be chosen from a stock in his office. The choice was of the London Houses of Parliament, the Eiffel Tower, St Mark's Square, Venice, and the Château of Chillon.

Her final piece of news was that Sebastian and Elvira had left her house. She made the announcement with a mixture of acrimony and relief for, with a faint smirk, and clutching suddenly with a huge paw at her belly, she gestured that Elvira was pregnant.

She directed me to Sebastian's place of work. By now I was ready for anything, and it came as no great surprise to find him sitting at a desk in the restaurant of the Brisas Del Mar hotel, taking slips of paper from a spike on which they had been stuck, and entering the information written on them in a book. It was about ten in the morning, hours before the restaurant opened, and for a few moments Sebastian did not register my presence, and when he looked up and saw me he seemed startled. He jumped up and we embraced. He was wearing black trousers and a black bow tie, managing to look at once jaunty and sheepish. Physically he looked in better shape than when I'd last seen him, and had put on several pounds, but was still thin, and there were slight shadows under his eyes.

We sat down together, and he explained, like a man in a confessional, the processes that had led to surrender. 'It happened before you went off, but I decided to say nothing about it. The head waiter who was here before was an old friend from the Figueras days, and I helped him out when he was ill. You know how much they paid me on the building site? Twenty-eight pesetas for eight hours. Every time you served a party in the restaurant you got up to 20 pesetas. There was no question of leaving the money because the tips went into a pool. The other waiter said, "If you don't want your share, don't worry, I'll have it". What was I expected to do? This year my friend was too ill with tuberculosis to start again and they asked me to take over.'

'And are you happy? That's the main thing.'

'In a way. You've got to give up the idea of standing on your dignity, that's all. At least we've got away from the Grandmother. We're in one of the chalets and we've been able to furnish a couple of rooms. You can't have everything. I miss the fishing. There's no time for it any more. I start making up the accounts at about eight in the morning and we don't knock off until midnight. I get tired of having to smile at people. You have to smile all the time. It's part of the tariff – that's our joke. We get a peseta a smile, and five pesetas for saying, "Good evening sir, good evening madam. It's nice to see you again." If a party orders a meal costing over 25 pesetas a head, we're allowed to give them a drink on the house, which usually means another 10 pesetas on the tip. You can safely say we've sold ourselves.'

'Let's talk about happier things,' I said. 'I was in Espalmador last week. You wouldn't believe anything like it existed. The water's so clear you get vertigo. It's like swimming through air. How's your diving these days?'

'I could get down to eighteen metres last September when we went out. I haven't tried since then.'

'In Espalmador you have a flat rock-bottom in about fifteen metres,

177

with deep grooves in the rock and fish by the thousand in the grooves. No sand. No weed. Just great big fish following each other nose to tail along corridors of rock. I couldn't believe my eyes. What was funny was this sensation brought on by the clearness of the water. It was like walking along the top of a wall. I was really dizzy, and the feeling only passed when some big fish came up to take a look at me.'

He grabbed at my hand. 'We'll have to go there together. That's decided it. As a matter of fact I'd already made up my mind. I was going to turn this job in anyway. Some heavy expenses coming up. Elvira's having a baby.'

'I know. The Grandmother just told me.'

'As soon as we've put that behind us I'll be free. Perhaps we could go to Espalmador this autumn.'

'Would they keep you on through the winter?'

'Yes.'

'Then you'd be making a mistake to leave this year. Let's be realistic. You can't afford it.'

'Right then, I will be realistic. I'll work on here until April, pay everything off, and get a bit of capital together. After that I'll be my own master. We'll go to Espalmador, right?'

'Absolutely.'

'It's agreed then. That's definite. In April, eh?'

'In April. It's a deal.'

He was suddenly overbrimming with enthusiasm. Miraculously the shadows under his eyes had vanished. I had even succeeded in convincing myself that he meant what he said.

A few foreigners were in the Alcalde's bar, talking in loud voices and gesturing in a way that Latins were supposed to, although only a small minority did. One of the foreigners was drinking from a *porón*, a vessel never seen in Farol until this time. There was a great variety of bottles on the shelf at the back of the new counter, and the old broken-backed, patched-up chairs that cast such wonderful shadows when put out in the sun had been replaced by new ones upholstered in starkly grained leatherette. The mermaid had gone, and so had the fishermen, and the foolish, giggling boy who had helped out behind the bar had given place to a sharp-eyed, unsmiling barman I had never seen before. Prices had been increased three-fold since the last year.

The local lad with the gift for mimicry, in particular of the caterwaulings of mating cats, chose that moment to come in. The original performance had failed to inspire the visitors' enthusiasm, so he had quickly taught himself to cluck like a hen, so convincingly that he was rarely free from the attentions of eager young cockerels, one of which followed him into the bar on this occasion. It was clear that this went down well, for he was greeted with shouts of delight and invitations to drink, but I could see that the Alcalde hated to have him in the place.

The Alcalde came over with two glasses drawn secretly from the Alicante cask. 'Muga has to be accepted as a fact of life,' he said. 'Something you have to learn to live with. If you go along with him you can keep him under some sort of control. If you start a fight you're done for. He came up with this offer. "Here's my money, take me in as a partner, or I'll open up in opposition." What would you have done? I wouldn't have lasted five minutes. By saying yes and giving him a forty-nine percent holding at least I have some say in the policy. I can insist on what we sell here being the real thing. Have you seen Sebastian?'

'I just came from the hotel.'

'Let me tell you how it works there. They buy casks of wine made up from what we call the ends, the dregs if you like, at one fifty a litre, put it in bottles with fancy labels and sell it for twenty. The brandy's the same. It says Jaime Primero on the label, but neither you nor I would want to drink what's inside.'

'Does Sebastian know about this?'

'Of course he does. He has to do what he's told. They serve up dogfish with sauce in the restaurant and call it merluza.'

'He told me he'd leave after this year.'

'Sebastian lives in Muga's house. How long do you imagine it's going to take him to pay back what he owes? When you come back next year you'll find him right where he is now. After that? Well, that's another story. I have my own personal theories about what's going to happen – but at this particular moment he's in a trap. The more money Sebastian can make the sooner he's going to be able to pay Muga off, and the way to make money fast is to go along with Muga's rackets. He pays a commission on all that terrible liquor they sell for him, and even if Sebastian wanted to say no, he couldn't.'

A brief quarrel had flared among some Germans who had been drinking steadily at the back of the bar. One man was on his feet, shouting, and his friends got up, imprisoned his arms, and dragged him back into his chair. Instant reconciliation was followed by laughter and urgent cries for more vino to be brought.

'How do you get on with them?' I asked, knowing the Alcalde's reputation for being a poor mixer.

'I think about mathematical problems. It takes my mind off them. Some of them are drunk all the time. The women are worse than the men – real animals. Never believe it to look at them, would you?'

'Do they give you a lot of trouble?'

'Not in here. I'm not talking about the drink now. Our problem is the way they go after the village lads. The night watchman up at the hotel fixes them up. Remember Lara? I had some trouble with him last year. He's always hanging around the foreigners. They say he's exceptionally well-endowed and has better than average staying powers. It's been officially reported to me that the night-watchman charges his fee then passes on 25 pesetas to Lara. Last year it used to be four pesetas for taking on some old French woman. Everything's gone up. I can't make up my mind whether or not to bring the police into it. It's something that goes against the grain, and in any case, what's the point? If Lara went they'd find somebody else.'

A German snapped his fingers to pay and the the Alcalde's sharp-faced waiter sauntered over, took the money and counted out the change. He waited in expectation while the Alcalde clicked his tongue, then used one hand to scoop the coins left on the table into the other. His expression was aloof, almost one of distaste. 'Notice,' the Alcalde said, 'not only does he take the money as something due to him, but there's no question of thanks. This is the measure of our moral decline. Although we've come to live off these people, we intensely dislike them. Why do we dislike them? Because we resent what they're doing to us. I have only one consolation.'

'And what's that?'

'That this won't last. It's a kind of sickness, an infection. In the past we suffered from the plague. Now we suffer from tourists, but like any other sickness it dies out in the end. We have these people for a year, and they corrupt us. Next year things are going to be better – I'm told the bookings are down by fifty percent. The year after it'll be all over. A thing of the past. This is only a passing fad with Muga too – like raising pigs. Next year or the year after he'll have had enough of it, and be looking for something else to turn his attention to. They'll all go and we'll be back where we were before. Do you know what I propose to do?'

'Put this place back to what it was before all this started, I would say.'

'You read my thoughts,' the Alcalde said. 'After that I'm going to live out the rest of my days in peace.'

'Where's the mermaid?' I asked. 'Very carefully stored away,' the Alcalde said. 'I'm looking after it, you can be sure of that. The day Muga comes to me and says he's pulling out, the mermaid will be back, and there it will stay.'

2

There were at that time as many foreigners as natives in Farol. Most of them were French, but there was a sprinkling of Germans and Scandinavians, and the first of the English had arrived. They had the loudest voices and the most forceful manner of all the visitors and, despite the never-ending, bustling activity of all those natives who had to do with them, they continued firm in their belief in the Spanish addiction to procrastination and sleep. All tourists accommodation was booked for the summer, and workmen were already digging out the foundations of two new hotels. It was impossible to find a seat in the Alcalde's bar or the Moorish folly at the end of the coast road after seven in the evening. A third bar, with restaurant, was about to be opened on the site of the old boathouse, from which I found Carmela had been ousted. Despite the unenchanting view from the hotel's verandah of Cabezas' house and the rubbish piled round it, it was thronged nightly with visitors who danced there until the small hours.

Muga watched over the tourists like a hen clucking after its brood. He opened all doors for them, and responded to every whim. A number of narrow-minded Spanish regulations relating to the conduct of the individual in public places were still in force and, single-handed, Muga tore them away. It was illegal to embrace or kiss publicly, but in the second year of the tourists it was not possible to go out on a moonlight night without seeing couples locked in each other's arms in the nooks and corners of the village, or in or under the boats pulled up on the beach. A professional bigot in plain clothes arrived with a tape-measure to spearhead a police campaign against off-the-shoulder dresses, but Muga soon got rid of him. In 1950 a male tourist was still not permitted in theory to go about in shorts unless he tied handkerchiefs over his knee-caps, but Muga had a Civil Guard who tried to enforce this regulation shifted to another area. In the same year a local girl was sent to a correctional institution run by nuns for wearing a two-piece bathing dress, but foreigners could wear what they liked, and even undress on the beach, although the spectacle could draw wondering crowds.

Down by the sea-front Don Jaime, having battered down all

opposition, reigned supreme. The narrow breaches opened in the fishermen's defences back in the autumn had widened through the surrender of more of the weaker elements, until the front had collapsed. Almost all the boats were now available for hire. Some foreigners had objected to the fact that the effort of climbing into a boat from a steeply sloping beach was too great, and that trippers invariably got wet, so government resources allocated for the promotion of tourism were provided at Muga's urgent request for the building of a jetty, to which the boats were now tied up. Of all changes this was the one the fishermen most deplored, and they discussed with relish the probability of its being carried away by the next severe storm due, according to past experience, in two years' time.

One outbuilding of the old slaughterhouse had been converted at Muga's expense to serve as a bar for the fishermen, and it was there that I discussed the fishermen's predicament with Simon, the survivor of the storm of January 1922, still believed to have retained through thick and thin some small residue of his communicable luck. Boredom, he said, was the enemy in this life. They took parties up and down the coast on picnic excursions, or to visit sites that might be expected to interest them, although they were all of them places that filled the fishermen with the profoundest of tedium. A few episodes had been good for a laugh. The tourists had insisted on being landed on an island and had been chased off by famished and cannibalistic dogs dumped there by the peasants of Sort. A girl had gone swimming in her pants and been stung across the bottom by a jelly fish. 'Do you take them to the famous cave?' I asked. Simon thought about this then nodded. 'They renamed it Sa Gruta Azul,' he said. 'The tourists go there because of the colour of the water. Personally I haven't and I wouldn't, but others do. The idea of it gives me the creeps.'

'And do they fish at all these days?'

'In a token fashion,' Simon said. Just to show they were still fishermen. The people from Palamos seemed to have the best of both worlds, but it didn't work out that way at Farol, owing to the irreconcileable timetables of tourists and fish.

But seen in the perspective of years, he insisted that what they were going through was no more than a temporary and unimportant phase. They were born fishermen, from innumerable generations of fisher-men and seafaring forebears, and this they would remain. Through the ungovernable forces of nature they had suffered a dislocation, but eventually the tide would turn again. In the meanwhile the easy money brought in by the foreigners should be taken, but only as a means to an honourable end. It was agreed by all that the cash windfall should be invested in the future, on the purchase of new gear, the rehabilitation of aged engines, and the major repairs necessary to the last of the three storm-damaged boats. Everyone proclaimed their faith that, re-equipped by the chance of foreign bounty, the little fishing armada would sail again in a rejuvenated form, prepared – in their own words – to 'overwhelm the sea' and wrest from it those great harvests of fish, those miraculous catches awaiting them when the shoals returned.

I ran into Carmela in the butcher's where I found myself standing beside her in the queue. She wore her bottle-green suit, carried her handbag, and I was amazed to see that she was attended by an errand-running girl holding the string bags into which her many purchases were dropped. The butcher's had undergone a spectacular face-lift. Gone were the bloodstains, the flowers stuck into jam jars, the artistic display of giblets, the be-ribboned tripes, and the severed heads presented on paper ruffs. The shop was as impersonal as a tax office. The customers no longer sneaked in carrying secret packages with which to bribe the butcher's wife, but formed an orderly queue to be served from a refrigeration room by a dispassionate young man in a surgeon's coat with well cared-for hands. The remembered smell of meat had been replaced by that of a perfumed disinfectant, called Floralia.

We left the shop together and Carmela gave me her news. She was now cook at the Brisas del Mar, and I could see for myself what had happened to the boathouse, where in any case it would not have been possible to stay on through the winter storms. She had a room of her own with running water and someone to do the donkey work in the preparation of the food, but it was a job that gave her small satisfaction. There were two problems, the first being the necessity to make the food sufficiently tasteless for foreign palates, and the second the camouflage of unattractive basic materials in order to make them acceptable. She found that the latter task came easier.

The small girl trundled at our side laden with the dubious bagfuls, while Carmela enlarged on her dislike of the people for whom she cooked. 'I'll say this for you, sir. You're prepared to have a try and you're not easily put off. If you had to, you closed your eyes, but you still went on eating. I got the impression that all foreigners like a good, strong flavour. I'd like someone to tell me how I'm supposed to cook an innard stew when they say, don't use herbs, and no garlic, eh?' The foreigners at the hotel were inhuman, she said, mere animals, devoid of moral sense. They infuriated her by sending food back to be reheated, or because something had surfaced from underneath the gravy they didn't like the look of, and if this happened she sometimes punished the offender by spitting in the dish before returning it, and if it happened a second time she called in one of the girls who helped out to contribute to the spittle.

Otherwise her news was good, above all the news of Rosa whose continued progress amazed all who saw her.

Was she at the hotel? I asked.

Well no, that wouldn't have been possible, but they had reached a much happier and better arrangement for all concerned. Rosa was in a home – well, not even a home, a sanatorium having all the necessary facilities for her treatment. It couldn't possibly have been a better arrangement. Mr Muga, who had been generosity itself, was paying, and he arranged for someone to take her over to Figueras to see the little girl once a fortnight.

'Is she walking normally now?'

'The slightest limp, that's all. Otherwise apart from a little trouble with her teeth that most people don't even notice, everything's cleared up. The doctor told me in some ways she's above average intelligence for her age.'

'Will she be coming out soon?'

'A year. Eighteen months at most. The time will fly. I tell you, sir, next time you see Rosa she'll be on the arm of her first boyfriend. I get down on my knees to thank God for such a miracle.'

I remembered the goat. 'What news of the goat?'

'The goat? Well that's a sad story. Mr Muga's been kindness itself to us but we couldn't expect him to have her here, so we invited a few friends round and had her for the feast of San Firmín. We all miss her, but it couldn't be helped. A pity you couldn't have been there, sir.'

No one could tell me anything of Don Alberto, so I trudged across the fields to his house in search of him. The windows were shuttered, with sparrows nesting between the wood and the glass, and there was no reply to '*Ave Maria purisima*' shouted at the top of my voice through the substantial opening where the double doors failed to meet. None of the peons was in sight and I made a note of the gigantic thistles growing up all over the place.

I made a small detour through the dog village on the way back and found it looking like an old film set from the American dust-bowl of *The Grapes of Wrath*. Sort was suddenly fragile and spent, and purposeless, waiting to be broken up. Its gates hung askew and its doors were nailed up, and tiles had slid from roofs to shatter into pink fragments in the rock-hard, grey earth. Some feather-duster chickens were scuffling in desperate hope through ancient refuse, but there was no sign of the dogs. The bar was closed, as was the church, with a notice posted over its doors. Huge piles of expertly stacked logs – all that remained of the oaks – overtopped the low houses, and phantoms of wind and grit moved up and down the empty street.

A man appeared from nowhere, wearing a military-style jacket, Texan boots, a big hat and, underneath the hat a blue eyeshade of the kind some journalists wear when at work in strong light.

He came towards me, then held out his hand. 'Julio Baeza, at your service. I'm Don Jaime Muga's number one. Can I be of assistance?' His voice held a faint transatlantic resonance, and he had rid himself of the *ceceo* – the famous Spanish lisp. A Spaniard, in fact, who preferred to sound and look like a South American.

'Does Don Jaime own this village now?' I asked.

'What's left of it,' he said. He twisted his lip into a half-smile of good-natured contempt.

'And all these houses are empty?'

'Put it this way, they're no longer tenanted.'

'Would the Alcalde happen to be about?'

'He's gone. This doesn't rate as a municipality any more.'

'Has everybody gone?'

'Not everyone,' the pseudo-South American said. 'One or two of the old timers didn't want to be moved, and we respected their wishes. We've settled all the rest on the model farm. It's just over the hill. Great place. We call it El Porvenir.'

'The Future', I thought. A good name for it.

'Run you over there if you'd like to look round.'

I could see El Porvenir in the mind's eye, and that was enough. 'Thanks all the same,' I said. 'I have to be getting back.'

The one person certain to have news of the old man was Don Ignacio, who had been out when I called earlier in the day. I found him in the church, and we strolled back to the house together. It seemed no longer important in Farol not to be seen with a priest. His servant brought glasses of *rancio*, and the cats, already unsteady on their feet, followed on her heels for their share. One or two new pieces had appeared on the bench top that Don Ignacio used to clean and restore his archaeological finds; a blackened crisp of leather – once part of a belt, Don Ignacio said – and real treasure in the form of a small, corroded spoon. It seemed that Muga had relented in the matter of the celebration of Mass, at least to the extent of fixing up someone to act as stand-in when Don Ignacio went off to recover the past from the salty wilderness of Ampurias.

Don Alberto, Don Ignacio said, had taken his aged girlfriend back to Madrid where, she announced, she was determined to die. The circumstances surrounding her departure had been a little theatrical. Don Alberto, he said, had gone off to Figueras to address a meeting of die-hard landlords determined to put a stop to progress and development of almost every kind, and above all the encroachments of tourism, when Gloria, who had not appeared in public for at least twenty years, walked out of the house. She walked two miles to Sort, sat in the little square there and ordered a drink of a kind no one had heard of, but accepted the inevitable *palo* in its place. Her appearance caused astonishment, and in the case of young children alarm, for she had dressed herself in a purple silk gown, wore a great deal of jewellery including a tiara, although almost bald, and had coated her face, arms and hands with stark-white powder.

The name Gloria, as applied to the aged creature I had only seen hunched in a corner over her gramophone, startled me. Don Alberto had always referred to her – even when speaking English – as *La Vieja*. How old was she? I asked. Don Ignacio said eighty, perhaps eighty-five. Having downed the *palo*, he said, the question of payment came up. She had no money, but offered the tavern-keeper a ruby ring. Someone fetched the Alcalde, and he came running to introduce himself. One of the onlookers told Don Ignacio that he went down on one knee, but Don Ignacio said that was a version he rejected. He invited her to his house where she shook hands with his goats. After that she went round the village with all the children trailing after her at a safe distance, picking the flowers in the gardens.

When Don Alberto got back she was waiting for him with an armful of roses. 'Alberto,' she said. 'I'm tired of this place, and I've decided to go back to Madrid. Please take me.'

'Well, of course my dear,' he told her. 'But what are we going to do when we get there?'

'I'm going to die,' she said. 'What you do is your own affair.'

'I went to the station to see them off,' Don Ignacio said. 'She was wearing a hat with plumes of the kind women must have worn at Ascot in the time of your Queen Victoria. Just before they went, she pushed a packet into my hands. "Take these and rebuild your church," she said. They were Imperial Russian Bonds. In 1916 we could have rebuilt it twice over with all those thousands of roubles. She was a beautiful woman in her day, and a witty one they say. I saw a picture of her in a gallery myself when I was in Madrid. They even say our late King had a brief relationship with her. *Sic transit gloria mundi*,' he said. I hoped it was not intended as a pun.

3

Slowly Farol began to adapt to the foreign presence, to do its best to accept the tribal customs of others and to cultivate a kind of holy indifference to endless assaults by foreigners on their own taboos. Police chiefs recalled the plain-clothes vigilantes with their tape-measures and told the rank and file of the Guardia Civil to look in the other direction when they saw a woman with a plunging neckline or split skirt. Soon there was a law for foreigners and another for Spaniards, just as in most places there is one for the rich and another for the poor. By and large communication remained a matter of gestures, smiles or frowns, and each side remained mysterious to the other, made what allowances they had to, and got on as best they could in that way.

Muga, steadfastly advancing the frontiers of his dominion, made a great leap forward by his purchase at a very low price of twelve thousand square metres of what was quickly becoming valuable land between his hotel and the sea. This had long been used as a rubbish dump and was cluttered as well with the remains of an old cork-processing plant; it was now overgrown with morning glory and offered sanctuary to numerous cats. Nobody had any idea in Farol who this land belonged to, but Muga eventually traced the legal owners, an aged brother and sister, to Figueras to which the family had emigrated some fifty years earlier. They were astounded to learn that they were property-owners, but coming from a background in which the conception of numbers above 100 was often vague, they were totally unable to conceive of the figure of 50,000 pesetas Muga offered. The problem was to present wealth not in terms of intellectual abstraction but reality, and Muga solved it by collecting 2,500 brand new 25-peseta notes from his bank, and covering the floor of the single room in which the old couple lived with several layers of them. The offer was then readily accepted, bulldozers moved in to clear the debris covering the land, and plans were submitted within the month for another hotel having a swimming pool and a complex of shops.

Muga now owned or controlled about two thirds of Farol and manipulated the lives of nine out of ten of its inhabitants. His one conspicuous failure had been his inability to acquire and demolish

Cabezas' hideous house. This stark, barracks-like building was more of an eyesore than ever in the context of its newly prettified surroundings. Worse than that, Cabezas in his half-witted fashion had given shelter in it to the gypsies and their performing bear, who failed to please the hotel guests overlooking Cabezas' patio with their demonstrations of the art of animal training, and kept them awake with their raucous singing that went on far into the night.

To Muga's amazement his planning application was turned down. An objection had been raised that it contravened a recent regulation by which in a coastal development area no building in excess of two stories could be erected in such a way as to deprive an existing habitation of its view of the sea. He was even more astonished when the author of the objection turned out to be the supposedly feeble-minded Cabezas, the habitation being his own house.

At the end of August there was more astonishing news: Mitzi was back, installed, alone, in Muga's hotel, and a day or two later I observed her, gold sandalled and white-gowned palely loitering along the beach. Distantly, all eyes were on her, and a small clique of young fishermen with too much time now on their hands were trailing along fifty yards in the rear. Legends had sprung up, for example that Muga, in preparation for a trip to Reno to divorce his wife, had invited her to join him. The Alcalde assured me that this was not so. He had stopped to welcome her back, then asked her where Klaus was, and had received a cold but penetrating look, and the reply, '*Ich weiss nicht.*' She was a person, the Alcalde said, who seemed to say the first thing that came into her head. The receptionist at the hotel reported her as replying to the same question, 'I doubt we will be seeing him again.' Talking to her had a strange effect on him, the Alcalde said. It was something about her eyes. Trying to describe the feeling he used the word *conjurado*, spellbound. The Civil Guards asked to see her and her story to them was that Klaus had turned up again in Germany and they had spent a few days together, after which they had finally gone their separate ways.

Mitzi kept strictly to herself, avoiding all social gatherings and excursions, the gala dinner, sardanas at Sort, barbecues and boat trips. She had adopted a collection of abandoned kittens and was to be seen sometimes, carrying these in a bag slung from her shoulder, as she paced softly along the beach down by the water's edge before the tourists took up their morning positions, and after they had left at the end of the day.

Any approach by a male was vigorously repelled. When Pujols

offered to take her to a secluded beach, she quelled him with a glance. If one of the boys who followed her wherever she went got too close, she swung round suddenly to swear at him in German, '*Du bist ein Arschloch*', making it a matter of simple statement. Faces appeared at windows and heads turned discreetly whenever she passed with her squeaking bagful of kittens. Her effect on the village came close to being hypnotic. My own feeling was that she was a little stupid, and whatever power she possessed stemmed from her inordinate self-confidence.

About the Sunday following her arrival there was a sudden flare-up in the village interest in Mitzi's affairs. Something had happened or was about to happen, but there was as yet no solid fact to be discovered among the muffled voices of rumour and hearsay. On the Sunday evening I settled in my usual place outside the Alcalde's bar, ordered a *palo* and watched the beginnings of the ritual promenade. Most of the foreigners were out of the village, away on excursions, and this was a nostalgic hour when Farol returned briefly to the past. According to custom the promenade began in a desultory and unplanned fashion, with the appearance of strolling groups of young people, and it would be a half-hour before the Grandmother and the butcher's wife made their entry on the scene like matadors in the ring after the preliminary cape-waving when the serious business was about to begin.

Almost immediately the white flash of Mitzi's Grecian gown caught my eye, and she came into view with Cabezas' son Pedro at her side. The promenaders following the couple had fallen back, and in distancing themselves in this way, Mitzi and Pedro were left to occupy the village stage.

I had never bothered to study Pedro, 'daddy's boy', closely before, but now I did in earnest. He was good looking in an oafish way, with thick lips, curly hair, and a vacant expression that matched Mitzi's. The couple walked past, looking straight ahead, and without exchanging a word or glance. They turned round by the church, walked the length of the street – over which a kind of hush had fallen – once again, then disappeared. Someone went for Cabezas, but by the time he reached the scene they had gone.

Next morning Mitzi and Pedro left Farol together for an unknown destination. Tiberio Lara, Pedro's only acquaintance, accompanied Cabezas – dressed in mourning – to the Alcalde's house to make a statement concerning the circumstances of the departure. Cabezas told the Alcalde of a heated and somewhat one-sided altercation with his son on the previous night when he had accused him of associating with a foreign prostitute, about whom there were strong doubts over the mystery of Klaus' disappearance. Asked what he proposed to do, Pedro told his father he was going – he had no idea where. Cabezas appealed to him, 'How can you go anywhere without money? I've got no money to give you. The house is all I've got, and it's yours. I'll call in the lawyer and sign it over to you tomorrow.' Pedro said he was going away with Mitzi whatever happened, and as he couldn't take the house with him he didn't want it. He would only take his guitar. Cabezas told the Alcalde that the gypsies had taught Pedro to play the guitar, and he believed it to have been the undoing of him. All Lara could add to this was that Pedro had told him that the German girl had come back for him, and that they were going away together, and would never be parted again.

Having finished his statement Cabezas, who seemed to the Alcalde strangely calm and resigned, asked the Alcalde if he had a fire, and the Alcalde took him through to the kitchen where two or three lumps of charcoal in the usual *cocina económica* were smouldering under a pot.

Cabezas asked if the Alcalde had any objection if he burned certain personal papers, and the Alcalde said, none at all. He lifted the pot off the fire, and Cabezas took a number of documents out of his pocket, including his birth certificate, his marriage certificate and his will and burned them one by one. The Alcalde got him a glass of brandy and he knocked it back. 'Well, that's that,' he said when the burning was over. 'Now I'm officially dead.'

'Not quite,' the Alcalde said, 'but I can see you're making difficulties for us. What are we going to do with the house when you go?'

'Whatever you like,' Cabezas said. 'I shan't be needing it any more. I lived in a cave for thirty years and I've never really got used to the place. Too hot in summer, and too cold in winter. I think I'm better off where I came from.'

4

I settled to an interlude of fishing, but there was less scope, variety or reward in it than in the past. Since nowadays so many of my friends were busied elsewhere I often spearfished alone, an arduous business entailing a long swim from the beach out to a suitable fishing ground, and the difficulty in the rare instance of a sizeable fish being taken of getting it back to shore. Nevertheless, constant swimming and diving practice was essential to avoid loss of form. Compared to some of the Spaniards who now, in the third season, were beginning to arrive as holiday-makers, I was never better than a mediocre diver. Many of these could easily, without an aqualung, reach a depth of twenty metres, and a few far more, whereas when one day in pursuit of a splendid mero I tried to exceed my limit of fifteen metres I suffered a ruptured ear-drum. The pain, although momentary, was intense, and the injury put me out of action as a diver for the rest of the year.

It was an accident that led to my first encounter with the cheerful and sprightly Dr Seduction. He had come a long way since the days when any youngish woman requiring his advice sent her mother to him, who would say, before hoisting up her skirts to subside on the fateful couch, 'Sorry, but you'll have to be content with a squint at my tripes. I'll tell you all about her symptoms and where the trouble is, and you can let me know what to do.'

Since then the doctor had made a fortune out of the visitors' stomach troubles and sunburn and invested part of it in a course in Barcelona, permitting him to display a sign: *Especialidad En Venereas, Sifilis, Vias Urinarias*. It was largely a matter of prestige since the merest sprinkling of foreigners took veneral diseases with them on holiday, but it enormously impressed the natives who credited him with the possession of secrets conferring a species of awful power. Few of the villagers would have disputed the existence in Barcelona of a hospital called La Merced (Mercy), in which terminal sufferers, whom Dr Seduction might well have saved if given the chance, were put out of their misery by stifling them under their pillows.

The doctor saw me in the breeze-block addition, acting as a surgery, to the windowless peasant house in Sort in which he lived, and he skipped about like a friendly kitten, kicked aside a shopping bag with a chicken's head lolling with eyes closed from among the purchases, snatched up a few tufts of bloodied cotton wool and dropped them into the waste-paper basket before attending to my injury. He shone an inspection lamp into my ear, and what he saw there clearly delighted him. A boy of about ten sat in a chair clutching his abdomen and groaning. He had been sent for something to ease his stomach ache, and the doctor called him over, handed him the auroscope and invited him to inspect my ruined ear-drum. It was effective psycho-therapy for the child's groans instantly gave way to exclamations of astonishment and delight, and soon after he ran off whistling.

Although we had never spoken before, the doctor knew all about me, treated me as an old friend and was quite prepared, after telling me there was nothing whatever to be done about the ear, to settle to a chat about our common interest in the local scene. We were like Stanley and Livingstone meeting in darkest Africa, he said, among pigmies and people who still practised trial by ordeal, and believed they could turn themselves into leopards.

'They can will themselves to die here,' he said.

'So I've heard,' I told him.

'I can tell you of a case of a man who's doing it at this very moment. Fellow called Cabezas. He was born in this very house. After that trouble with his son he decided he didn't want to go on living. The neighbours asked me to talk to him, but he wouldn't see me. So now he's dying. Of no disease known to medicine – unless you include a broken heart. I give him a month at most. Did you know Pablo Fons?'

'Don Alberto took me to see him last year,' I said. 'The great family man.'

'I signed his death certificate on Monday,' the doctor said. 'It's something that could only happen here.'

'He was the kind of man you'd expect to live for ever. What did he die of?'

'His wife polished him off. He treated her like an animal, and she just took it quietly and waited her time. She used to be a nym-phomaniac and he kept her locked up in an outhouse at night for twenty years. I can tell you this as a positive fact. You know they lost everything?'

'I knew Muga took over the farm.'

'He had to find something to do, so he took up dynamiting wells. It's risky work, but the pay's good. She used to go with him and carry the gear.'

'And she pushed him down a well, I suppose. The usual thing.'

'No, she threw a stick of dynamite down while he was working. Or so they say. These things can never be proved.'

'What did you put on the certificate?'

The doctor spread his hands and twinkled. 'Accidental death,' he said. 'The police don't like to be bothered with borderline cases. Who can blame them?'

Apart from token sorties by the big boats undertaken to reaffirm the fisherman's belief in their true purpose and destiny, little fishing was done now except by one or two hard-core specialists, working singly or in pairs. Men such as my neighbour Juan, and the crab-eating Pujols – with whom I worked from this time on – not only fished for a living, but were addicts and enthusiasts of their profession, and the many skills it drew upon. When they were tired of the routine with the palangres or the nets, they took days off to fish with the raï, or illegally at night with the trident and a torch. Accompanying them on such expeditions, I learned something, caught nothing, but shared to the full in their excitement.

Juan and Pujols were adventurers, full of curiosity. They could always have rowed out and fished within a mile or two of shore and left it at that, but something lured them on to explore the deep and uncharted waters which yielded surprises in plenty, but little in the way of extra profit. The sea had its sierras, its ravines and its great divides, and Juan and Pujols explored its secret geography just as their forebears had explored new continents, sounding great depths with their nets and hooks, never exhausting their capacity for wonder at the deep-sea monsters they occasionally caught.

There had never been much money in fishing of this kind, and now there was less. A number of fish, as the Grandmother had made clear – including such innocent varieties as rays of all kinds (skate) and eels – came under some taboo or other, and could not be sold at any price, and nothing was regarded as edible in Farol if it was not recognisable. Many of the fish taken in expeditions with Juan or with Pujols were not – they were strange goggle-eyed scowling creatures, some with heads like the fronts of the very first motor cars, that had come to the end of their evolutionary journey millions of years ago, perfectly adapted now to a crevice in near-darkness at the bottom of the ocean. The flesh of such fish, able to withstand pressure that bruised and dented wooden components in Pujols' nets, was almost incredibly tough, but made exquisite soup, as I had learned from Carmela who possessed no reservations of any kind where food was concerned.

Pujols was glad of my company and my assistance because his brother was one of those who had gone off to join the Palamos smuggling fleet, and he could not handle his large net without assistance. The recent changes in the life-style of the village had brought its compensations for Pujols. His diet of raw crabs, originally prescribed by the Curandero who believed him to be suffering from tuberculosis, had had the side effect – or so he thought – of increasing his libido, with its attendant problems following the loss of Sa Cordovesa and Maria Cabritas. Now with the advent of several lively and unattached ladies from the north, things were beginning to look up again. Although cadaverous and hollow-chested, Pujols remained an imposing man, and shortly after my return, a relationship developed with a buxom Swede who had accompanied him on several trips to secluded beaches.

While telling me of this success he groped in his pocket, and pulled out a small crab, tore off a leg and began to chew, inadvertently bespattering both of us a moment later with its fragments as he was racked by a fit of coughing.

'Do you do that when she's with you?' I asked, as Pujols replaced the lost leg with another. 'I mean chew raw crabs?'

'Why? Shouldn't I?'

'You never know with women,' I said. 'They can be funny creatures.'

'She doesn't object,' Pujols said. 'I explained to her I have to eat crabs for my health, and she was very understanding. Foreign ladies seem to be about the bodily needs.'

5

At six-thirty every morning the Alcalde put out a couple of tables for the early risers, and by a quarter to seven as usual I was seated and ready for the exquisite experience of coffee from the finest of newly-ground black-market beans on the fresh, morning palate.

The first days of autumn had begun to pour colour back into the surroundings, speckling the greyish glitter of the beach with soft, yellow highlights, and revarnishing the purple of the boats. Green and indigo medallions the sun could no longer burn away floated on the sea's surface, marking the presence of weed or a twist of currents in the depths.

The coffee came, unfolding its perfume against the Farol background odour of mature sewage. The old chairs set out in the morning for such regulars as myself sent their spindly, noble shadows down the street. A few villagers appeared, walking and talking very softly as if still overshadowed by the experience of sleep. The canary cages were being put out, each shaded by a canopy woven from grass. The sea-front was quieter than it had been in the early morning. A year before Maria Cabritas would have passed at this hour, prodding her goats along with one of her many umbrellas on their way to the scrawny pasturage offered by the cliff ledges. A year before the boats would have been coming in, and the nets spread out to be mended on the beach. Now the fishermen slept through the barren nights, and their work by day, they said, deprived them of the bodily rhythm of exhaustion and recovery to which they had become accustomed. On this morning I noticed for the first time that there appeared to be far fewer cats about than in the past, then I remembered the sinister rumours of death squads at work at night.

At seven-fifteen or thereabouts, the church bell clanked a half-dozen times, and a few minutes later I saw Don Ignacio sneak out of a side door of the building and make off, having done his duty for the day. There followed a short interval of silence broken only by the sound of the pebbles shifted by the tide, then I heard the unmistakeable puttering of Don Alberto's Levis, and in a moment, turning the corner at the far end of the street, he came into view, perched as it always seemed precariously on his machine, looking at that distance like a simple Meccano model.

He stopped a few yards away, dismounted, put his motorcycle on the stand, and joined me at the table. 'I felt sure I'd find you here,' he said. 'I got in yesterday.' He was trembling as he always did for the first few moments from the vibration of the worn two-stroke engine, but clearly in excellent form.

'What news of Gloria, Don Alberto?'

The Alcalde brought his coffee and Don Alberto took a sip, leaving a small, vivacious stain on the cup's rim. He gasped his appreciation, then re-arranged the cup, saucer and spoon for a better display of the treacly morning reflections.

'We went to Madrid,' he said.

'I know.'

'It was her idea, but it turned out a success. Took us out of ourselves. I was going stale in this place. She was too. Do you know Madrid?'

'I'm afraid I don't.'

'You should go there. It's not to be missed. The air's different. The climate's different. The people are different. It's a civilised place where you can have a drink and listen to good music. Madrid refreshes the soul. It did us a world of good.'

'Don Ignacio mentioned that Gloria hadn't been well. I imagine she's her old self again.'

'No, she died last month. We went out for a night on the town, and she had a heart attack in the cab on her way home.'

'I'm sorry,' I said. 'Very sorry indeed.'

'She was rather under the weather when we left, but she brightened up as soon as we got there. The fact of the matter is, we both overdid it. One tends to over-estimate one's powers. It was as good a way to go as any.'

I nodded, remembering with sorrow the terrible delay the long dark years of waiting death had imposed on the old woman.

'It was impossible to imagine La Vieja would ever depart this world,' Don Alberto said. 'I found it hard to get used to the fact that she was no longer there. It made me take stock of my life and come to a decision as to what was essential and what could be done without. All this land of mine, for example, I thought. I only hold it in trust. I don't really *own* it. How can anyone own mountains, rivers, trees? If anything it owns me. I decided it was about time that the people I spent most of my life looking after stood on their own feet. Let them carry the responsibility, I said to myself. I made a decision on the spot. Remember those seven peons of mine who came to see me that day you were there?'

'Very well indeed.'

'They were the ones who'd stood by me, I thought. Why not turn the land over to them? They'd probably be just as happy to have it as I would be to get rid of it. I went to one of Madrid's best lawyers to discuss with him how these things are best done, and we got the preliminaries under way. You'd be astonished if I told you how complicated it is to stop being a landowner. Have you by any chance been anywhere near my house in the past few months?'

'I called over there to see if anyone had news of you a couple of weeks ago. There didn't seem to be much going on.'

'There wasn't,' Don Alberto said. 'I left a steward in charge of the place but he never bothered to go there. My peons charged up their wages for clearing and ditching, ploughing, sowing the crops, pruning and spraying the vines, and the steward paid out. He paid out for the seed that wasn't sown, a pump for a well that had dried out, and for veterinary treatment for animals I never possessed. They must have vaccinated every cow in the province and put it down to my account.'

'In other words you were taken for a ride.'

'For some reason or other my peons took it into their heads I wasn't coming back. Perhaps someone told them I wasn't. I happened to arrive at the very moment when two of them were busily taking down one of the outhouses and carting the stones away. When I asked them what they were doing they said, "The place was falling down, anyhow."'

'What are you going to do about it, Don Alberto?' I asked.

'Nothing,' he said, 'and they know it. Corruption doesn't come naturally to the poor, as it does to the rich. The people hereabouts have always been cruel, mean and litigious, but they were never corrupt until those they looked to for an example set them one. You see corruption wherever you look these days. You breathe it in with the air. It's not something you whisper about any more. It's accepted. Respectable. How can I really blame my peons for cheating me, when cheating's become a game everybody plays at? At the moment they're picking up potatoes for Muga, and I'm left with 200 *caballerías* of land I don't want, and no one to give it to.'

'You could make a fresh start. Hire labour in Figueras and go in for mechanisation.'

'I wouldn't even dream of it,' Don Alberto said. 'I prefer to let it go. When my ancestors got their hands on this land by whatever means they did, it was a beautiful place. It may take a decade to recover, more, because they cut down too many trees – but in the end it will. They can turn it into a national park if they like, but no one will ever grow potatoes on it. There used to be wild goats up in the hills in my father's day. Perhaps they'll come back.'

Some scrounging sparrows alighted on the table and Don Alberto watched with affection as they pecked at the husk he broke up for them. Suddenly the day had begun in earnest. The shopkeeper a few yards further on unbolted his door with a great rattling of iron and lumbered into sight carrying the table on which he would set out his newly acquired display of stuffed Pyrenean weasels, believed everywhere in Spain to be irresistible as tourist souvenirs. Each weasel was rapped sharply on the wooden edge to dislodge the tiny silverfish moths its fur harboured, then wired to a length of branch nailed to the table top in a characteristically aggressive posture. Next door on our left, the butcher's wife took down the shutters on a window display of plaster piglets, hygienic little pseudo-corpses, each throat slashed and reddened with a simulated wound. Someone had suggested to her that she should change the title of her business – *Carnicería* – to make it more comprehensible to foreigners, and her sign-board now read '*Carnage*'. Juan's Francesca, her face sharpened, as it seemed to me, with new purpose, pedalled past on a brand-new bicycle garnished with all the trimmings that could be bought for it. As a result of a Figueras schooling she was the only person in the village apart from the Alcalde able to cope with simple arithmetic, and had been appointed book-keeper to the Muga enterprises. Sebastian followed her almost at a trot. He stopped to reach for our hands, sat to gulp down a coffee, got up again and pulled me after him, and we walked a few yards together out of earshot of Don Alberto. 'I need your advice,' he said. 'I've been asked to sign a contract. Everybody has.'

'What does that mean?'

'It's for a year from the first of September. It puts paid to our plans. Muga says he's invested money in our training, and he wants to be sure he gets it back.'

'You *could* say no, I suppose.'

'I'd be back on 28 pesetas a day. At the moment I average 150. Our furniture's on credit, and if we leave the chalet we've nowhere to go.'

'Then you've no alternative. You have to sign.'

'I can see that,' Sebastian said. 'I just wanted to talk to someone. One more year. It's a bit like facing a prison stretch.'

I clapped him on the back. 'We'll go to Espalmador the year after next. The fish will still be there.'

'You really mean it, don't you?'

'Of course I do,' I said.

'It'll be something to look forward to.'

He broke off for a moment, and we listened to the sweet solemn hooting of a conch shell blown twice, distantly. 'Someone bringing in fish,' Sebastian said. 'That's something I haven't heard for weeks.'

'Do they give you any time off?' I asked.

'Sunday afternoons, if I ask.'

'Let's go calamar fishing,' I said, 'and talk about old times.'

We clasped each other's shoulders, and Sebastian dashed off, nearly colliding with Don Ignacio who had been hurrying to join us. He and Don Alberto had spent the previous evening together, locked in discussions largely concerned with the past, but a bright morning steered them back to present times. Barros was inevitably dragged in to support the new line both had taken. 'Don't force me to listen to people who tell you yesterday was better than today,' Don Alberto said, and Don Ignacio nodded his agreement.

'Does it ever occur to you that we're dinosaurs?' Don Alberto asked him. 'Creatures of the past? Could we be so soaked in prejudice that we can't accept the virtue of change of any kind?'

Don Ignacio smiled. 'When you and I are gone people may look back on this as a golden age. As Barros says, "Why speak of truth or lies? It all depends on the colour of the glass we look through." I must apologise for quoting a heretic once again.'

We had shifted our chairs so that the village and its invasive barbarities were at our back. The sea view was as it always had been at the beginning of any good autumn day, full of the tricks of light and of substance, the semblance of fire in the rocks, the pines tufting sashes of morning mist, the slow leaden curl of water on the grey beach. 'Here comes Juan with his boat,' Don Alberto said. 'Let's go and see what he's caught.'

Don Ignacio got up to join us, then sat down again, regretfully. 'I was forgetting I wouldn't be welcome,' he said. 'Tell me all about it.'

Don Alberto and I walked down to the beach. By the time we had surmounted the obstacles of Muga's road and wall Juan had pulled up the boat and lifted out his catch. He looked up and waved. 'You didn't show up this morning,' he said to me.

'Sorry, I overslept. I'll come tomorrow.'

The fish were arranged like over-elaborate, watery jewels in the shallow baskets. He had caught them in a spirit of adventure at great depth, in what he called a hole in the sea. Their colours were strong and dark, the deepest of blues and yellows and reds. They had morose, distraught expressions, and the heads of dogs and bulls. Eyes, released from the pressure of the depths, bulged hugely, and a few mouths still opened and closed in a thin frothing of black blood.

'No sale for them any more,' Juan said. 'The foreigners run away when they see them.'

'What do you do with them, then?' Don Alberto asked.

'Give them away to my friends. Help yourself.'

'Thank you, but I eat very little. Why go on fishing at all if there's nothing in it for you?'

'I have to keep my hand in for the better times to come,' Juan told him.

A few minutes later we rejoined Don Ignacio, and Don Alberto reported what had been said. 'When he began to talk about good times ahead, I could hardly stop myself from telling him, "Make the best of it, these *are* the good times."'

'I'm glad you restrained yourself,' the priest said. 'Sometimes it is necessary to believe things that are absurd. When an illusion dies, a hope is born. He has as much right to his hope as we to our resignation.'